Urban Bush Women

Society of Dance History Scholars

The Society of Dance History Scholars (SDHS) advances the field of dance studies through research, publication, performance, and outreach to audiences across the arts, humanities, and social sciences. As a constituent member of the American Council of Learned Societies, SDHS holds wide-ranging annual conferences, publishes new scholarship through its book series and proceedings, collaborates regularly with peer institutions in the United States and abroad, and presents yearly awards for exemplary scholarship.

Urban Bush Women

Twenty Years of African American Dance Theater, Community Engagement, and Working It Out

Nadine George-Graves

The University of Wisconsin Press

This book was published with support from the Office of the Dean of Arts and Humanities at the University of California, San Diego.

The University of Wisconsin Press
1930 Monroe Street, 3rd Floor
Madison, Wisconsin 53711-2059
uwpress.wisc.edu

3 Henrietta Street
London WC2E 8LU, England
eurospanbookstore.com

1 3 5 4 2

Printed in the United States of America

Library of Congress Cataloging-in-Publication Data
George-Graves, Nadine.
Urban Bush Women: twenty years of African American dance theater, community engagement, and working it out / Nadine George-Graves.
p. cm.
Includes bibliographical references and index.
ISBN 978-0-299-23554-3 (pbk.: alk. paper)
ISBN 978-0-299-23553-6 (e-book)
1. Urban Bush Women (Dance company)—History.
2. Dance companies—New York (State)—New York—History.
3. African American dance—New York (State)—New York—History.
I. Title. II. Series: Studies in dance history (Unnumbered)
GV1786.U73G46 2010
792.809747′1—dc22
2009041985

For

GIDEON, MAYA, AND ZORA,

who help me keep

all things in perspective

As soon as healing takes place, go out and heal someone else.
Maya Angelou,
quoted in Iyanla Vanzant, *Acts of Faith*

Dance is vulnerability; it's about giving your love, light, generosity.
Judith Jamison,
quoted in Dorothy Winbush Riley, ed.,
My Soul Looks Back, 'Less I Forget

There is a purifying process in dancing.
Katherine Dunham,
quoted in Diane J. Johnson, ed., *The Proud Sisters*

Black dance itself embodied a resistance to the confinement of the body solely to wage work.
Tera W. Hunter,
To 'Joy My Freedom

Sisters say to me,
"One day I'm gonna be a woman in the bush."
That's when I say,
"Sister, you don't know.
You already are a woman in the bush.
You already are a woman in the bush.
You already are a woman in the bush,
living on the frontline."
On the street, alleyway, on the street, on the roof.
On the street, alleyway, on the street, on the roof.
Carl Hancock Rux,
"Woman in the Bush"

Contents

Illustrations

The first chapter analyzes the ways Urban Bush Women develops pieces. The remaining chapters examine the choreography around central concerns—the body, the word, the world, the soul, and the community. In "The Body: Divided and Conquered," I examine how Zollar lays out the negotiation of the black female body, a highly contested site. In "The Word: Black Magic Realism," I discuss the use of narrative, mystical beings, ancestors, and supernatural plots to create scenarios for conquering hardship. "The World: Shelter from the Heat" concerns pieces in which women must deal with contemporary social problems. I detail how these pieces outline real survival strategies and argue that the performances provide a rehearsal for reality. In "The Soul: The Spirit Moves," I look at pieces that interrogate spirituality as a tool for strength and solidarity. In "The Community: In Theory and Practice," I look at Urban Bush Women's activities in support of community empowerment. It is in these settings that the company most directly translates the choreographic aesthetic into actual problem solving. I end the book with a short coda in which I examine Urban Bush Women's twentieth-anniversary season.

Acknowledgments

I owe thanks to many people and institutions for their support. Without this strong community this book could not have been written. Yale University provided much needed time and financial support in the early stages of my research by awarding me a Morse grant. The University of California, San Diego, also provided research grant money and course relief. Thank you to Seth Lerer and the UCSD Division of Arts and Humanities for additional grant support. I have found homes in several professional organizations: the Society of Dance History Scholars, the American Society for Theatre Research, the Black Performance Theory Research Group, the Association for Theatre in Higher Education, the Black Theatre Association, Performance Studies International, and the Congress on Research in Dance. I credit these groups with helping to influence my development as a scholar. Thanks also to the many librarians (especially Robert Melton and the librarians at the New York Public Library for the Performing Arts) who have graciously honored my every research request.

I am indebted to many colleagues, particularly Ann Cooper Albright, who read countless drafts and generously devoted much time and energy to helping me shape the final project. I am grateful for a large company of brilliant minds and supportive energy, including Joseph Roach, Thomas DeFrantz, Susan Manning, Una Chaudhuri, Robert Vorlicky, LeAnn Fields, Sandra Richards, E. Patrick Johnson, Deborah Paredez, Margaret Werry, Anthea Kraut, Shannon Steen, Catherine Cole, Patrick Anderson, Rebecca Schneider, Jorge Huerta, Caroline Jackson Smith, Soyica Colbert, Hazel Carby, James V. Hatch, Elizabeth Alexander, Anita Gonzalez, and Harry Elam. Thank you to all of my colleagues at Yale and UCSD. My students (undergraduate and graduate) are a constant source of academic inspiration.

Thanks to everyone at the University of Wisconsin Press, especially Raphael Kadushin, Nicole Kvale, Sheila Moermond, Carla Aspelmeier, Anna

Catherine Gollmer, Sheila Leary, Katie Malchow, and Rebecca Pioreck. Thank you to Bette Marshall, Jane Hoffer, Mike Van Sleen, and Cylla von Tiedemann for allowing me to reproduce your stunning images. Thank you to Naomi Linzer for the indexing. And thank you to Aimee Zygmonski and Melissa Wolff for research assistance.

My husband, Cebra, has made the work-home balance not only possible but also enjoyable. Words can't express how much I owe him. He has helped in every aspect of writing this book, and I would not be who or where I am without his love and support. My children (Gideon, Maya, and Zora) give me measureless joy. Seeing them "work" on my computer and explore in their creativity reminds me of why I do what I do. I look forward to a lifetime of watching them grow. My aunt Ruby Rowe is my anchor, connecting me to family, my past, and my future. Thank you for all of your sacrifices, your goodness, your prayers, and especially your stories. Everything I have ever done and will ever do is in honor of my mother, Lorna George. I hope to live up to everything she wanted for me.

Last but certainly not least, thank you to Jawole Willa Jo Zollar for being an inspired artist and an inspiration to so many artists and scholars. Thank you for welcoming me into the community and for supporting the project by granting me interviews and opening up your rehearsals, workshops, and archives. Thanks also to all Urban Bush Women dancers (past and present) and all the collaborators, administrators, staff, interns, and volunteers for the formal interviews and informal chats. In particular, Amy Cassello, former managing director, enthusiastically helped with my research. Vanessa Manley, former special project manager, and Christine King, former dancer and current production coordinator/associate artistic director, were also generous with their time. From the moment I saw my first Urban Bush Women piece, *Shelter*, I knew I wanted to learn more about the energy that went into making such a profound work. The more I studied the company, the more I became convinced that more people in the world needed to know about the important work happening both on the Urban Bush Women concert dance stage and in the community projects.

Urban Bush Women

An iconic Urban Bush Women image. Photo by Dona Ann McAdams.

Introduction

Working Dance

I chose the title *Urban Bush Women: Twenty Years of African American Dance Theater, Community Engagement, and Working It Out* because Urban Bush Women, one of the most important contemporary dance/theater companies, "works" on many levels, and my project here is to analyze and contextualize these different levels. "Working" became the major motif as I was writing this book. First, I am interested in the ways the company's founder and artistic director, Jawole Willa Jo Zollar, works on (i.e., develops) choreography. Second, I want to analyze what "works" choreographically in her aesthetic and why. Finally, and most importantly, I am interested in how she works *through* choreography, uses dance to dialogue with society, and "works" an audience. Critics and scholars of Urban Bush Women generally argue that the company's repertoire is politically activist and resistive. This is certainly true, but I believe the work is much more complex. Urban Bush Women forces us to view/read/understand dance differently by using dance as a mechanism to work through important issues. In Urban Bush Women's repertoire there exists a physical rhetoric or corporeal argumentation that attempts to activate audiences to attend to the complexities of daily life in terms of race, gender, spirituality, social relations, political power, aesthetics, and community life when we are often reluctant to do so. The strategies by which Zollar opens up these dialogues I term "working." Urban Bush Women's choreography is emblematic of how individuals and communities work though social anxieties using layers of performance. In other words, Urban Bush Women is changing what it means to watch certain bodies perform. Performing artists can speak politically or socially and culturally in a way that no others can.

Black female herbalist healers are also called root workers because they take what nature provides and work it into healing substances. I argue that dance, particularly the work of Urban Bush Women, has a metaphorically similar impact. When we talk about healing, we talk in terms of the body—illness, health, scars, fitness, et cetera. We also talk in terms of the soul—spiritual and emotional wellbeing. Likewise, the dances of Urban Bush Women attend to the bodies and souls of individuals and communities. Healing happens when one works the roots, works the body, works the soul, works the tangles out. Perhaps this is too intangible a prospect for an academic investigation. Nevertheless, I detail how the Urban Bush Women's choreography is political, unapologetic, provocative, and ultimately healing.

"Working" is also central to the way Zollar conceives choreography. In the autobiographical and improvisational piece *Working for Free*, Zollar uses choreography to explain her methods for working a movement. Zollar uses the spirits of music, mood, and rhythm to work through movement, which she ultimately shapes into choreography that works on audiences. For example, in the first section of the piece, "The Spirit of Music," Zollar begins by walking around the space. She states "I feel the spirit of music move me. . . . I gotta move" and begins walking around in circles, creating sinuous shapes. Though there is no music playing, she moves to the music inside of her, experimenting with movement. The audience sees her thinking through movement, using the spirit of the music in her head to inspire her. She tests various combinations and then goes back to simply walking in a circle. Unafraid to show an audience a stage in her work in which she has nothing but a tune in her head, Zollar urges attention to the impetus, the first steps that lead to the journey. Similarly, in the second section, "The Spirit of a Mood," Zollar uses emotions as the impetus to guide her discovery of movement. She says: "Sometimes I'm moving and feel a mood come down on me. . . . When the spirit of a mood comes down, you just gotta ride it out." She poses with one hand on her hip and the other over her head and face. She looks to the side and walks around, anxiously wringing her hands. Her energy heats up as she flails her arms, confronting an unseen force. She says, "Forget you!" as she stops, with her arms akimbo, staring down her enemy. She switches and begins exploring a seductive mood but cuts it off abruptly, saying that she can't get too far into that one. By taking an emotional exploration to the edge and a bit beyond, Zollar exposes a vulnerability avoided by many contemporary choreographers and highlights it as an essential ingredient in working choreography.

Finally, in "The Spirit of Rhythm," she talks about the uncontrollable feeling one has when a rhythm grabs hold. One cannot help but move. She vocalizes "ah"s as she plays with rhythm by snapping and bouncing up and down. She says "Some brothers got the omni-directional rhythm" and begins moving in a slick strut. Further experimenting with the embodiment of gender, she claims "Men from St. Louis got a special kind of cool" and shifts her rhythm accordingly. She goes on to explain and work the rhythms of Kansas City, St. Louis, and New York. Here Zollar argues that, as opposed to psychological realism methods, a corporeal-focused technique can also get at character. It is from the body that she finds these different types of men.

After singing and dancing to a P-Funk song, like she is in her living room rather than on a concert dance stage, she reveals a bit of herself and explains that funk makes her think of childhood memories and the stories her grandfather told her. This revelation of personal memories in the form of verbal storytelling is central to the work. It is another way to connect to the audience that resists distance and detachment. It requires investment not only in the movement but also in the emotions. Zollar often works out of her childhood memories and finds ways to validate what others might not recognize as valuable, like childhood ways of moving and the profundity in "simple" reasoning (right and wrong and the ways we should treat one another). These moral lessons might be passed down through the generations, and this traditional history becomes both oral and physical epistemology for Zollar. She acknowledges that there are bodily ways of knowing, with sense memories that speak to truth, inspire, and influence.

Later in the piece, she talks about how Joseph Stevenson Jr. introduced her to improvisation. He explained that to improvise one must take one movement and *work it*—explore it from all angles, try it out in different positions, get a sense of what succeeds choreographically. Zollar's favorite movement, she tells us, was the shake. As children, she and her sister developed a shake routine in which they would "get up underneath the movement and work it!" From this autobiographical tidbit, Zollar builds the foundation for an aesthetic that uses dance theater to engage communities. Like working a movement, Zollar challenges individuals and communities to take an issue, get up underneath it, and work it. This is an avenue by which her performers find the motivation behind the steps. It is also present in her community engagement work, where Zollar has non-professional performers take an issue and process it physically as well as intellectually.

Music, emotions, and rhythm—the basic building blocks through which Zollar works through the initial impulses of choreography—are not unique to contemporary choreography. Certainly other choreographers begin here, rather than, say, with geometry. Zollar's particular intervention comes from the ways she combines this impulse with movement genre, collaboration, and content. This juxtaposition creates an aesthetic that pushes dance past a cool disinterest and unabashedly into social discourse.

Audience members are asked to work during Urban Bush Women performances. We are then asked to take the material or information from the shows

Urban Bush Women publicity photo. Photo by Cylla Von Tiedemann.

and work on our environments and ourselves. In the following pages I argue that this functions choreographically through a number of "unsettling" rhetorical arguments. Specifically, the company unsettles notions of blackness in terms of the body, storytelling traditions, oppression, spirituality, and communities in order to encourage its audiences to effect social change.

Through a postmodern blending of styles and juxtaposition of choreography, music, text, history, culture, and spirituality, the members of the company challenge their audiences to reimagine society and renounce old definitions of black dance, and indeed, black identity. As Brenda Dixon Gottschild observes, Zollar and others like her "preserve Africanisms in their particularly postmodern styles."[1] By attending to Diaspora traditions that are complex, blended, ambiguous, and constantly shifting, they challenge notions of fixed racial identity. In that challenge, they then indicate alternate modalities.

This resistance to fixity and embrace of flux in terms of identity politics is echoed in her eclectic choreographic influences. Zollar fuses classical, modern, postmodern, African, European, and Eastern movement traditions. Because she is not tied to a particular tradition and moves freely through several, she resists pigeonholing her dances, pushes boundaries of accessibility, and creates a dynamic in which traditions not only coexist but lean on and comment on each other—all while creating an Urban Bush Woman style. This provides a recipe for working an audience and opens up dialogue. One reviewer claimed that "the lines of communication between [Urban Bush Women] and audience are so direct and clear, you blink as if seeing daylight for the first time."[2] The choreography of Urban Bush Women embodies the contradictions of memory, identity, and heritage for many demographics. Of course, nothing speaks to all constituents, and the company's in-your-face attitude puts off some people. However, what some find threatening is precisely the kind of stakes-raising necessary to create empowerment and effect change. Interestingly, Urban Bush Women is popular with both the patrons of Jacob's Pillow and the kids at the Brooklyn Y. Through her work on the concert-stage and with neighborhoods in community building projects, Zollar demonstrates a dedication to individuals and societies. These are not easy lines to navigate, and the dialogue does not always produce harmony. However, Urban Bush Women presents an important methodology for negotiating the intersections between dance theater and discourse.

1

Development

Core Values, Process, and Style

A brief word about Zollar's impetus for starting the company, a description of its early years, and an introduction to the company's core values are necessary for later analyses. Zollar began dancing when she was about six years old in Kansas City, Missouri. In the 1950s and 1960s, her neighborhood in Kansas City was completely segregated. "We children thought the city was all black because that was our world. The schools were all black; the teachers were all black. I didn't realize we were confined to certain boundaries. So my cultural world and the models in it were all black."[1]

A pivotal exception to this all-black experience came when her mother took her and her sister to the Harvard Conservatory for Music, in the white part of town, which had ballet classes. Her mother targeted this school specifically because she wanted her children to learn ballet. It had a new teacher from Russia, and Zollar's mother hoped that this foreign-born teacher (i.e., someone removed from U.S. racism) would accept black students. She was correct. There were three black children in the class.

However, ballet training didn't appeal to Zollar, so she soon switched to the neighborhood dancing school, the Joseph Stevenson School of Dance, where she learned a form of Afro-Caribbean Dunham technique. Joseph Stevenson had studied with Katharine Dunham and had also been a ballroom dancer. He taught Zollar to dance from the "inside out" and to develop her own style. The classes were conducted to drumming or jazz by musicians such as Art Blakey and Ahmed Jamal. Zollar was already familiar with these rhythms since her mother was a jazz vocalist, and the movement styles inspired by these rhythms were comfortable to her.

Stevenson also had a cabaret ensemble, in which some of the students provided the entertainment at social gatherings. These floorshows were popular in her community, and whenever a black social club was hosting an event, it hired a floorshow. In this variety-style show, Zollar, her sister, and several others would perform the children's act by improvising to live music. Other performers included a comic, a female impersonator, a stripper, an emcee, and a flash act (highly charged acrobatic tap dancing like the Nicholas Brothers). Zollar has said, "That kind of dance helped shape my aesthetic. Stripping was my first accomplished dance, and that's what I wanted to be when I grew up. Sometimes the stripper was a female impersonator and we understood that was all right, too."[2] One of the dances Zollar and the other children did was called "The Sacrifice": they were dressed all in white and performed a sacrifice dance involving a chicken and a volcano. They would get paid relatively good money, and she performed like this until she was about eighteen years old. Then she went to college at the University of Missouri, where she studied theater and dance and earned a bachelor of arts in dance. Later, she had a company in Kansas City called Black Exodus, which (along with a gospel choir called Voices of Black Exodus) combined dance, text, and live music. Through this company, Zollar deepened her commitment to black liberation and contemporaneous social movements. During this time, she also came under the influence of the writings of many 1960s artists and intellectuals, including Amiri Baraka, Larry Neal, Deborah Hay, Trisha Brown, and Steve Paxton. Influences of the civil rights movement, the Black Power movement, the Black Arts movement, and second-wave feminism began to permeate her choreography. Even in these early years, the elements of movement vocabularies that would contribute to defining the Urban Bush Women style, particularly the combination of "high" and "low" and "black" and "white" art forms as well as the commitment to social consciousness, began to surface.

Zollar went on to earn a master of fine arts degree in dance from Florida State University, where she now teaches when she is not choreographing. In graduate school, she was involved in many communities that influenced her work, including women's support groups, the Black Theater Guild, the dance department, and the local Yoruba community. She also read Antonin Artaud and decided that she wanted dance theater to have an impact. She studied the work of Peter Brook as well as that of the Free Southern Theater. She studied Haitian, Cuban Brazilian, Congolese, and "what we thought was African" dance. Of those, she studied Haitian the most deeply. She studied with an Algerian company for a while and was influenced by Nontsizi Cayou, a Bay Area choreographer, and her company, Wajumbe Cultural Ensemble. During this period she deepened her desire to combine African dance forms and more Westernized contemporary dance expressions.[3]

In 1980 she moved to New York and studied with Dianne McIntyre at Sounds in Motion. There, Zollar worked extensively with live music and was

Jawole Willa Jo Zollar. Photo by Dona Ann McAdams.

introduced to jazz improvisational aesthetics in modern dance. Of the experience, she has said: "I knew I wasn't going to be an Ailey dancer. I didn't have the feet or the legs. So I had to find some other way to live in this love of dance. And when I saw Dianne's company, I thought, 'Ah, it's possible.'"[4] Zollar has carried this philosophy over to her own company in the embrace of strong dancers with different body types. Many dancers in her company have expressed similar awakenings to the constructed physical limitations of professional dance aesthetics.

Also in these early years, she saw Blondell Cummings's work and experienced the possibilities of using personal narrative in choreography.[5] From Kei Takei, a Japanese dance experimentalist, Zollar was given affirmation to incorporate her own culture and developed an appreciation of the importance of moving naturally. She says, "Some people are natural dancers, but many good dancers have to be trained to find that natural movement impulse because it has basically been 'trained' out of them."[6]

In 1984 she and six other dancers (Terri Cousar, Anita Gonzalez, Christine Jones, Viola Sheely, Robin Wilson, and Marlies Yearby) formed a company and called themselves Urban Bush Women. The name of the company suggests African women warriors, savvy city street women, untamed growth, as well as the female anatomy. It also implies a reexamination of the colonial "subject." Whatever the interpretation, the attitude is provocative. The name is so threatening to some that a number of promoters and venues have objected to booking the company because of marketing difficulties.[7] The name reflects how the company members think of themselves as a group. It recognizes the parts of them that are African, American urban, and Black-Southern rural. Also influential in her choice of names was one of Zollar's favorite albums in college, *Harlem Bush Music*, by Gary Bartz. This is a rearticulation of 1960s liberation attitude, negritude, and Afrocentrism read through dance. Also, in 1981, the jazz group Art Ensemble of Chicago put out the album *Urban Bushmen*, an album that emphasized ritual, range, and improvisation—all hallmarks of Urban Bush Women's style.

Zollar also chose her own first name, Jawole, which means (she found out after making the change) "she enters the house." She found the name in a book of African names. Instead of entirely renouncing her given name (Willa Jo), Zollar retained it, along with her last name, and added her African name. Many African Americans who came of age during the 1960s chose African names in order to self-identify with their African heritage (examples of other artists include Amiri Baraka and Ntozake Shange). Though this philosophy is born out of a particular moment in the late 1960s and early 1970s, an emphasis on self-determinacy as an avenue to strength is still central to the work of the choreography.

Core Values

From the beginning, Zollar wanted a company that challenged contemporaneous notions of dance and social politics, particularly in terms of African American identity. She wanted to create dances that showed how African Americans perform themselves "when not in the presence of whites."[8] The first members of the company were black women over the age of thirty. Zollar considered this "the prime performing time in terms of the physical kind of performing nuance. . . . As a dancer, maybe you can't do what you did when you were twenty . . . but what you can do is extremely powerful—if you use it for what it is."[9] More recently, however, the company has been made up of a combination of older and younger performers.

The company performed its first concert in July 1984 in New York City. The cognoscenti told Zollar that she was foolish to mount a concert in July because everyone would be in the Hamptons. Zollar thought "Nobody in *my* neighborhood was in the Hamptons" and scheduled the concert.[10] This off-season arrangement proved advantageous. Hers was the only dance concert that weekend, and Jennifer Dunning, dance critic for the *New York Times*, came and reviewed the work favorably: "It isn't often that a loft dance performance brings an audience spontaneously to its feet in a standing ovation, then sends that audience out singing. But Urban Bush Women did just that."[11] After the rave review, more and more people came to Urban Bush Women shows and the company quickly developed a reputation.

When I asked Zollar what her best experiences were, she spoke of the early days of touring: "We were just wild and having fun. But we were also damn poor and when we got per diem we were living like queens. We were existing on two or three dollars a day. You'd go to Kiev and you'd get the dollar bowl of mushroom barley soup and the challah bread and you'd fill up off that. After each gig we were going out and hanging out and going to the club and going partying and dancing. Those were really fun days." Also on the early years of the company, Zollar says, "I think you would say it was a combination of a lot of things. There was a lot of dedication in the company members . . . 'cause nobody was getting paid then. They were just doing it from a belief in the vision."[12]

The experiences of the first company members influenced the focus of the work in many ways, particularly the female-identified nature of the company. Women of color, mostly black women, have historically made up the core of the company. Initially, Zollar did not intend for the company to be composed solely of women and many men have performed with Urban Bush Women.[13] Zollar has said that the female makeup is "by default, almost."[14] Because male dancers are rarer than female dancers, they are in high demand. Men would come in to the company, do a project, and then leave for more lucrative and prestigious opportunities; Zollar found that the women were much more committed to the ensemble. They became the heart. Female energy led to the development of some pieces, like "Girlfriends," that would have taken on a much different tone if there were men in the core. However, Zollar says that she loves male energy (especially competitiveness, bravado, and machismo) and likes to work with men, but she takes pride in the fact that a female energy is at the center of the company's work.[15]

Gender and race are crucial defining categories and critical lenses through which to view this work. The negotiation of Urban Bush Women's repertory with the different interpretations of feminism is complex, and different value judgments are attached to the different labels. Some label the work feminist, some womanist, some resist the exclusionary and combative histories of white feminism and black feminism, and others claim it is not feminist enough. The perception of the company as feminist depends upon which ideology one holds within these shifting matrices. Nevertheless, the tools of these theoretical models are valuable in analyzing the work, and I find womanism the most helpful, because a major tenet of womanism is the recognition and celebration of the strength of women of color that is not at the expense of men or white women. Womanism is a concept that appeals to many women of color as a refinement of white feminism and black feminism that rejects their problematic histories. Alice Walker introduced the term in the early 1980s, and it has experienced varying degrees of influence in critical discourse since then. Urban Bush Women's work is rooted in this philosophy that is "committed to survival and wholeness of entire people."[16] I would push these ideas further and argue that not only is Urban Bush Women's work a significant model of womanism, but it also challenges us to redefine all of the terms of gender-based ideologies and their relationship to the performing arts.

Zollar herself tends to resist labels but she readily acknowledges that as she creates works reflecting her concerns, she touches on many feminist/womanist issues (especially the struggle for gender equity). As a child she recognized gender-based double standards, and in college she helped form a black women's support group. When I asked her if she thought her work was feminist, her answer echoed Walker: "Yes, because that's me. Now I don't know what that means to some people, and I'm not sure what I think about that. I'm not sure that I separate feminist from human, or that the fact that I'm concerned about what's happening to black men is outside of feminist thought."[17] So, although Zollar did not necessarily set out to create a black feminist company, black women's issues and the legacy left by black foremothers are part and parcel of her company's work. The healing work of the choreography has a political agenda (with all of the implications of the loaded term)—sometimes implicit, sometimes explicit—and this work is undeniably racialized and gendered as it resists oppressive hegemonic structures. The part of Walker's definition most salient to this study is the modeling of "whole" people surviving in a troubled world. Affirming women of color also affirms the larger project of global, intercultural progress.

Zollar's interest in gender is also a part of her larger connection to heritage. She has said: "Whether it's the ancestral memory or not, I certainly believe there is something about spirit and memory on an ancestral level. It's very powerful. Why does break-dancing look like some of the forms of dancing in

Africa when the kids didn't know anything about that?"[18] She has also said: "I very much believe that there is some type of memory, whether it's gender or racial. There is some type of memory that we tap into. I don't think it's only black people that tap into a black memory. I don't think it's only white people that tap into a white memory. I don't think it's only women that tap into women's memory. I think that they're there, those memories are there."[19]

In his seminal text *Cities of the Dead: Circum-Atlantic Performance*, Joseph Roach investigates the tenets of memory for peoples along the Atlantic rim. These people invent themselves "by performing their pasts in the presence of others. They could not perform themselves, however, unless they also performed what and who they thought they were not."[20] Similarly, Urban Bush Women pieces are mechanisms for tapping into the past, into this memory, to create a future. I do not believe we will discover a genetic marker for break-dancing. Rather, ancestral memory is a performance, a will to remember across generations and oceans. Heritage moves though overt interactions as well as in encounters not recognized as moments of memory-transference. Access to memory along racial lines is one of the most important debates in critical race theory. Zollar complicates this debate through her choices in style and content that vex notions of ownership and authority. The past pushes the future and gives fodder to a progressive aesthetics that simultaneously accesses and constructs memory. These memories (even the ones particular to black female experiences) are global, implicating and challenging all.

At the heart of the core values of the company is the validation of individuals. This operates on numerous levels—experiences, perspectives, relationships, et cetera—forming an epistemic base. Significantly, there is a corporeal foundation for this individualism. It is rooted in the body. This is crucial for the dancers as well as the audience. According to Zollar,

> The individual experience, background, history, who you are, working from an authentic place of your individuality is very important. The technique work, it's going to mean that you're inside your body having your experience and it has nothing to do with the person's body next to you. You can learn from it, but you each have something to offer in terms of dance. You know, maybe somebody's legs will be really high. Then you have somebody . . . like Nora [a company member]; Nora doesn't have high legs . . . but there's a beauty because she's so grounded in her own sense of herself, and that's what makes her powerful. That's one of the core values. Celebrating culture after the Diaspora, which means validating body types or just the way we use rhythm, and the use of the body. In jazz dance, when you do the pelvic thrust and the rib cage, it's more about selling something. This is not about selling. This is about just expressing.[21]

Stemming from her experiences dancing with a body type not considered ideal for concert dance, Zollar has worked with many different body types.[22] As Brenda Dixon Gottschild explains, "There is an exhilarating democracy in the UBW collective dancing body. Short, tall, slim, stocky, light-skinned, dark-skinned, new and mature dancers are represented at any given time in the company roster."[23] According to Zollar, "In some ways, interestingly enough, in the early years we caused all kinds of mischief, but we didn't fit into any place. Robin Wilson had this really idiosyncratic movement style, and she was a large woman, and . . . we didn't fit into the mold. I didn't realize that that would later really become part of the identity."[24]

Company member Christal Brown echoes this sentiment: "I work with what I got. . . . I can't put my knee in my ear, I don't have a developé to die for. . . . I got something else."[25] Maria Bauman, another company member, also speaks to this as she recounts her first experiences with the company in a workshop when she was in high school. Instead of focusing on typical ballet technique, which she had associated with professional dance, Urban Bush Women paid attention to a different type of strength that she could more readily access. "I still remember . . . it was just fierce. It was really athletic. And I think that's what spoke to me the most, because starting dance 'late' I think I was really trying to make my body fit into this mold of what I thought dancing was. I was looking around me and the girls that I saw [were] the ballerinas, which I really respected and that is something that I value in dance. But when [Urban Bush Women] came it was just really affirming. It's something I can sink my teeth into."[26]

This attitude about the body and individuality translates directly into the choreography and the message the dances convey to the audiences. Also, a philosophy about the way individuals connect with other individuals is affirmed in the dancer's working relationship as well as in the content of the choreography. There is a mutual respect of that individuality that is demanded among participants in order for the choreography to succeed. Dancers readily lean on each other and support each other's weight. They often form semicircles and, together with the audience completing the circle, provide a ring of support for a soloist. The individual is affirmed by the group and becomes a part of a community.

Zollar refers to her aesthetic that "is not about selling." This is an important claim for this provocative aesthetic. It is too easy to simply embrace the obvious freedom of loose hips. It is dangerous to watch the looseness of the Urban Bush Women dancer's hips decontextualized. Though the choreography resists a purely sexualized reading, Zollar's need to verbally articulate the distinction between selling and expressing bespeaks a culture still fraught with representations of oversexualized women of color. In the Urban Bush Women style, body

Urban Bush Women in *Bitter Tongue*. Photo by Cylla Von Tiedemann.

affirmation of the individual is often read in the raised chin, the forward solar plexus, and the free hips, as well as the movement quality and energy. In many master classes, Zollar helps dancers locate the difference. In that difference also lies technique. Novices tend to go to "selling" when instructed to thrust the pelvis or isolate the rib cage or shoulders. Much richer and more vulnerable is a movement born out of accessing experience, even if that experience is sexualized. This accessing, as well as the narrativized content of many of the pieces, pushes the aesthetic to dance theater. As it relates to the core values of the company, however, Zollar utilizes the combination of dance and theater to create performers armed to use performance to build up individuals and communities.

Rehearsal Process

A dancer's individual talents and strengths are not the sole qualification for an Urban Bush Women dancer. Along with training and a strong personality, the dancers must be able to work collaboratively. The company functions as an ensemble, though Zollar makes the final decisions. She tries to maintain a less hierarchical milieu than other choreographers and welcomes the input and feedback of the dancers: "There's collaboration between the dancers and myself constantly. I'll throw out an idea, we'll improvise on it, we'll talk about it. Somebody will bring in some information they know.[27] Empowerment becomes part and parcel of the process as well as the product: "I want to build a company on participation [not] victimization."[28] Choreographic solutions are achieved through processes similar to those advocated in the group's community work. By respecting individual contributions, the company endeavors to create a working atmosphere similar to a larger vision of community engagement.

Bauman explains how this works in rehearsal: "It's no accident that all the dancers have something else that they do outside of dance: capoeira, yoga, Pilates. And they all come from different socioeconomic, religious, geographic locations."[29] If a dancer actually choreographs a piece (as they sometimes do in Urban Bush Women's community work), then Zollar makes sure to credit that dancer in the program. Zollar encourages the dancers to draw from their personal histories and experiences and bring these stories and feelings out in a way in which they can be shared with others. She also tries to keep the focus of her rehearsals and classes on process over product. She explains: "Everything is the journey. Now, that doesn't mean that you don't have a goal for your product, but the journey is where you find out all your information. . . . I think that's one of the harder things when a dancer's training has been something more like Horton. Horton [technique] is what I call 'You're here, you're there.'"[30]

Many of the dancers I interviewed testified to the supportive, encouraging nature of the company and the strength that provides to each dancer as an artist. Of course in any collaborative situation there are going to be tensions between Zollar and the dancers or among the dancers themselves. Dancers bicker about casting choices, favoritism, touring conditions. For the most part, however, those I consulted emphasized the value of working in the company of other strong-willed women of color and the emphasis of support within the working relationship. This attitude is a metaphor for the broader work of the company.

Zollar gives her audience a glimpse into the Urban Bush Women creative process in the meta-theatrical autobiographical piece *Self-Portrait*, which is quite open and self-reflexive about the creative process and identity. In the opening, she and her codirector, Steve Kent, talk through their process, assessing the dancers' embracing of the work. They also discuss the more challenging material and the significance of the piece for Urban Bush Women and their larger mission. It is noteworthy that the piece begins with a reflection on the meaning behind the work and on its meta-performative significance rather than a preoccupation with technique or execution. In other words, in terms of content and context, very little is "thrown away" or left unexamined.

The lights come up on the dancers scattered throughout the stage, warming up and practicing. Each dancer, in her own space, does wide swings with her arms and legs to loosen her limbs in their sockets and find under-curves, contractions, extension and alignment. Some stretch. Some do floor-barre work. Some practice steps from the dance. Some do vocal warm-ups. This is a moment of individuality as the dancers get centered and prepared to give to the group. Zollar enters the space and introduces the work. She reads from what seem to be her rehearsal notes, which sound like a thought poem: "Section one—a portrait. Three letters. A dance to do. Spoken. Figure one. Untitled soul transition. Self-portrait. As critical paradigm within this un-mirrored vacuum called 'earth,' called 'society,' called 'community,' called 'the bush.' Mixing flesh colors with earth tones, women compose languid librettos."[31] Like a euphemism in reverse, "the bush" comes to represent the space gone too long without self-reflection. This piece is a portrait of Zollar's process as well as of a community including Zollar, Kent, and the dancers. Like the women in Shange's play *For Colored Girls Who Have Considered Suicide/When the Rainbow Is Enuf*, women of many stripes and sizes come together to push against old orders. They are at once individuals and representative of larger segments. "Languid" is a provocative adjective to describe the resulting artwork; meaning both "unenergetic" and "graceful," it suggests both the slow-moving pace of progress and the patience needed to effect change. Librettos, the stuff of the traditionally white, western, high-brow art forms like opera, rest uneasy with these women. The piece asks: How do we work within and without "traditions"?

By this time in her speech, the dancers have come together. Still sitting on the floor, they lean into each other like girlfriends listening to stories. Zollar then instructs one of the dancers, Christine, to lead the company in the "Satisfied" warm-up song. All the dancers jump up and begin to sing:

> Early in the morning—satisfied!
> Early in the morning—satisfied!

Not until after the company members have warmed up vocally to an inspirational song and reached a place of understanding intellectually and emotionally do they begin to dance. Zollar has the company move in intricate combinations across the floor to a quick $\frac{4}{4}$ drumbeat. She continues to share her reflections on the work: "Just transcendental dreams, looking for lessons in combat and meditation. Dance as normalization process." Opposite ends of the spectrum, combat and meditation find equal places within her process. These are both strategies for resisting oppression. Through dance, through the body, they will work to create new models.

Then Zollar asks another dancer, Carolina, to work with the rhythm. She agrees but first requests to do sun salutations. Zollar is enthusiastic about the idea, and the company moves through several yoga positions to come to a more centered place before launching in again. While they move, Zollar continues to speak: "Self-healing women. Women squeezing strong-backed bodies, made for evangelism and warfare—into gentle arabesques. Unregulated hips and thighs. Voices long-groomed to sing beautifully off-key. Constrained to fit fragile arias. You breathe with them, you stretch with them, you close your eyes with them. You breathe with them, you stretch with them, you close your eyes with them." The contradictory images of women of color and beauty ideals are negotiated. These are the women who, though not the dominant image of desirability, inspire Zollar. Working through dance, Zollar reconsiders the "strong black woman" read against conventional standards in dance as well as life. It is a struggle familiar to women bombarded with mixed messages about how to conduct oneself on and off stage. Zollar moves the piece into an understanding that out of these contradictions could come empowerment. Carolina then leads the dancers in vocalizing different rhythmic patterns using a "ga" sound. Once they have the rhythm, she asks them to put it in their bodies and move with the sounds. The text continues:

> ZOLLAR: They never excuse themselves from your eye!

All of the dancers run forward to the lip of the stage.

> ZOLLAR: These dancing women!
> DANCERS: Dancing women coming to town!
> ZOLLAR: These grandiloquent girls!
> DANCERS: Women!
> ZOLLAR: Women! In workshops. Inventing sestinas. Sestinas!
> ALL: Women. Women in the bush!

She then asks the women to hold the fierce pose they have created on the last line. This, she tells them, is their character portrait for the "Alleyway Women" sequence. Working from the body, she helps the performers find the emotional energy to put forward. Running to the edge of the stage, albeit under the metatheatrical performance, the dancers pose a confrontation. Freezing in a severe pose is at once a performance, a rehearsal for performance, and a rehearsal for life. The gestures live in a physical vocabulary known in American culture, coded with attitude. Coupled with loud feminist affirmations, the bodies put forth the strong woman image that has come to symbolize Urban Bush Women.

The dancers next practice a fast-moving capoeira sequence while maintaining the discovered attitude. They then shake off the tension and let go of the rage. Zollar has them soften the energy. They move on again to practice a section titled "Moanin', Wailin', Sanctifying Women." They stand in a line and moan together in harmony, building in intensity as Zollar coaches them to open the backs of their throats and find a weighted breath. They each find ways to express their anger and pain. Zollar freezes them again because she thinks they have found the perfect "sassy" character portrait for the "loquacious Harlem women" sequence. This time, like Stanislavskian actors, the performers are expected to affect and recall emotional responses. They must move through emotional shifts in order to execute choreography. Though some may rely on the "magic if" that allows a method performer to ostensibly create any role, most are required to recall and build upon personal experiences. Zollar's exercises are meant to bring certain aspects of the performer's personalities to the fore. Unlike many other choreographers, Zollar asks her dancers to bring their total selves (i.e., not just their bodies) to the process.

They next rehearse the loquacious Harlem women section, moving through sequences that express inner-city "home-girl" attitude—Harlem and East Harlem. Zollar pushes a possible stereotype using specific experiences. One dancer breaks out, sits in a wide second position, and proceeds to explain how everyone needs balance in life. The other dancers quickly stand on one foot and try to stay balanced. She tells us that we all should be thinking about the future by investing in mutual funds, 401ks, IRAs, et cetera. Zollar tells her to find something else in her voice. She and another dancer work through the speech and find different qualities and accents to express how the starving-artist lifestyle is not going to work. They continue vocalizing until another dancer breaks out and in a lightning-fast speech talks about her new boyfriend and her ambivalence about where the relationship is going. She doesn't know if he is the one because there are so many other men in the world. She gives the pros and cons about staying with this man while some of the other dancers encourage her and some dissuade her. Zollar angrily stops the action and chastises her for blowing her lines. She wants them to focus and take it again. Lest we get too caught up in the portrayals, Zollar breaks the illusion, reminding all that this is a performance. It is at once real life, rehearsal for performance, rehearsal for life and performance. The dancers get giddy and unfocused. Zollar loses her wits, rushing into the space as the dancers scatter in "fear." In her rampage, she screams about how *she* is the choreographer and nobody is listening to her or understanding her art. She launches into a hysterical solo in which she kicks and throws her hands up wildly. With one foot planted, she takes large steps with the other—pivoting around in a circle as if she were trying to move forward but kept getting thrown off course. She screams several times, stands still, takes a deep breath, and pulls herself together. The voiceover comes back in, and Kent and Zollar talk about where the dancers are, how they can personalize the material, and how she can translate the character portraits into choreographic language appropriate to the lives of these women—the essence of Urban Bush Women. While this conversation happens, the live Zollar works through choreography.

She moves back to her position on the side and calls out to the dancers that the break is over. She assembles three dancers to work on the alleyway women character portraits. One walks across the stage, wailing in torment, "Oh, damn! Why now! Why now!" Another moves as if to slit her wrists, and a third cowers in fear. Eventually the second dancer lies down, dead or exhausted. The first keeps keening while Zollar coldly asks her to move to different parts of the stage so that she can see how it looks. The result is comical, and the dancer Amara finally breaks out of character to tell Zollar that it is extremely difficult to maintain such an intense emotional state while she is experimenting with blocking. Unsympathetic, Zollar tells her that that is what needs to happen. Amara takes her anger at Zollar and channels it into the character, who suddenly shifts from helpless to irritated. She paces back and forth in a huff, expressing her disgust at being so mistreated. "Oh, damn! Why now! Why now!" Zollar likes what is happening, despite the fact that the anger is largely directed at her. In the move from victimhood to anger, an activated agent occurs when the dancer is asked to shift physical position. Staying in one place breeds repetitive, stagnant suffering. When she has to deal with Zollar's requests to move physically, the dancer moves emotionally to a more empowered place.

It is not the case that grief and suffering have no place in Urban Bush Women's work. Without this side of the coin, the dangerous stereotype that women of color are superwoman, able to miraculously withstand all adversity, is perpetuated. An important motif for the company, though, is that during times of suffering, women can and should look to each other for support. For example, at this point, Amara breaks down again, falls to her knees, and begins to sob and hum softly. Zollar recites "Alleyway Women" while the other dancers enter the stage and try to comfort the three, helping them to stand up. They all chime in "Alleyway women" while Zollar recites her poem about the power of dance to transform. The dancers mill about in different characters, chanting, "On the street, alleyway, on the street, on the roof." In the final moments, a dancer screams out "Jinga!" and the dancers execute the capoeira they rehearsed earlier. With a final shout of "Women!" they all freeze in squats, hands in fists, ready to do battle. Zollar freezes them one last time, tells them that this is the final moment, and instructs them to take a bow.

I describe this piece at length to illustrate part of the Urban Bush Women process and to begin to consider the larger implications. Zollar works both alone and in collaboration. She takes the dancers through physical and emotional exercises. She utilizes several motivational techniques, from inspiring words to anger. She asks them to commit personally and emotionally. The blending of process and product echo the Boalian rehearsal for real life that is part and parcel of the choreography. As Alison Lee Bory states, "*Self-Portrait* suggests that identity, in every articulation and construction, is always in process."[32] The individuals find solidarity in the group—they find themselves by working with and against each other. Eventually, they come to a vocabulary of strong movement, read strong senses of self. The piece is about how an Urban Bush Woman is created, onstage and off, and who controls the image and the implications of that negotiation. One of the last lines of the piece is "Get used to being outrageous!" It may be seen as a mantra for the work of the company in process, product, and result.

The Style

I asked Zollar and several dancers for adjectives to describe the style of the choreography. Some of their responses were: "strong," "relevant," "attainable," "athletic," "infused with popular culture," "dangerous," "grounded," "soulful," "thought-provoking," "authentic," "liberating," "native," "unapologetic," "powerful," "strong," "inspiring," "comforting," "challenging," "trusting," "empowering," and "healthy."

The movement quality of Zollar's choreography is based first in her own body type and style, and many of these elicited words describe the way Zollar herself moves. Speed was an early defining characteristic of the movement that came easily to Zollar. Her small, muscular frame allowed her to move in ways different from typical modern aesthetics. An interest in speed led her to other discoveries about movement. She states: "What I like about a certain kind of speed is that the dancer also has to let go of formal training because you can't hold onto it once you get to a certain kind of athletic speed."[33]

Even though sometimes required to let go of formal training, Urban Bush Women dancers are well trained in West African dance, ballet, modern, capoeira, Feldenkrais, yoga, qigong, acting, and vocalization. Zollar eclectically combines these styles to produce her aesthetic. This repertory serves as another social metaphor: by integrating seemingly disparate techniques, Urban Bush Women's choreography moves them all in interesting new directions. They work together, and the whole is more than the sum of its parts. For example, Zollar's dancers might commingle ballet and modern with Brazilian capoeira

Urban Bush Women publicity photo. Photo by Cylla Von Tiedemann.

and West African koo koo in a single piece. Zollar says of her methods for working with different styles: "I think that . . . if you don't fragment yourself, if you don't fragment your knowledge, then it can be seamless."[34]

In rehearsal she also freely borrows from different traditions. For example, she uses counts and ballet terminology but usually rejects extension, the pointe shoe, and turnout. Her adagios are contrasted with quick percussive African movements, especially ones that use legs that kick out and jut in quickly and feet that pound into the ground in a "down and down and up and up" motion. Some of Zollar's movement style may be described as having balletic energy, in the sense that it is lyrical and airy and the body is held and suspended. The dancers seem ethereal and otherworldly. Her movement style may also be described as having African energy in the sense that the movement is weighty, grounded, and heavy. The energy goes down into the earth so the dancer may build from that secure foundation to leap up, spin fast, and toss limbs through the air with seeming abandon but precise control. A third way of moving is rooted in release work, based in Eastern styles of moving and martial arts that emphasize naturalness, breath, release technique, managed collapses, and visualization.

The marriage of these traditions does not expose their contradictions but rather highlights ways they complement each other. Urban Bush Women dancers are as comfortable pointing (ballet) as they are flexing (modern and Eastern) or relaxing their feet (African and Eastern). The movement is alternately angular and curvaceous, controlled and flyaway, cool and passionate, extended and contracted, patient and quick, airy and grounded, tight and loose. The choreography also blends formal dance (African, ballet, modern, et cetera) with relaxed, "everyday" movements (e.g., pedestrian actions, club dancing, and social dance). Zollar also sees dance in places not usually associated with it and draws materials from these alternate sites. For example, in her introduction to the piece *I Don't Know, but I've Been Told, if You Keep on Dancin' You Never Grow Old*, she talks about seeing dance in public schools:

> This is a piece that grew out of a conversation with some funders and policy makers in dance in Washington, D.C. They were lamenting over what they thought was the lack of dance going on in the public schools, a lack of art going on. It is a statement I strongly disagree with. I think there is a lot of dance, a lot of art going on in the public schools. But I think there's a failure on our part to recognize, honor, celebrate, and come to terms with what is going on. So this piece is dedicated to cheerleaders, majorettes, drill teams, Double Dutch jumpers, line dancers, fraternity and sorority step dancers, rappers and their fly-girls, people who dance in bars, people who dance in the street, people who keep the spirit of dance alive all over the world.

She then looks to the dancers and calls out in a low singsong, "I don't know but I been told, if you keep on dancin', you never grow old!" and the dancing begins—an abstract representation of all of the styles she mentioned, arguing that the dances or movements of everyday life are or should be the stuff of the concert dance world.

The individual personalities of the dancers are essential to the aesthetic. Many times in Zollar's choreography a soloist will perform in the center with other dancers supporting her from the side. The others allow the soloist to define her space, explore the boundaries, and break free of imposed limitations. Zollar's aesthetic can be a challenge for dancers unable to take on this individual responsibility and for those unwilling or unable to pick and choose when they display technique. She describes such moments working with dancers: "I don't want your foot pointed. I don't want your back straight. I want it to come from a different place, and they're like, 'Well, what the hell have I been training for all my life?' And then there are times when I want it. I've had dancers that really just couldn't find that duality. They couldn't find that place where both things exist." She recalls a conversation she had with the dancers from the Dayton Contemporary Dance Company: "I was telling them to let go and to just physicalize that movement of dance. [I said] 'Are you concerned that people

Joy Voeth and Francine Sheffield in a publicity photo. Photo by Cylla Von Tiedemann.

won't know that you have ballet training? They've seen you in the other piece earlier. You can let go of that.' I'm asking the dancers to go beyond [technique] and sometimes [that creates] a tension within the dancers."[35]

For some dancers, however, Urban Bush Women's style is liberating in its seeming simplicity. Christine King says, "People tell me that they like watching me on stage because I make it look like . . . it's just second nature. Not like I'm showing off a technique, because I'm there and the whole body, the face, everything is there and that's how I feel."[36]

Perhaps the first thing an audience member notices, though, is the strength of the dancers.[37] Though they all have different body types and some are more muscular than others, they all look very strong and they all move from a strong core. The choreography demands it. This just touches on the negotiations of power in the work. It is useful now to touch on strength as central to the style of the aesthetic. From the dancers' muscularity to the public's perception to the energy of the choreography, power and strength permeate the choreography.

There is a tradition (to some a stereotype) of muscular black dancers.[38] With that image comes the danger of exploiting an image with mixed messages. Zollar states, "I want the strength because I think a value in African American culture is strength."[39] Strength in the stories of African Americans' struggles has become fodder for many movements. Though not all Urban Bush Women pieces tell the same story of rise to empowerment after struggle, enough of them play into the narrative that it becomes a hallmark of the choreography. The manifestation of uplift is perhaps more valuable than more complicated messages. The works of Urban Bush Women do not exist for their own sake or as museum pieces interested in historical accuracy. Rather, they are means to ends that use aesthetic currency to galvanize audience members. The image of strong black bodies is key.

There is a connection between this power and perceptions that the company is lesbian. It has earned the nickname "Urban Butch Women." Zollar embraces the mislabel and uses it to advocate for lesbian and gay empowerment. When I asked Zollar about it, she replied:

> Well, it's several things. . . . I'm a heterosexual woman, but calling me a lesbian is not an insult. . . . Nor do I think it's something that I need to confirm [for] people. When I audition people, I do not ask them, "Do you sleep with men or women?" 'Cause that's not my business. But I did learn to, in the audition, sometimes talk to women and say, 'Urban Bush Women is women of many different sexual preferences, although we're often identified as lesbian. How do you feel about that?' Because I did have a problem when people were very homophobic. And sometimes our publicity advocates for lesbian and gay rights, so I ask [auditioners how they] feel about that. I did learn to ask people about that. It's just more of a statement about our society that a strong woman is considered butch. I've heard that all along. The funny thing, when we were hearing that, the company was all heterosexual. Every woman in the company was heterosexual. So it was so funny that that was the identity. I mean it was really funny to us. Because at that time we were flamingly heterosexual! [But] I don't care if that's what you think.[40]

They have faced homophobia on a number of occasions. For example, a New Haven, Connecticut, church group uninvited them for a project because they were "lesbian" (one company member at that time was gay). Ironically, that particular group was the most Christian of all of the company's configurations.

There is also an interesting connection between this strength and perceptions of training. Zollar told me in an interview that her dancers are often asked whether they have any training.

> Back stage we joke, no, we just jumped up out of the womb, leapt across the stage, and our feet pointed. Wow, it was a miracle! But I think what people are responding to is that there's a visceral way the dancers move that makes it look like it's being made up on the spot and it's coming out of a different kind of place. It's coming out of the place of an actor, where you're accessing the moment and you're using your resources to communicate that moment through a detailed set of decisions. And they're maybe not used to seeing that in a dancer, so the question comes out, do you all have any training?[41]

As a follow-up question, I asked Zollar if she thought part of the questioning of her dancers' training stemmed from the old stereotype and romantic myth that black people just dance naturally. She responded:

> As a black artist you always get "Do you have any training?" That's so interesting to me. One person really said this to me, he said that "you should put a white person in your group so that people can see that there's a technique behind it." Ach! And I thought, if it's a white person in my company, it's because they come to the audition, and you know, actually white, black, male, female, I don't really care. It's 'cause they can do the work. But that was so interesting to me that they said that. That in order to prove . . . because then people could see that it's a technique and it's not just natural. . . . And I've had that happen when there's been light-skinned or a white woman up there. People came up to me. They were so excited about that. Or there was a woman in the company who's biracial, and so from the stage she looked, you know, whatever that concept of white is. . . . "Oh, I'm so glad you have a white woman." But I mean, then, on the other hand, we all want validation of ourselves. When I go to see a white company, I see a black person, I'm excited . . . so we all want that validation.[42]

In addition to Zollar's style, which requires dancers to sometimes let go of training, improvise, or put their personal touch on a movement to make it appear raw and individual, the history of assumptions that people of African descent are "natural" dancers certainly plays a role here. Disguised as a compliment (and often perpetuated and marketed by people of African descent themselves), the perception has the danger of denying skill attained through hard work. I argue that even cultures that maintain dance as more of a part of everyday life than those in the United States provide more continuous training (much perhaps occurring outside of a technique class, but training nonetheless). Dangerously, labeling people of African descent as "natural" dancers implies a biological essentialism and allows for a failure of valuing physical accomplishments coming out of such traditions. Improvisation in dance, considered the stuff of social dance or specialized technique (like contact) in traditional Western dance, does not lie in the same space in West African dance and therefore has a different value judgment placed on it. In West African dance, improvisation is more ubiquitous and, therefore, to some, considered more natural. Historically, the emphasis on these "natural" techniques has served to disenfranchise dancers and cast black aesthetics with lesser value in some forums. Zollar's experiences attest to the longevity of the perception. Her movement between techniques deemed more and less "natural" serves to challenge audiences and complicate their understanding of the black female moving body. This move to complicate reception further moves the aesthetic beyond entertainment.

Breath is also very important to the style of this choreography. Certainly, by breathing together, the collection of women becomes an ensemble. But breath not only keeps the dancers connected, it also brings out tone and mood. It is often through the dancers' breathing that the full weight of the dance is conveyed to the audience. Audience members can hear the dancers breathing; when things heat up, the breaths may become grunts and then yells. It is no coincidence that the etymology of "breath" (i.e., to inspire) is linked to inspiration and spirit. Inhalation opens up the chest, diaphragm, and whole body. It allows the dancer to move and be moved (inspired) by others and go to the necessary emotional places. According to artist Riua Akinshegun, "Spirituality can't be separated from breath, let alone art."[43]

Too, the choreography often requires the dancers to maintain the "aesthetic of the cool," an African Diaspora performance trope that calls for discipline and control during even the most chaotic moments. Also a social metaphor for a way to conduct oneself during trying times, "cool" results in expressions that are in command while bodies move with abandon.[44]

Zollar uses acting techniques to tap into her performers' emotional resources. This has proven to be a challenge in rehearsals. Choreographers aren't typically trained as directors who work to elicit certain emotions from their performers. As such, in the early days Zollar would demand things from her dancers emotionally and would get frustrated if they couldn't give her what she was looking for. Eventually, she developed a training technique that includes theater methods to elicit the aesthetic she wants from her dancers in terms of acting as well as movement. Urban Bush Women dancers are expected to dance, sing, act, and occasionally play instruments. Since few dancers are trained in these other arts, Zollar builds this training into her technique classes and rehearsal exercises. King, who has a strong signing voice, told me that before working with Urban Bush Women she didn't think her voice was very good, though she loved singing. "When I first started into the company I was like a little mouse. . . . I

Makeda Thomas, Sita Frederick, Wanjiru Kamuyu, Millicent Johnnie, Shaneeka Harrell, and Liria Guambe in *Shadow's Child*. Photo copyright by Mike Van Sleen.

would sing in the back, in the shower, with records." As far as singing on stage, "[Zollar] had to crank the sound out of there."[45]

Many of the pieces require the dancers to create believable characters and deliver lines loudly enough to be heard over several booming drums. Some are very presentational, and the dancers are required to speak directly to the audience either as characters or as themselves. Someone is often on a microphone reading poetry while others dance. All of the pieces are emotionally charged. One reviewer remarked on how this translated to the stage, noting that in a world where much of our art is distanced from passion or pathos, the company "exhibited no embarrassment in a richly expressive display of feeling. Quite the opposite. They rejoiced in it."[46]

This process of working is unusual and often challenges the dancers to access different parts of themselves. Christal Brown describes Urban Bush Women's character-based, collaborative process: "A lot of it for me is characterization. To find these characters [you need to] figure out where the character is in you. [In rehearsals] you have to be open to a lot of different things."[47] Christine King echoes this when she talks about acting in *Bones and Ash*: "[You learn to] use a part of you that's already there and brings about another side of you that you never thought was something you could do."[48]

The musical rhythms that accompany Urban Bush Women performances usually stem from the African matrix. West African drumming, jazz, funk, and hip-hop help set the tone for many of the performances. *Hair Stories* is set to James Brown funk, jazz creates the mood for *Heat*, and Southern rural folk music accompanies *Praise House*. West African drumming often kicks in as an emotional trigger and reminder of how these styles are connected to African roots.

A brief examination of one of Urban Bush Women's earlier pieces is helpful for understanding how the stylistic elements discussed so far come together in the choreography. The first section of *The Thirteenth Tribe, Nyabinghi Dreamtime* is an excellent example of much of Urban Bush Women's style, particularly the ways the aesthetic flows between modern dance tradition and African Diaspora cultures. It is based on Zollar's research into Jamaican Rastafarian traditions that combines political protest and resistance with Old Testament teachings. The Nyabinghi ceremony is a Rastafarian rite that lasts anywhere from three to twenty-one days. Rather than re-creating it, as Katherine Dunham might have done, Zollar uses this research to inspire original choreography. The result is an illustration of the Urban Bush Women style (technique blends, pedestrianism, strength, breath, pace, and emotion).

The piece starts with the sound of many feet stomping, ringing out in the darkness. Low lights come up to reveal six dancers dressed simply in sports bras and shorts. They circle their arms around their heads, slap their chests, and lower themselves to the ground. Immediately, a grounded aesthetic is established. One dancer gives a vocal cue, aurally connecting them all, and they all spin on the floor. As a single drum comes in, the dancers rise up and swing both arms around their heads while taking a step and rolling through their chests. The single African drum acts as a call, lifting them from the ground and moving them forward. They pause, sink down in their plies, and coolly isolate their pelvises by rotating their hips several times. The gestures are not for sale, as Zollar might say, and combining them with the aesthetic of the cool empowers these provocative acts by leaving no doubt that they are not cheap gestures, even if sexualized. They chassé with their legs extended in arabesque, turn with their legs in back attitude, and spin to the floor. From the floor, they move out of a ballet aesthetic by kicking out their feet, spinning, and hopping into splits and low, crouched positions. The choreography continues in this vein for several minutes. Meanwhile, male and female voices emerge softly, chanting, intoning, and moaning. The vocalizations add another layer to the performance that suggests an evocation, a summoning of spirituality and power. Further blending technique, the dancers stand, plié, rond de jambe, reach out, then flex their

Christine King and Treva Offutt in *Bones and Ash: A Gilda Story*. Photo by Cylla Von Tiedemann.

feet and stomp. With limp upper torsos, they point their feet, extend their legs, and step forward. They spin, jump, slap their arms, roll their shoulders, and drop in the waist. It is a Garth Fagan–like deconstruction of the elements of African Diaspora dance as well as an exploration of lines, shapes, and directions in ballet and modern dance tradition.

At one point, the dancers hang their heads forward, bend at the waist, and swing their arms prosaically. They "step out" of the choreography and walk around in a pedestrian manner popularized by 1960s postmodern dance. Moving separately and no longer dancing, they each go through different sequences of freezes, runs, turns, kicks, and extensions. They give and take weight and support each other in lifts. They then walk around cautiously as if preparing to defend themselves. They move into a line, and each dancer places her arms around the back of the adjacent one. For the remainder of the piece, the dancers share weight, spin, and leap. They move individually and as a unit, alternating smoothly among modern choreography, African steps, and pedestrian running and walking patterns.

Many significant parts of the Urban Bush Women aesthetic are demonstrated in this piece. As a community and ensemble, the performers use breath to control the piece's energy and pace. All of the actions and attitudes are rooted in a cool strength. Emotionally, they charge the space to allow for possession and calm it to allow for personal reflection. They alternate between moving as a group and as individuals by dancing closer together or farther apart. If one or two people break out for a solo or duet, the group supports them. Above all, this dance displays many influences from different African Diaspora traditions (including the storytelling, chanting, singing, and, of course, dances of African, Caribbean, and African American people), as well as European traditions (ballet, modern) and postmodern pedestrianism.

Another important part of the Urban Bush Women style is a sense of playfulness. Zollar uses play in strategic ways. At some points, she breaks up tense moments by having the dancers abruptly shift to children's games. At others, she uses playful styles to lull the audience into a false sense of security before hitting them with a poignant moment. The sharp contrast that manifests as she raises the stakes emphasizes her points. She believes that the playful girl exists alongside the warrior, and she constantly reminds her dancers to make sure their warriors are in their back pockets, even when they are playing. She asks them to access both sides of themselves. According to Zollar, "It's not a disconnect. It's the same person. I think we create duality where there is none."[49] Brown adds: "Once you find those characters within you, it is not hard to switch them on and off. If you have a hard time having those characters at your beck and call, in your back pocket . . . once you find those people, it's okay."[50] Bauman agrees: "I think they're connected. I don't find it really hard to switch, because we all have all of those things in us all the time."[51] Zollar suggests that the experiences of African American women and their ancestors may help them tap into their warrior side more easily: "I think the hardest thing in terms of what I see of the white dancers who come in to do the work or in the classes is [accessing] 'the warrior.' So maybe that's ancestral? Or maybe it's a connection to oppression. There's something about that that's developed. It's in the music and it's in the language. Our language has it sometimes, that fierceness in it, you know, like a wave. It's not in white language, or . . . the way white people speak standard English." This is not to say that Zollar thinks it's impossible for white women to channel their inner warrior: "We had a white woman in the company, working with us for a while. A fierce warrior woman. Oh my God. . . . I mean she was just kick-ass power!"[52]

That access often comes through vocalizations that create and sustain the power in the movement. Many of the pieces have the dancers vocalize, chant, sing singsongs, hold a note, call out. Much of this work comes out of African Diaspora tradition. Singsongs and vocalizations, like children's games, offer an important contrast to the intense moments in the choreography. The voice and the body are connected, and both are crucial to the aesthetic. Vocalizations enhance the movement and help motivate the performers. By combining voice and movement, Urban Bush Women evoke a nommo force. Nommo, the power of language to create that which it names and to endow an individual with control over her/his life, helps Urban Bush Women create ritual.[53] The use of voice comes out of not only Zollar's work with Dianne McIntyre but also her theater background and her interest in exploring the connections between sound and movement.

Sections of the piece *Vocal Attack* provide excellent examples of Zollar's use of sound and movement in her choreography. In one section, a dancer wearing a simple Urban Bush Woman T-shirt and black shorts executes simple playful steps, isolations, and skips while matching vocalizations to her movements. A hop might be matched with a whoop sound, a leap with a yell, and shivers with staccato vowel sounds. She performs accents both vocally and physically. This opening section sets the vocabulary of the piece and eases the exploration of body and voice.

As she makes her way offstage, two more dancers walk on casually, as if they were two girlfriends walking down the street. They "talk" to each other using a nonsense language. One points to something on the side and they decide to walk over and check it out. They each take an audible breath, in unison, while shrugging their shoulders. They pantomime choosing various items from a table and express their love of the items with sighs of satisfaction. At one point, each tastes something that causes her so much joy that she falls to the floor and, leaning on one hand, writhes in delight. They grab at something and giggle as they back up offstage, waving.

A dancer then enters from stage right while a drummer enters from stage left. With about six feet between them, they face each other and lean in. The drummer plays a short rhythm, and the dancer mimics the sound while moving her body to her own vocalization. The dancer turns and hums a tune while spinning and stomping out a rhythm. The drummer responds by also humming along and playing the beat. The dancer hums, "um hum," to indicate that the drummer is correct. She passes him another rhythm, and he returns yet another to her—a playful call-and-response exchange. They continue until the dancer gives a rhythm that the drummer joins. They begin dancing, chanting, and drumming together. She moves closer to him, and as they join forces they move offstage together. Though there is very little distinguishable dialogue in these two sections, there is communication, and the vocalizations are integral to the movement. Though not in a typical manner, the dancers do converse, using their bodies and their voices. Physicality and gestures fill in so the audience gets a fuller understanding of the connections between the performers even though they can't understand the "words." Linguistically, the vocalizations not only underscore movement, but they also substitute for words and together with movement effectively communicate. The body "translates" for the voice, and vice versa. They riff, scat, talk, embrace, comfort, goad. In short, all of the elements (body, drum, and voice) celebrate each other. There is a meeting of music, movement, and voice. Vocalizing and moving together create a sense of community and support.

The final important element of the Urban Bush Women style that I want to introduce is the focus on energy sources, the wells from which the performers draw to access all of the other elements. For example, at a rehearsal for *Bitter Tongue*, Zollar asks the dancers to focus on their lower chakras. She has the dancers walk around the space feeling their weight in order to settle down into their bodies before dancing. They do some qigong breathing exercises and use the sigh to conjure the right kind of energy. Zollar emphasizes that this dance requires a particular kind of energy, one rooted in the chest and collected in the sockets—dropped, grounded, and fiery. Emotionally, the dancers need to be in the right place, because when the energy is not dropped they risk looking like little girls instead of the determined women Zollar wants for this piece. The dancers go through the process individually and come together and into their opening positions when they are ready. One dancer begins a rhythmic vocalization of grunts and groans, and as the other dancers join in, the sound turns to screams, as though they need to get the sound out of their bodies. After all of the dancers build up this energy, they draw upon it to bring them to the emotional state necessary to perform the piece. They need the energy that lets them and the audience sense that they are "about to kick butt," as Zollar puts it. They must maintain the intensity throughout the piece so the audience senses that there was a dispersal that is now coming together over the course of the dance. Everyone feeds into and feeds off of the group dynamics. While they dance, Zollar asks the dancers questions and gives them directives to keep them focused on maintaining the emotional and physical qualities she wants: "How old are you?" "Get that knee up!" "Engage the legs quickly!" Zollar wants the dancers to hold onto the ferocity in a delicate balance of drawing energy in and letting it out. There is a moment when they all move backward in a triangle to bring the energy in, slam it down to the ground, and move their arms to the side and turn their heads as if they are defending themselves and moving away from a slap. On top of all of this, they are using breathing techniques, especially when they need to drop their energy even further. Rather than lighten the mood, the breath gives them power. On this particular occasion, the techniques create a dangerous energy. It is evident in the dancers' faces, in the quality of their movement, and in their offstage demeanors. For the dancers to switch gears and go on a break, Zollar has them walk around the space again to let it go. In studio, the dancers practice accessing that energy so that they may transfer it to the audience in performance.

To summarize, the major elements of style for the Urban Bush Women aesthetic are technique blends, pedestrianism, strength, breath, pace, emotion, playfulness, vocalization, and energy. These are the tools Zollar and her dancers use to create their art and communicate their messages. In the next four chapters, I will discuss content in terms of the themes of the concert choreography and their significance. In each of these chapters, I analyze the important choreographic motifs and describe how they work in larger social contexts. Some of these include finding the strength to survive adversity; calling upon the spirits and ancestors; overcoming violence and pain; reclaiming heritage, history, legacy, and memory; claiming agency and authenticity over the female identity (voice, body, and spirit); using the personal to connect with the universal; connecting to everyday life; and connecting to others.[54] A critical analysis of content, along with the above discussion and an analysis of the company's community work, provides the support for my claims about the company's work in creating a mechanism to do things with bodies that move spectators to reconsider movement, activism in the arts, and the role of dance in projects of social healing, awareness, and change.

2

The Body

Divided and Conquered

The concert dance world has historically ghettoized ways of moving that are labeled "black." Although attitudes are shifting, many mature dancers and choreographers grew up knowing the stigma of black dance and make conscious choreography decisions with that in mind. Different ways of moving certain body parts are still loaded with prejudices about race, class, and gender.

It is not inconsequential, nor is it happenstance, that Urban Bush Women's image is of the strong black female body. Zollar embraces ways of moving that many African American women were and still are taught to deny. For those fortunate black women who have not been subject to this, she further affirms the aesthetic value, clearing the way for the next generation of black women to look at their bodies in a new, affirmative manner. Much of Zollar's technique focuses on the isolation of body parts that enables the dancers to move various parts in different styles and tempos. Often, in class and in choreography, Zollar has dancers begin a movement in one style and switch mid-motion to complete it in another style. For example, a dancer might start a balletic rond de jambe en l'air. As she moves her leg to the back, instead of supporting her torso and extending forward to smoothly rotate her leg in the hip socket (often displacing the socket so that buttock sits back in it unnaturally but beautifully), an Urban Bush Women dancer might break at the waist, contract the torso, flex the foot, and exhale.

One cannot overemphasize the importance of individual body parts in Zollar's work. Not only does her technique often require the dancers to isolate different parts, but many of Urban Bush Women's pieces also thematically draw our attention to a particular part of the body. Zollar separates the parts to analyze the social significance of the body for black women. She acts like a scientist, putting a part under a microscope for examination and experimentation. She unpacks the history of coding and the connections between the body

Kenya Massey, Christine King, Dionne Kamara, Michelle Dorant, Carolina Garcia, and Jawole Willa Jo Zollar in *Bitter Tongue*. Photo by Jane Hoffer.

part and the process of identification, subjection, and objectification. As she asks us to take another, more considered look at the black female body, she pushes our knowledge and understanding about the power of ocularcentrism and the manipulation of the visual aspect of identity. Ultimately, Urban Bush Women moves toward putting the black female body back together, healing the old wounds and creating more complete, positive images of black women. As Zollar's movement style is highly charged, by watching it we are forced to renegotiate and reconsider the power of the black female body. I asked her how she came to address the different parts of the black female body. She replied:

> With *Batty Moves*, that year I had gone to Jamaica, Nigeria, and Brazil. One of the things I was really aware of is how easy the buttocks moved and how easy that movement was part of the dances. . . . Everyone did it. It didn't have the [stigma] that this is bad. I used that in creating this work and then I started reading about Venus Hottentot and got pissed off about that and so then it became boxing movements. It was kind of an evolution. And the piece "Hand Singing Song"—even when I was in school, I wanted to do a piece based on an album that Bernice Johnson Reagon had made, called *Give Your Hands to Struggle*, and I always loved that. And then

> Adam Clayton Powell had this speech called "What's In Your Hands," and . . . he talked about David and Goliath and the people—you're facing this mighty enemy but you have the power in your hands.[1]

Control over the images surrounding the black female body has been continually negotiated since the first slaves were brought to the shores of the Western Atlantic. A number of Urban Bush Women's dances deal with different parts of the black body—hair in *Hair Stories*, the buttocks in *Batty Moves*, and the hand in *Hand Singing Song*. In this chapter, I examine these dances and discuss the work the choreography does to make audiences reconsider the black female body. Several theorists offer helpful frameworks to analyze the ways Zollar breaks apart the body to empower each part and ultimately put the body back together again. It is beyond the scope of this project to engage in all of the writings of each theorist. Rather, I will focus on the topics most germane to this study. Foucault's thoughts on subjectification and discursivity, for example, are particularly useful.[2] The basis of this work lies in a suspicion of claims to universal truth, utopian schemes, and essential human nature. More important to Foucault are the ways these ideas have been used as tools of power in society. The greatest influence comes from that which develops out of notions of subjectivity; it is crucial to examine the modes of objectification that are techniques to define who we are in the name of truth. In other words, Foucault is interested in the ways human beings become subjects, which is often through the exercise of power through discursive modes.

Paul Rabinow separates Foucault's process of objectification into three distinct but interrelated modes. The first is "dividing practices," in which the subject is separated from others and/or from her/himself. The second mode is "scientific classification"; this comes from modes of inquiry that try to give themselves the status of sciences. These disciplines function to order, label, and compartmentalize various ideas (like madness, health, sexuality) in the name of science and knowledge. Foucault points out, mainly by looking at abrupt shifts in certain systems of classification, how these practices serve power more than truth.

The third mode of objectification, "subjectification," is the most important to the study of Zollar's work. It concerns the ways a human being turns him/herself into a subject. The difference between this mode and the others lies in the power of agency. The first two are processes of domination of the individual from the outside. The third implies agency for the individual, though the degree varies and is itself a negotiation of power. Rather than passively being divided and labeled, a person is an active participant in creating and understanding him/herself.

These modes of objectification can happen simultaneously or discreetly, and distilling the nuances of each category is probably impossible and/or maddening. What is important is to understand that all of these modes go into the creation and definition of self for the purposes of negotiating with society for power, in many arenas to varying degrees of explicitness.

The body is at the center of these processes because it is the location of much of the justification and consequence of objectification. It is from the body that studies and experiments base conclusions, and it is on the body that treatments, remedies, and beliefs about normality are instilled. It is primarily the *body* of the prisoner, patient, sexual being that must be ordered, understood, and controlled. The body is a thing to divide and conquer.

The black female body can serve as an excellent example to understand these processes and relations. Few would disagree that the black female body is a discursive site (a locus of ideological debate) of power struggles for the ability to control the process of objectification. Slave owners controlled not only the productive labor of their female slaves but also the reproductive labor. And though those women struggled to hold onto a modicum of power and dignity over their own bodies, the slaveholder and hegemonic forces controlled how this body was viewed and used. We are still negotiating the effects of hate, violence, stereotyping, and exploitation on the black female body. Since they stepped onto the slave ships, Africans in the Diaspora have been trying to regain control of their bodies.[3] They have done this is many ways—among them, breaking shackles, running, fighting, defying fire hoses, sitting in the front of the bus or at the lunch counter, committing suicide, committing murder.

Again, these negotiations can happen in different venues: the work place, the neighborhood, school, et cetera. Dance, too, can be seen as a discursive site, an ideal one for these negotiations, I argue, because dance directly engages/reengages the body. To hold onto their senses of selves, slaves danced despite legal prohibitions. Early black female pioneers of concert dance (Edna Guy, Pearl Primus, Katherine Dunham) engaged in power negotiations from the moment they stepped onto the concert dance stage, and black female choreographers have been similarly engaged ever since, even those who create works not explicitly about race, gender, identity, or other such issues. However, those who try to assert the third self-empowered mode of objectification inevitably run into the other two, usually in the form of critics, scholars, and audience members whose role is often to divide and label, regardless of the choreographer's intent. Much of this boils down to control. Control of the black female body has both a physical sense, in terms of making the body do something (like hard labor), and a representational one, in terms of how the black female body is perceived and what judgments are made about it. This is a political, social, and personal struggle. Historically, control has not rested with black women. Many choreographers such as Zollar perceive that black women do not have complete control over their bodies and through choreography attempt to regain control by revealing the myths and the truths about the body. By exercising this kind of agency, Zollar promotes a relishing of the body, trying to take the body back.

Judith Butler's work is also pertinent to this analysis. Her philosophical treatises on agency, identity, power, and performance are persuasive, though controversial. Generally speaking, Butler is interested in the ways aspects of identity (particularly gender) manifest as products of power relations between individuals and hegemonic forces. She is also skeptical of the "universal truths" of identity and sees identity as a process of becoming through regularized and repeated norms and expectations. Like Foucault, Butler focuses on the body as the site of this process, and the facts and circumstances of materiality are at the crux of her analysis.

Two key concepts for Butler are "performativity" and "citationality":

> Performativity is thus not a singular "act," for it is always a reiteration of a norm or set of norms, and to the extent that it acquires an act-like status in the present, it conceals or dissimulates the conventions of which it is a repetition. Moreover, this act is not primarily theatrical; indeed its apparent theatricality is produced to the extent that its historicity remains dissimulated (and, conversely, its theatricality gains a certain inevitability given the impossibility of a full disclosure of its historicity). Within speech act theory, *a performative is that discursive practice that enacts or produces that which it names.* . . . The process of that sedimentation or what we might call materialization will be a kind of citationality, the acquisition of being through the citing of power, a citing that establishes an originary complicity with power in the formation of the "I."[4]

If we push the statement "a performative is that discursive practice that enacts or produces that which it names" to include unspoken language, particularly dance, we can translate this concept to Urban Bush Women's work. We can examine the movement of the body alongside the words spoken by the performers (and the music played) as acts. Speech act theory, such as nommo, claims that words do; so too movement, so too music. Through choreography, taking on centuries of counter-productions enacted and written on the body, Zollar attempts to produce that which she dances: the strong, whole, healed black woman. By analyzing the performativity of her performances, we can unpack how the choreography works. It is important to remember that performativity is not primarily theatrical, though we are looking at a theatrical site (the concert dance stage). There is a dual performativity at work, further complicating the analysis, since the negotiation for groups like Urban Bush Women is metatheatrical. In other words, an aesthetic use of performativity in a performance site implies awareness and agency. We may examine artistic intent or outcome (citationality) as criteria, but the negotiation itself is most salient to this study.

Scholars of theater and performance studies are fascinated with these concepts. They provide a way for us to interrogate the performativity of performance and meta-theatrical significance. Butler sees sex as a Foucauldian regulatory ideal; I argue that race is a regulatory ideal as well. Both of these produce the bodies over which they hold sway. For the performing arts, this means that audiences create the bodies as well as their readings of the bodies as they witness a performance. Since Zollar and Urban Bush Women are primarily concerned with the black female body, it is over this body that these ideals clash. Foucault and Butler help us understand that the materiality of racialized (colored) femininity is the effect of power. In other words, we might perceive that individuals are a particular race and gender (as well as other markers of identity) but what these theories suggest is that it is more the case that one *does* and is *compelled to do* race and gender.[5] Butler is far more political than Foucault, however, and more likely to point out the destructive consequences of these processes. In many ways Urban Bush Women *does* black femininity. The company members perform (in all senses of the word), create and construct gendered, raced bodies that trouble stereotypes, celebrate neglected strengths, and expose the social circumstances of many black women.

The scholar/artist Coco Fusco explores the relationship between the body and the mind for people of color on a transcultural scale. "It is historical memory that I live as both a psychic and bodily experience," she says. This work is useful for examining Urban Bush Women in the context of the black Atlantic world, past and present. The dancers move through ancestral memory, often compelled by the force of past generations. The cultural divisions between African American, Caribbean, and African blur. As a postmodern dance company, Urban Bush Women participates in contemporary conversations on otherness in the arts. New struggles based on race and gender emerge on a global scale to attend to current oppressions. Symbolic visibility takes on new meaning, and the associations between art and political power shift. In her choreography, particularly the three pieces I analyze below, Zollar attempts to claim political power for women of color by healing the body physically, emotionally, and spiritually. She takes on the outside institutions of racism and sexism by championing the individual to resist all forces that seek to redefine her identity. Only by creating and knowing the self can the individual confront the other. This resistance is, of course, met with resistance. Fusco exposes the backlash against politicized art and theorizes on strategies for artists: "To focus on the

Urban Bush Women in *Nyabinghi Dreamtime*. Photo by Dona Ann McAdams.

imbalances of power and institutionalized racism has been deemed anathema to beauty, championed once again as the essence of art. . . . Postcolonially identified artists know very well what to avoid and take a strategic approach as to how they present themselves in such a climate in order to survive and thrive. But some of them keep trying to go against the grain, to unleash the demons that others try vehemently to hide."[6] The members of Urban Bush Women are such artists. They are exposing the demons by exposing the body.

The black body was first divided and conquered in the slave system. Slaves were institutionally alienated from the productive and reproductive fruits of their labor. Slavery literally attempted to dis-own the slave from his/her body. As Fusco puts it, "Black people's entry into the symbolic order of Western culture hinged on the theft of their bodies, the severing of will from their bodies, the reduction of their bodies to things, and the transformation of their sexuality into an expression of otherness."[7] Much of the postcolonial project is reclamation of the black body. Zollar redivides and reconquers the black body through dance. She shifts the power dynamics through which we come to know the black body and reaffirms African Americans' sovereignty over their own bodies.

Hair Stories

And keep your heads nappy!
The Fugees,
"Nappy Heads"

The natural Respect of Self and Seal!
Sisters!
Your hair is Celebration in the world!
Gwendolyn Brooks,
"To Those of My Sisters Who Keep Their Naturals"

We teach you to love the hair God gave you.
Malcolm X,
The Autobiography of Malcolm X

Urban Bush Women took to collecting hair stories while they were on the road. Company members and people involved with producing a show would talk about early childhood memories of getting their hair done or share stories about making personal choices in hairstyles that signified their life choices. Zollar decided to create a piece using these stories as the source material. The company started hosting more formal hair parties, in which men and women of all races could gather specifically to discuss the social significance of their hair, enter a dialogue about hair and life, and perhaps persuade each other to change their minds about hair. The parties continued after the piece premiered, making new ideas for the piece constantly available. They also served an end in themselves as part of Urban Bush Women's community work.[8] The artistic end product is the piece *Hair Stories*. With this work, Zollar joins a larger company of artists who have addressed hair issues.[9] The importance of this work has led Zollar and the company to be featured in the book *Queens: Portraits of Black Women and Their Fabulous Hair* by Michael Cunningham and George Alexander.

For *Hair Stories*, Zollar interviewed many women and men, and some of these interviews appear on-screen during the performance. These personal anecdotes make clear how much of our identity is braided into our hair. For some women, dealing with hair becomes a way to love oneself and create an identity, a way of creating beauty for people systematically made to believe they are not and never could be beautiful. In one example, a woman discusses how upset her father was when she decided to get dreadlocks.[10] The decision became a way for her to take a stand as her own person.

Performatively, it is an error to dismiss the importance of hair in the creation and performance of black female identity. True, just about everyone has (or had) hair and a personal relationship with their hair or lack thereof. For many black women, though, hair is vitally linked to the experience of self in a unique way. Since the antebellum era, black women have had to figure out ways of dealing with their hair, and since they walked off the plantation they have spent much time, energy, and money on it. Be it wrapped, braided, twisted, relaxed, curled, or dreadlocked, the constant shifting of preferred styles tells us much about selfhood. *Hair Stories* tells us that black women are sometimes afraid to see the knots, the roots of who they are. They have asked and have been asked that telltale question, "Is that your *real* hair?" They have been trying to get rid of the nappy edges for over a hundred years and have only recently embraced them. Hair has been both a source of oppression and a symbol of freedom. For many black women, hair crowns the concept that the personal is political. According to Ayana D. Byrd and Lori L. Tharps, "Ever since African civilizations bloomed, hairstyles have been used to indicate a person's marital status, age, religion, ethnic identity, wealth, and rank within the community. In some cultures a person's surname could be ascertained simply by examining the hair because each clan had its own unique hairstyle."[11] *Hair Stories* interrogates how hair affects black women's notions of race, gender, class, sexuality, images of beauty, and power.[12]

Black women have many strong opinions about and deep emotional connections to hair. There is a larger conversation about hair, and everyone from journalists to novelists to scholars to musicians to children's book authors to film directors and, of course, choreographers are addressing the topic. On her motivation for creating the piece, Zollar has said, "I want to create a world in which every little Black girl, every little girl, every child can feel comfortable being himself or herself."[13]

Hair Stories had its world premiere at the Doris Duke Studio Theater in August 2001 as part of the Jacob's Pillow Dance Festival. The first thing the audience experiences when viewing a performance of *Hair Stories* is the familiar soulful beat of a James Brown song, which brings them back to a particular time and spirit—whether the actual 1970s or what we of the retro-flashback-postmodern era style as the spirit of the 1970s. We know that the tone of the piece will have attitude—negritude. What follows is a roller-coaster ride through the trials and tribulations, sociology, history, and drama that is the relationship black women have with their hair. Zollar and her dancers (with the help of director Elizabeth Heron) deconstruct black female hair in order to force us to reimagine the construction and performance of identity for women of color.

Hair Stories emphasizes the importance of hair for black women, the convictions and contradictions of ideology pertaining to who black women are and how someone's hair can make a statement even if the person never utters a word. Images speak, and words act. Speech is not a luxury for black women; black foremothers fought to be heard in politics, academia, the boardroom, the arts. At the same time, black women today often feel pressure to constantly "speak for their people" and carefully select conversations in which to engage in order to keep sane. One powerful strategy lies in letting their hair speak for them. In *Hair Stories*, hair takes on personality; it becomes a metaphor for life. It is a key player in all aspects of life; it has a long, complex history that is both a disturbing socio-psychological paradigm and a testament to the battles won. The performance becomes at once a purging ritual and a house party.

There is, as Dr. Professor, the first character on stage, explains to us, a phenomenology of hair. Dr. Professor, played by Zollar herself, is a parody of a college lecturer and, as the redundancy of her name suggests, she is an über-scholar wrapped up in jargon that profoundly confuses common sense.[14] She is both fascinating and full of herself. Though she is over the top and absurd in a sense, she does make a point. Through humor, Zollar seduces the audience into thinking about hair; they become students being asked by a professor to engage in dialogue. In this meta-academic mock lecture, Dr. Professor lays out some of the important issues for the audience to consider concerning race, class, gender, and the political mythology of "good hair" and "bad hair." Ultimately, we come to understand that one's personal appearance is a political statement, particularly for African Americans, and one's hairstyle can advance a political and cultural agenda.

We love to hate our hair, and, as Dr. Professor points out, a value construct is supported by the good hair/bad hair dichotomy: long, straight, manageable hair that can be tossed around like white women's hair and run through by a lover's fingers becomes desirable. Think of the Whoopi Goldberg character who puts a towel on her head and tosses it to and fro to pretend that she has "long, luxurious blond hair."[15] It is funny because it speaks truth for many black women. Good hair becomes associated with a constructed whiteness or the desire to be as close to white as possible. In contrast, nappy hair (or bad hair) is linked to default blackness. That is, of course, until the late 1960s and the rise to status of the Afro, when "bad" became "good" or "baaad."

Many of the interviewees for the piece discussed early childhood memories of getting their hair "done" or "did." One woman talked about "back in the day" when she got her hair pressed and a "big thick sister" would come at her, brandishing a hot comb. She recalled the smell of burning flesh, the sound of the iron meeting grease and hair, the singeing, the itching, her inability to scratch—in other words, the beauty pain.

These tales inspired Zollar to create "The Hot Comb Blues" and "The Lock Down," sections of the performance in which the dancers feverishly twitch to funk music. They perform a fervid combination in which they jerk their bodies wildly while patting and rubbing their heads like mad to get at the itch. The frenetic energy comes from the pain and the frustration of these early memories. At one point in "The Lock Down," five women line up behind a young girl sitting on the floor, rev up, and pantomime pulling and tugging her hair as she writhes and screams in pain. They yell at her, "Come here, girl! I said, 'Come here, girl!' You better give me your hair!" In this moment the young girl has the force of centuries of maternal history behind her, inflicting pain so that she can look presentable. Zollar comes running out on stage, the escaped child with her hair half done, fleeing the mother/torturer. She looks crazy: one side in tight braids and the other in a big 'fro with a comb sticking out. At one point they send up the James Brown cape moment, the child's mother entering on stage with a bright red towel and covering the exhausted child to bring her back offstage to continue the torture. The child acquiesces for a few steps then turns dramatically and pleads with the audience to help her. The action is repeated until the child is brought finally offstage; this is all performed to "You've Done Me Wrong." Interestingly, there is little actual dance in this section—the movement is more stylized pantomime. With this, Zollar lays out the movement vocabulary that will recur in more abstract, dancerly versions.

Many who address black hair issues focus on the experiences of children. Besides the pain of having their hair pulled, pressed, and/or tightly twisted, myriad beauty myths threaten the healthy development of young black girls. These focus on the belief that "good hair" (straight hair) will attract a man, lead to a good career, and in general symbolize privilege. Children's book authors Carolivia Herron and bell hooks attempt to remedy this damaging image by promoting the beauty of natural hair in their respective books, *Nappy Hair* and *Happy to Be Nappy*. In her first autobiography, *I Know Why the Caged Bird Sings*, Maya Angelou describes the pain of growing up as a black girl trying to discover who she is and the role that her hair played in that process. Like Herron, hooks, and Angelou, Zollar attempts to move beyond this pain. *Hair Stories* tackles the demons in some closets. By calling them out, Zollar hopes to create a space in which black women can undo some of this childhood damage, recognize self-hate, and conceive positive, healthy self-images. The underlying message of the piece is that we must move to a place that accepts a diverse beauty standard and promotes personal creative expression through hair that is loaded with meaning and thus celebrated, and this work must start with the youngest girls.

For Zollar, the story is far more complicated than the simplistic narrative that black women put themselves through hell to attain a simulacrum of the white female beauty ideal. Over time, attitudes about hair (for both the individual and the collective) shift. Later in the piece, Zollar reveals this by reminding us that the term "nappy" contains a negative connotation for some and simultaneously embodies strength and empowerment for others. Embracing and loving nappy hair becomes a means of reappropriating the tools of the oppressor. As Audre Lorde taught us, we cannot use the master's tools to take down the master's house. However, according to Zollar we can deny the tools the power to take us down. In other words, we can take that power, reverse it, and reinscribe it.

During the performance, Zollar steps out and asks audience members for other definitions of "nappy."[16] In doing so she is asking them to move from being passive spectators to active contributors. She thereby cleverly implicates us all in the "phenomenology of hair." We have knowledge of or are actively perpetuating the myths by which we define ourselves and others. When she asks the predominately white Jacob's Pillow audience for other definitions of "nappy," the spectators are hesitant to speak at first. Anxious thoughts probably run the gamut from "I don't know. Is that bad?" to "I don't know. Is that good?" to "I know a few, but should I say anything? Do I look racist if I say something? Do I seem ignorant if I don't?" Women of color might be more comfortable speaking up in general, but the racial makeup of an audience at Jacob's Pillow undoubtedly yields different vibes and different responses from the black women in it than an audience in Harlem with a majority black presence. Whatever the response, the audience is put on the spot, implicated, possibly even incriminated. As opposed to Dr. Professor lecturing at the audience, Zollar here turns the onus back on the spectators, challenging them to think about not only the different definitions but also the social influences that construct those definitions and their political implications. At the Jacob's Pillow performance, Zollar received a few tentative responses: "wooly," "bad hair day." At Long Island University in Brooklyn, audiences were far more forthcoming.

This race-based anxiety is illustrated in one of the most comedic moments of the performance. This section is divided into two parts. In "Hair Hell Moment #1," a black woman with a shaved head enters an elevator filled with white women. She turns to face the audience with the other dancers behind her. The air is thick with tension as the white women (played by the black dancers) discretely stare, wonder, and ponder this choice.[17] Though the bald woman cannot see the others behind her, she knows that they are staring at her hair. She rolls her eyes, which the audience can see but not the white women. Opening up a dialogue about hair is untenable in this moment and probably not one the bald woman wants to engage in at the moment. Instead, she deftly turns around and the white women quickly adopt oblivious attitudes. The comedy is in the truthfulness of this moment of interracial tension. "Hair Hell Moment #1" examines where that anxiety and curiosity goes when there is no hair to reach out and touch—it gets at the unspoken dialogue, the continued misunderstanding, and the reluctance on all sides to work it out because of anxiety, anger, and complexity.

The dancers turn around and adopt neutral stances. In "Hair Hell Moment #2," the scene is replayed as the bald black woman enters an elevator filled with black women. As she announces that this elevator now contains black passengers, the dancers sharply sink their weights and adopt attitude, they roll their heads and openly stare as the woman enters the elevator. Here Zollar makes an important strategic move: she resists a simplistic message in which the black women create a supportive atmosphere and celebrate the diversity of hair options as opposed to the ignorant and oppressive white women. The black women begin talking to each other, loud enough to be certain that the bald woman can hear them. One wonders if there is a draft. Another replies that she feels a draft but wonders if "she" feels a draft. They begin subtly chanting, "You think she feels a draft? I know she feels a draft." Again the woman rolls her eyes. The woman, fed up with the taunts, turns abruptly to face them, snaps a finger to silence them, and abruptly turns back with her own attitude. She folds her arms and rolls her head. The women behind her, after being snapped into silence, also roll their heads and softly continue to whisper their chant as the lights fade. The bald woman is just as tormented by the black women as she is by the white women, albeit more overtly. In both instances, she turns sharply to confront them with a powerful gesture. Through her choreographic choices, Zollar emphasizes the complexity of these negotiations, the impetus toward confrontation, and the difficulty of working through issues.

A poignant moment in *Hair Stories* occurs later, when Zollar reads a letter she has written to Madame C. J. Walker, the woman who introduced the French hot comb to African American women, became the first black female millionaire, and, some say, caused generations of African American women to despise and alter their natural hair. Zollar expresses the ambivalence many black women feel toward Walker and the idea of getting their hair "done." Walker should be recognized and applauded for her accomplishments; it was no easy task for a black woman to become a success in the business world at the end of the nineteenth century. At the same time, her success is at the heart of much black female self-hatred. Zollar blames Walker for the burns on her scalp, ears, and neck but she also fondly remembers the rites of passage that occur in black beauty shops as important times for female bonding. While her hair was

Jawole Willa Jo Zollar. Photo by Dona Ann McAdams.

being fried and flattened she learned how to become a woman. Zollar imagines the little girl who tries to get her hair to go a way it does not want to go. Then she tries to imagine a little girl proud of the beauty in her nappy hair. It is a harder image to conjure. As the controversy over the teaching of *Nappy Hair* illustrates, African American women have very different opinions about nappy hair. At the end of this section, Zollar imagines a scenario in which Walker championed the different ways to wear nappy hair and sold the idea that black women should be happy to be nappy.

In the "Aunt Bell" section, Zollar further aestheticizes the performativity of ethnic identity through hair when she talks about visiting her Aunt Bell after having just cut off ten years of dreadlocks. She had decided to just cover her hair with a scarf because Aunt Bell was "old school" and Zollar did not want to have to explain why she had nappy hair. More than any other, this section deals overtly with identity and hair. Making a direct link between self-determined identity and hair, she talks about giving herself the name Jawole. She is proud of having taken her own identity by naming herself, but she is also proud of, and uses, her given name: Willa Jo. People call her either or both, she tells the audience. Her family calls her Jody or Jody Pody MacAsody.

She then becomes a little girl learning the children's game "Zing Boom":

Pull it up
And Snap it Back
Zing Boom!

She stands in the center of a circle of friends (played by the dancers) as they sing, "She got nappy nappy nappy hair!" "Zing Boom," the audience learns, is Aunt Bell's description of nappy hair. It describes what happens when one pulls on nappy hair ("zing") and snaps it back ("boom"). The children wonder "how you gonna be happy with your hair all nappy."

The trajectory of *Hair Stories* demonstrates Zollar's skill at taking an audience on a dramatic journey, even without a conventional plot. By giving us lighter and comedic takes on hair issues in earlier sections, Zollar eases us into a comfort zone so that in the "C. J. Walker," "Grief," and "The Zollar Sisters" sections she can take on these matters more seriously.

In "Grief," women briefly talk about the pain of having hair fall out due to harsh chemicals or cancer. It is at these times when we most realize how important hair is to us; the whole discussion of what to do with one's hair is rendered moot, and the devastating loss must be reckoned with instead. In "The Zollar Sisters," Zollar recounts a personal story about growing up with her sister Donna Rae, whose hair was significantly shorter than her own. It is a painful account about the search for dignity and identity. The dancer playing Donna Rae desperately pulls her hair to make it grow; the movement is hunched over and persecuted. Though Zollar tries to comfort Donna Rae, it is clear that hair issues have created a wedge between the sisters. They are pulled apart; as the chasm that separates them grows, they reach out longingly to each other. The dancer playing Donna Rae is deeply afflicted. She hectically alternates among a blonde wig, a redheaded wig, and a wig with dreads—desperately trying to fit in, find a positive identity, be accepted, and attain the ever-elusive beauty ideal. She is ultimately overcome and defeated, and the audience is left with a bitter reminder of just how deeply these wounds cut.

Other issues tackled in the piece are Afrocentrism; hair as a marker of the one drop of black blood that many whites, like former president Clinton, may

Christalyn Wright, Gacirah Diagne, and Beverley Prentice-Hall in *Bones and Ash: A Gilda Story*. Photo by Cylla Von Tiedemann.

have; spiritual awakenings and beauty images articulated in self-help talk shows; and dreadlocks. Ultimately, Zollar here tries to get at the complexities of black female identity made manifest by hair. Although many experiences involve physical and emotional pain, the hair stories are also filled with fond memories of deep female bonding, stories of empowerment, and tales of economic success. *Hair Stories* attempts to embrace the positive experiences, expose the negative, and create dialogue about the controversial in order to foster healing so that all hair stories can have happy endings. The solution to the pain and anxiety is implied. Though not overt in its politics and ostensibly a celebration of the ability to choose one's hairstyle as an act of agency, the piece does implicitly advocate a politically informed attitude about hair, particularly "natural" hairstyles. Though the hair parties foster fruitful discussions, the company members have to negotiate two important balances: the degree to which they promote the non-altering of hair and the amount of argument between participants about good and bad they allow before the discussion becomes unproductive.

The piece promotes a natural approach to hair care and styling, one without chemicals, which does not privilege approximations of white styles. This message is not unproblematic, however, and is played out in other examples. The rhetoric that natural hairstyles are positive, life-affirming choices exists in many forms. Zollar is less adamantly proscriptive than many, yet she too posits a natural approach to hair and life.

"Natural" is a vexed concept, however, particularly in terms of political economy. Much time and money is spent on Afros, twists, braids, dreads, and other "natural" styles. It may be argued that though fewer chemicals are used, these hairstyles are still manipulations intended to attain an ideal. This belief system as the "solution" to black female identity issues is, I maintain, unresolved and dialogic. By laying out inter- and intra-racial dialectics on hair and gender, Zollar runs the risk of "airing our dirty laundry" for white audiences. Close to this fear are the beliefs that black women need to mount a unified front and that external obstacles take precedence over such quarrels between black women. In essence, by making an intra-racial conversation interracial, Zollar takes on an even more complex task. Ingrid Banks received this criticism for her book *Hair Matters: Beauty, Power, and Black Women's Consciousness*. One of the women she interviewed claimed that she was just adding to the controversy, implying that such discussion is dangerous, since people other than black women would read the book. Zollar's varied audience bases guarantee a multiple and complex spectatorship. To give these audiences opportunities to more overtly enter the dialogue, she often hosts post-show discussions, and, unlike most, these often include heated debates between people who have very strong opinions about hair. At one event a woman defiantly argued that she is not an assimilationist because she straightens her hair. Another passionately claimed to take strength and spirituality from her dreadlocks.

Regardless of one's personal feelings about hair, Zollar highlights that hair is dialogic. Black women are having a conversation through and about their hair. Hairstyle has become a gesture of freedom, a personal statement, and a creative act. As the funk music returns at the end of the performance, the dancers, confident in their ability and right to make decisions about their hair and by extension their lives, dance joyfully to the lyrics "one nation under a groove, getting down just for the funk of it."

As a coda to the performance, Zollar comes back onstage and relates the story of friends who were traveling in West Virginia and stopped at a diner. There, the waitress, amazed at their long locks, called to her husband to come out and take a look at "these women's hairstyles." Because they were in a good mood (and this is crucial, because the scenario could have gone a very different way), the women took up the task of explaining to this black woman and her husband the matting process of locking one's hair. Enthralled, the waitress exclaims that she thinks it's beautiful and is delighted that ordinary "kinky hair will do that" and that other people (presumably meaning herself) could achieve the same look. She wonders if everybody knows this. One is left with the sense that this woman might just reevaluate her relationship with her hair and soon add to her own hair story a personal awakening to her beauty.

Batty Moves

> The rear end exists. I see no reason to be ashamed of it. It's true there are rear ends so stupid, so pretentious, so insignificant that they're only good for sitting on.
>
> Josephine Baker,
> quoted in Phyllis Rose, *Jazz Cleopatra*

> Since my own genitals are public
> I have made other parts private.
> In my silence I possess
> mouth, larynx, brain, in a single
> gesture.
>
> Elizabeth Alexander,
> "The Venus Hottentot"

Perhaps the most well known Urban Bush Women piece that focuses on isolating and deconstructing one part of the black female body is *Batty Moves*.[18] In this piece, Zollar calls attention to the personal and political relationships black women have with that part of the body. The title says much. Descriptively, the dance will be a series of moves one can do with one's buttocks. Declaratively, it is a statement that the nether regions can be isolated and can, indeed, move. It also serves as a metaphor in the dance world; it is a message to forms like classical ballet, reminding it of a long-forgotten body part. Not only does the batty move, but it can also communicate a message and fight for a cause—corporeal rhetoric. Zollar has said, "Whenever you see African peoples you see movement in the hips. . . . I wanted to continue that tradition with this piece . . . to celebrate what is just a glorious, wonderful, beautiful, and fun part of the body."[19] Personal and social issues around ethnicity and the buttocks are quite complex and deeply connected to notions of personal identity and sources of political power. At the heart of the piece is a reexamination of this hotly contested site and an empowered re-inscription of it. During the panel "Directions of Choreographers for the 21st Century/Perceptions of Dance in the Black Community" at the International Association of Black Dancers' Conference in 1995, Zollar laid out the stakes of the project: "Most young women I've talked to have been through some very strong, traumatic, sexual abuse. I think there comes a way that you want to reclaim your sensual being through dance. In Nigeria, shaking the butt is raised to a powerful level of artistry. We have to work with that energy here, and raise it to a higher level so that we can begin a healing cultural momentum."[20] There are many reasons why interrogating the trope of the black female posterior is so highly charged. Throughout history, particularly from the nineteenth century forward, scientists, social theorists, and cultural critics have seen the backsides of black women as discursive sites from which judgments and conclusions about the place of black women in society may be made. Zollar herself met resistance to her desire to become a professional dancer because of her body type, particularly her hips. This led her to do drastic things to lose weight; at one point she weighed just ninety-five pounds. Eventually, she learned to embrace her body and even toyed with the idea of naming her company "Thunder Buns and Company." She claims that being rooted in African dance helped her accept her body image, particularly that of her rear end.[21] Here, I examine where that awakening about body image has taken Urban Bush Women and the work being done through the piece. I contextualize the piece with historical and cultural examples and base my analysis on the assumption that the choreography reaches beyond the stage to comment on and change contemporary attitudes about body image, sexuality, and authority.[22] The piece works to undo the damage of sexual abuse and to challenge audience members to imagine new relationships with their bodies.

The opening sequence of *Batty Moves* suggests a powerful journey for an individual. There may be audience members unfamiliar with the term "batty," and this opening sets their expectations. Although the dancer does not seem frightened at the beginning of the piece, her steps are tentative, the music is halting, and she needs to find her groove. It is an awakening, a testing out of a body. The music supports this process, drawing the dancer in to its rhythm. The dancer takes minimal steps in moving across the floor. Her hair and arm tosses punctuate the tone. But it is the hip swings and lower-torso rotations that truly draw our attention. Two moments in particular—the single beat/double beat percussive swings to the side with a funky attitude and the moment she stops, takes her time, and executes a slow, full hip rotation—emphasize the importance the piece attaches to the lower extremities. Her pleasant, hip, assured demeanor communicates the ultimate message of the piece—black women should accept their posteriors despite what history and society might try to dictate.

In many ways, this journey is an inscription of the message of the piece that exhorts us, especially black women, to celebrate all parts of our bodies, particularly those that have been taboo. It is an attitude that encourages playfulness, sensuality, self-assurance, sexuality, and power. In the next section, the rhythm shifts so that African and Southern beats are more pronounced, and singers come in. The dancer does small skips to the lively beat, making full commitment to an energy that radiates with poise and conviction. It is as if the dancer has blessed the space, claiming ownership over it and her body. Some yells are heard from offstage in celebration of her accomplishments and encouraging her. At one point she stops abruptly, starts swinging with a very cool aesthetic, and, isolating her buttocks, looks over her shoulders as if to see what they can do. The piece that began from a tentative impulse ends in affirmation, joy, and fun.

This attitude flies in the face of centuries of negative representations of black female bodies and the damaging effects of racist, sexist conclusions drawn about black women's place in the world. I pause here to contextualize the black female bottom as a discursive site. It has a long and vexed history, and it is in light of many nuanced and loaded meanings that we must understand Zollar's constructions. Not just any body part, the buttocks have served as a central image for African American female sexuality since the antebellum era. Large hips are a vital part of the stereotype of the slave woman, paradoxically both grotesque and sexually enticing. A site of desire in and of themselves, the buttocks also conceal an even more "mysterious" site—the labia. According to Gottschild, "Indeed, the buttocks stand as a secondary sexual substitute for the real thing."[23]

The most powerful and devastating example of the legacy from which Zollar draws is the story of Sarah (aka Saartjie, Saartje) Bartmann (aka Baartman, Bartman), a black woman believed to be from South Africa who was brought to London in 1810 by William Dunlop, a British ship's doctor, as both a scientific curiosity and a circus freak.[24] She was lured with promises of riches but upon arrival was forced to exhibit herself, scantily clad even in the cold months, as an exotic aberrant in circuses, museums, bars, and universities. Endowed with what were considered abnormally large buttocks and genitalia (a condition known as steatopygia), she was given the labels "The Venus Hottentot" and "Black Venus." Steatopygia eroticized women and became the "scientific" explanation for prostitution and for Freud's later diagnosis of nymphomania. She was one of a number of such exhibitions.[25]

After her "success" in the English provinces, in 1814 she was taken to Paris, where an animal trainer exhibited her daily, from eleven in the morning until ten at night, for fifteen months in a shed in the Rue Neuve. She was then given to a wild animal showman. By November 1815, she was gravely ill and could no longer be exhibited.

Her double status as freak and symbol of love, femininity, beauty, and purity (Venus) epitomizes the contradictions of desire in her relationship to Western constructions of the exotic/erotic, though Western men of science remarkably failed to acknowledge the erotic tension. The Black Venus is a vexed label that may hold more value than originally admitted. The contradictions in the colonial mind between the black and the Venus image may not be as stark as believed. Roland Barthes suggests that it would be absurd to conceive of her as the object of desire, but as the longevity of her legacy attests, there is something about her (especially her buttocks) that continues to intrigue and entice.[26] Stereotypes and cartoons were created in order to reinforce this relationship. She has had a profound effect in many spaces, according to poet and scholar Anca Vlasopolos: "Venus has exerted immense erotic fascination for the Western world, reflected for two centuries in fashions, paintings, and literature." We see this in the voluminous addition of padding (the bustle) and adornments in the form of ribbons and bows to the backs of European women's dresses in the nineteenth century, blurring the boundaries between the normal and the deviant, the sacred and the profane, the divine and the bestial. Vlasopolos put it well: "*La Vénus Noire* embodies, after all, the unsuspected desire of white men, poets, painters, civil servants, and of women, 'slaves' of fashion models, muses, for a fetishized Other, dis-embodied in the Venus Hottentot."[27]

Bartmann was ultimately given to the anatomist and zoologist Georges Cuvier, who (despite the fact that she was dying) commissioned a painting of her in the nude at the Jardin du Roi for "scientific" purposes.[28] After her death on December 29, 1815 (sources vary about whether she died of smallpox, exposure, syphilis, tuberculosis, or alcoholism), Cuvier made a plaster cast of her body and conducted experiments on her body in the name of science. She was approximately twenty-five years old.

Because Cuvier writes of his surprise upon examining her labia postmortem, we can deduce that Bartmann successfully resisted this invasion while she was alive. However, upon her death her entire body was at his disposal. He used Bartmann as a case study to "prove" hypotheses of racial inferiority as well as sexual proclivities.[29] Eventually, Cuvier cut her body into pieces, jarred the parts in formaldehyde, and placed the jars on display at the Musée de l'Homme in Paris. She was reduced to a collection of sexual parts. Somehow divorced from moral responsibility (no doubt under the illusion of science), the museum allowed spectators to gaze upon her dissected body relatively guilt-free. In 1974, due to public pressure, the jars were removed from public viewing and put in storage. In February 2002, after about six years of concerted efforts by the government of newly liberated South Africa, France finally returned Bartmann to South Africa (two hundred years after she left).

In a very direct way, Bartmann's story illustrates Foucault's first two modes of objectification of the subject through the exercise of power on the body. Bartmann was separated from her land with promises of riches and separated from herself as she came to comprehend how others viewed her. In the name of science, she was classified as abnormal and became a thing to be looked at and studied. To the world, she ceased being a person with interiority and became solely a body. The pseudoscientific fascination with the different served a pathological desire of the power structure to define normality by dissecting that which is considered abnormal in order to solidify its own place as normal (and, by extension, better, just, and good). P. T. Barnum made a career out of taking control over others' performances of identity. The exploitation of Sarah Bartmann lies at the nexus of performance, medicine, anthropology, zoology, Darwinian evolutionary biology, comparative taxonomy, colonialism, and tyranny.

In *Difference and Pathology*, Sander L. Gilman gives an account of the historical and psychological creation of stereotypes based on race and gender. Chapter 3, "The Hottentot and the Prostitute: Toward an Iconography of Female Sexuality," is devoted to an explanation of the role played by representations of blackness and female sexuality during the eighteenth and nineteenth centuries. This sexuality was inextricably linked in popular conception to animality, particularly wild, apelike lasciviousness. Rumors spread that black women actually did copulate with apes.

Foucault's process of classification plays an important role when one looks at the myths created by the Venus Hottentot situation. As Gilman points out, the labels of the primitive and hypersexual black would not have held were it not for the system of "science" that developed to "prove" the conclusions through evaluation and experimentation. Sarah Bartmann provided the definitive case study in this skewed scientific system of sociocultural Darwinism. Cuvier's description of Sarah Bartmann after her autopsy concluded that she was part of the lowest form of human species. According to Gilman, "If their sexual parts could be shown to be inherently different, this would be a sufficient sign that blacks were a separate (and needless to say, lower) race, as different from the European as the proverbial orangutan. Similar arguments were made about the nature of all blacks' (not just Hottentots') genitalia, but almost always concerning the female."[30]

So, black women have had to contend with the legacy of this stereotype of pathology that has stigmatized their very existence in western society.[31] Indeed, the true pathology might be Europeans' and North Americans' simultaneous attraction to and repulsion from the black female body through a fictionalized construction of black female identity. This complex, distorted desire conflates everything in the lower regions (the buttocks, genitals, hips) as the locus of the mysterious, primitive, wild, animal, grotesque, risqué, dangerous, and base. This process of classifying and stereotyping was a way for whites to define their identities against blackness. By retaining control of agency in this relationship, they could assure themselves that nobody would challenge this system and that their senses of self were secure. Today, black women still have to contend with these representations, stereotypes, and power dynamics. As black women gain power in this dialectic, artists, theorists, and scholars tend to agree on the desirable power of representation, even if they are still debating the pros and cons of specific images and the real political process toward improving the relationship black women have with their bodies. This is the project of *Batty Moves.*

In its second section, the lights come up on eight women calmly walking with a slight swagger onto the stage. They get into a line parallel to the audience facing upstage, and as each steps into place she punctuates her arrival by swinging her hips on her final two steps. These women move with a mixture of sensuality, power, and attitude. The woman stage left begins a chain in which each dancer swings her hips quickly (punctuated with arms and torsos), rotates her head to the woman on her left, and, giving attitude, yells to her, "Say what?!" Each woman's bottom, more than her mouth, seems to be doing the talking. "Say what?!" becomes question, commandment, and exclamation and responds with indignation to whatever was just said. Each woman responds with surprise and offense to the audacity of the statement or request that precipitated it. I imagine somebody has just asked them to wash their floor or stated that they were not permitted to do something or go somewhere. These women are having none of it. The last woman gets the message and replies, "Say what, honey-child?!" "Honey-child" then travels back in the other direction to the same charged gesticulations, as if the women are telling their girlfriends about the outrageous thing that happened to them and reassuring each other. This "conversation" through the buttocks emphasizes the attitude needed for resistance; it begins a build-up of empowering energy.

Throughout this section the dancers mostly keep their backs to the audience. In unison, they sink into their hips, bounce down, and as they rebound they look over at their bottoms, alternating sides with each bounce. On a yell from one of the performers, the women crouch even lower, further punctuating the buttocks, in case there is any doubt about where the audience should focus. For two counts of eight the dancers hop backward (toward the audience) and push up their bums on each beat. They march back upstage, posing in different stances as one woman turns to the audience, calls out to it, and turns back around with a head roll and a snap up (one of the most powerful gestures of attitude in the black female movement arsenal). They move into a sequence of fast-paced, hard-hitting steps and shakes and begin the phrase again, looking over their shoulders as they bounce. Zollar is making a statement simply by having the women keep their backs to the audience for so long. Rather than a position of vulnerability, having their backs turned to the audience becomes one of strength. More dancers enter, and the movement shifts between pounding, weighty, muscular, confrontational movement to one that is casual and social, more like nightclub dancing. The juxtaposition of the in-your-face attitude and relaxed self-assuredness sets a strong tone for the performance, both mindful of the audience to the point of sassy defiance and indifferent to outside judgments. This is an important postmodern embrace of the both/and and a rearticulation of Du Bois's concept of double-consciousness. They exist on the stage *both* as to-be-looked-at *and* as ends in themselves. They perform with *both* a self-conscious awareness of the implications of taboo and codification in their movements *and* a cool dismissal of them (as opposed to an anxiety-ridden suppression).

At the end of this section, the dancers spread out into a traditional circle (they stand in a semicircle, with the audience completing the circle) to allow soloists to come out and improvise. It is as if Zollar left this space in the piece open for the spirit to catch the dancers, allowing them to riff on the batty theme. The dancers on the side clap and shout out support for each one in the center, and they take turns showing the audience their stuff. After the final solo, the group comes together again. As the lights come down, the sense is that they are each grooving to the rhythms, power, and joy of their own bodies with the support of other women around them.

The firsthand accounts of the Bartmann spectacle are mainly given through the eyes and writings of the white men who gazed on, dissected, and labeled her: she was literally divided and conquered. Now there is a desire to get at the woman behind the image, however impossible that project may be. What was she thinking? What was it like to be *that* objectified? It is almost as if contemporary artists are doing battle with the extant record to counter Cuvier's assessment. The contemporary project becomes a metaphorical reassembling of her body. Though we may never be satisfied with these attempts, and they will perhaps always be surrounded by controversy, they serve a healing purpose for contemporary black women, and *Batty Moves* directly participates in this project. That Bartmann was and is distinctly without voice or personal story is catastrophic. It is for humanity's sake that so many have tried to give her voice and dignity, reimagine her as a whole self, and re-empower the body parts whose treatment was the source of her tragedy.

We may also wonder what lies behind the continued obsession with black women's buttocks; they have always held power for women of color, be it as the control others took to define them or as the source from which they now gather strength. In the twentieth and early twenty-first centuries, women of color have found various ways to use their buttocks to claim agency and authority over their lives. As Vlasopolos points out, "[This] nexus of sex, climate, race, class, anatomical stigmata, mental illness, ethical lapses, deviant sexuality and endangered/ing reproduction has been examined and unraveled again and again."[32]

In this context, *Batty Moves* again asks its audience members to reevaluate their notions about the significance of the buttocks. Importantly, this is in the context *not* of increasing one's desirability to men or of being young and current with popular trends. Rather, it is a celebration of the individual without validating dominant culture. As part of Urban Bush Women's project toward healing, *Batty Moves* is a highly politicized reassessment of the body. We are asked to celebrate the body part for ourselves, not others. Ananya Chatterjea states that this type of representation "springs . . . from an ability to love and value our physicality and a calm assertion of our need to have control over our representation. . . . In such choreography, subversion and critique are braided with celebration and creativity."[33] Similarly, Thomas F. DeFrantz articulates this: "[Zollar] means to heal the dancers and the dance by reminding us how our bodies are profound not just in the metaphors they inspire, but in the memories they contain."[34] The dancers take the term "reversing the gaze" in a new direction. Like staring back at the camera in film, turning their backs to the audience and emphasizing their rear ends is a politically charged move. They "stare" back at the audience with their backsides in a power play that renegotiates control of their bodies.

Hand Singing Song

Dance is the fist with which I fight the sickening ignorance of prejudice.

Pearl Primus,
Dance Magazine interview, 1968

I am black and I have seen black hands
Raised in fists of revolt, side by side with the white fists of white workers,
And some day—and it is only this which sustains me—
Some day there shall be millions and millions of them,
On some red day in a burst of fists on a new horizon!

Richard Wright,
"I Have Seen Black Hands"

I believe in the magic of the hands.

Assata Shakur,
"I Believe in Living"

> Look at me! Look at my arm! I have plowed, and planted, and gathered into barns, and no man could head me—and ain't I a woman?
>
> Sojourner Truth, "Ain't I a Woman?"

Isabella Baumfree (later Sojourner Truth), an escaped slave, spiritual leader, and activist, addressed a women's rights convention in 1851. She pulled up her sleeve, made a fist, and displayed the muscles shaped by years of slave labor in the field. She stood over six feet tall and to one master was "better . . . than a man" because of her ability to do both "women's work" and "men's work." Though her hard work for her masters led to ridicule from her fellow slaves, she proved that she was no complacent mammy by escaping the terror at the first opportunity when things became unbearable, despite the fact that the New York State emancipation laws would take effect just one year later. In 1826 the strong hands that had gotten her through life became badly diseased. Her master used this as an excuse to renege on his promise to set her free. Fed up, Truth escaped with her baby in one arm and a few provisions in her other.

Throughout U.S. history, the image of muscular black woman has pervaded popular culture. At its worst, it is a misleading stereotype. At its best, it is a source of inspiration for women the world over. As in the 1940s poster of Pearl Primus dancing in *The Negro Speaks of Rivers*, dance and power often go hand in hand. Caught in an attitude leap so high the floor is not visible, Primus raises her head proud, eyes open wide, chest broad, and, most germane to this discussion, fists clenched and muscles flexed.

With her concert dance piece *Hand Singing Song*, Zollar claims a place as Primus's heir. The piece serves as a monument to the resolve and strength of black women using the image of black female hands as a metaphor. These hands comfort, pray, and punch. *Hand Singing Song*, a reach back to history and a call to future triumphs, is a forty-minute performance divided into six sections. The first section, "Give Your Hands to Struggle," begins with calls out to the ancestors. Voices in the dark proclaim the names of historical figures who were or are leaders in the struggle for freedom and equality: Sojourner Truth, Frederick Douglass, Harriet Tubman, Nat Turner, Sitting Bull, Medgar Evers, César Chávez, and Leonard Peltier. As the audience listens to the names, a circular spotlight comes up on a soloist, front and center. Her movements are slow and sinuous, weighty and requiring a great deal of strength to execute. Her arms circle the space, her chest expands, and her head reaches back. Upstage right of her, another spotlight reveals a small group of people dressed in red robes, calling out the names, standing as symbols of her ancestry, giving her the strength she needs to go on and build on the works of those who've gone before. She does not acknowledge them physically or verbally. They are like the voices in her head, the stories in her memory that empower her. The group supports her by swaying and moaning a spiritual, bringing her a certain surety and peace; several times she is able to simply walk forward, hands raised to her chest as if she is taking a precious piece of herself and offering it to the audience. From this base of support and through this gesture, she allows the spirit of the movement to possess her, and her movements become freer. She steps out of this to slowly assume the familiar Black Power liberation posture—feet in a wide, secure stance, muscles tense, head down, right arm raised up and out, and hand in a tightly clenched fist. This gesture echoes throughout the entire performance as a reminder not to give up the struggle for liberation. This first moment is in the context of African American heritage as the source of power. From her ancestors and the spirit, she acquires the strength to struggle and survive. With them, she is a force to be reckoned with. The music builds, and the spirit takes increasing possession of her body, until she at last fully abandons herself. Her head commits to the actions so that she need not look everywhere she is going, checking in with the ground. Rather, she trusts that the ground will be there to support her. She raises her hand up in glory, and as the spirit washes over her, the audience sees the wave course through her body. As the possession ends, she moves more calmly, walking in circles, arms raised up, head back as if taking in the sun. The lights come down as she brings her hands to her heart.

By beginning the piece with this look to history, Zollar connects it to the long line of figures in the struggle for freedom and equality. She claims this connection through the hands. In addition to washing, ironing, and cooking, slave women's hands were put to use hoeing fields and picking crops, sometimes while nursing, thereby creating both productive and reproductive labor for the plantation.[35]

Slaves were literally considered "hands." This synecdoche defined the "worth" of many field slaves. In a Foucauldian exercise of power, masters classified hands according to individual strength and endurance. Contrary to contemporaneous beliefs about the delicate female constitution, reserved for white women, black women were not exempt from this classification. According to Jacqueline Jones:

> Judged on the basis of a standard set by a healthy adult man, most women probably ranked as three-quarter hands; yet there were enough women like Susan Mabry of Virginia, who could pick 400 or 500 pounds of cotton a day (150 to 200 pounds was considered respectable for an average worker) to remove from a master's mind all doubts about the ability of a

> strong, healthy woman field worker. As a result, he conveniently discarded his time-honored Anglo-Saxon notions about the types of work best suited for women.

Black men were three-fifths a man, and black women were three-quarters of that. Pregnant and nursing women were typically considered half hands if they picked less than the average 150 pounds of cotton per day. By doing what they were forced to do, Jones explains, slave women gained a reputation for being abnormally suited for manual labor, unlike their white counterparts: "White men and women from the North and South marveled at the skill and strength of female plow hands."[36] The image of the strong black woman developed into an overpowering national myth and stereotype; we are still wrestling with the ramifications of this. The myth, according to scholar Michele Wallace, is that she is "too domineering, too strong, too aggressive, too outspoken, too castrating, too masculine."[37]

Somewhere between superhero and victim lies the truth of African American female subjectivity. Black women's victimization serves an argument for their strength. But without strength, how could Harriet Tubman have escaped slavery and keep returning to the South to rescue others, victim though she was? Slave women were, above all, victims of an oppressive regime. Nevertheless, we cannot ignore the strength it took to survive. Slave women were more likely than slave men to stand up to their masters in verbal confrontation and by striking them, although fewer of them ran away, probably because of their family obligations.[38] They often worked as hard as men, they nursed the other slaves, they pilfered food to feed runaway slaves, and they bore children under impossible circumstances. For all these reasons and many more, many people, including those in the concert dance tradition, have taken pride in the physical, emotional, and spiritual strength of these women. Rejecting the idealization of the frail, airy nymphs of classical European ballet, African American female choreographers like Pearl Primus, Blondell Cummings, and Zollar prefer grounded, weighty, and strong physical vocabularies.

Hands appear as important images throughout African American cultural history. Hand jive is a language unto itself, and the high five (along with other black "handshakes") is a powerful greeting, loaded with implications about status and coolness. These are such strong gestures that they have permeated mainstream U.S. society. Some African Americans shake their hands instead of or in addition to their heads to indicate a negative response. The hands of black boxers like Jack Johnson and Mohammed Ali became symbols of the potential of the race. In black and Latino gay culture the snap is a powerful retort, an exclamation point that punctuates and closes a discussion.[39] Fists and violence are

Christalyn Wright, Gacirah Diagne, and Beverley Prentice-Hall in *Bones and Ash: A Gilda Story*. Photo by Cylla Von Tiedemann.

also an important part of African American history, and the image of black fists breaking chains abounds. In his autobiography, Frederick Douglass talks about striking his master as being the moment he moved from slave to man. Malcolm X rejects a guidance counselor's suggestion that he make his living working with his hands. Black grandmothers' hands dexterously knit, sew, quilt, testify, pray, and comfort. Booker T. Washington extolled the virtues of manual labor. In Lorraine Hansberry's *Raisin in the Sun*, Mama Younger talks about the pride her late husband had in turning the earth with his hands. Writing became a means to freedom for many slaves, and slave autobiographies that were "handwritten" by the slaves are prized.

Zollar uses the title of the second piece to name the entire performance. In "Hand Singing Song," Zollar lets the hands do the talking. The focus is on the hand gestures and movements that resonate particularly for African Americans.

The piece opens with five women standing casually in a line. There is no music. Each dancer moves through a series of pantomimed gestures that isolate the hands, abstractions of everyday movements—showering, cooking, shaking a finger at a naughty child. After a time, the dancers freeze. Then, in unison, they walk toward the audience, each bringing a hand forward, palm up as if offering something to them. The other hand swings around from the back and slaps the palm. The dancers walk backward upstage, hands raised as if they are being arrested or want to show that they are unarmed. This opening sequence raises the seemingly banal to the symbolic. The level of isolation and abstraction, together with the silence, focuses our attention on the ways the body (particularly the hands) carves through space. The gestures, the varied rhythms, the play with unison, and the contrasts create "music" enough.

The overhead floodlights darken so that the dancers are isolated center stage, illuminated only by sidelighting. They lean toward the audience, touch their fingers to their mouths, and whisper, "Shhh." They repeat the various gesture sequences in silence with a serious, committed tone. The mood abruptly lightens as the dancers begin doing the Hokey Pokey, a release of tension and an embrace of the playfulness of everyday gestures. Yet this sense of security turns out to be a false one as the children's game suddenly turns violent. The first dancer in line turns, looks up sharply, and asks, "What?!" Her eyes widen, registering some frightening force. The dancers hide their faces and cower in fear. Operating under that oppression, the first dancer in line grabs the right arm of the next dancer, pushes it forward while commanding her to put her right hand in and out, in a violent round of Hokey Pokey. The first dancer does not appear to want to be inflicting this pain on the next but is compelled to do so by the force. The invisible hand of oppression is forcing one dancer to torment the next. Each dancer takes a turn being her neighbor's torturer, always with an awareness of the governing force. When all the women scream "That's what it's all about!" the last woman is forced to repeat the scenario with a significant change. The final dancer reverses the in/out action so that when she says "I put my right hand in," she plunges an imaginary knife into her heart. She pulls it out on "I take my right hand out," and then with both hands around it, she plunges the "knife" into her stomach on the second "I put my right hand in." The harmless children's game has transmogrified into a vignette of torture, self-inflicted wounds, and suicidal gestures. A barrage of insults begins traversing the line to the accompaniment of slaps. The damage of affronts like "You so black and ugly!" "Nappy-head!" and "Big-lipped!" are played out on each dancer emotionally and physically as she alternates between being oppressor and oppressed. The hands are the means by which violence is inflicted. Each dancer then twists her open palm into a mock gun that she points at the audience and fires. The guns are transformed back into open palms and the gesture of offering repeats.

The piece "On the Black Hand Side" is an homage to race pride and creativity as expressed with hands and the elaborate handshakes and gestures developed by African Americans throughout history. Zollar explains that rather than adopt European methods of physical contact during greetings and leavings, African Americans developed new forms in order to claim separate space, assert self-determined identity, and show solidarity. Developed by musicians, the handshakes indicate liberation from oppression through style. For the simple gestures to be improved on, they must be complex and labyrinthine. Each position must be hit precisely, as the dancers demonstrate by yelling "Bam!" each time they strike a pose in the process of shaking hands. Each "Bam!" becomes one more blow to the power structure. The handshakes are firm, and precision and confidence are hallmarks; there is no room for shakiness or sloppiness in the struggle.

All of this happens under the aesthetic of the cool, of course. Jazz music begins to play and the traditions of black greetings from slipping skin to high-fiving are connected. The revolutionary spirit of the late 1960s and early 1970s is connected to the spirit of the 1920s and 1930s. By participating in this intricate ceremony, the individual dancers become a part of a larger project. The hands move through ritualistic twistings, and handshakes lead to hugs—bodies touching heart to heart. Finally, these gestures lead again to the Black Power sign. They are part of a community in which members support and nurture one another. From this foundation, the next several pieces explore guiding hands as the means toward self-discovery.

In "Hands Singing Hallelujah," a woman remembers her grandmother reaching out her hands to her, saying, "Come, give grandmother a hug." The hugs were warm and cuddly, and the woman always felt secure in her grandmother's arms. She strokes her chest as she remembers times when she was sick and her grandmother would smooth vapor rub into her chest, promising that she would feel better in the morning. Her grandmother's love and care manifested through her hands has made a deep, lasting impression on the woman, inspiring her to sing:

> I think I saw my grandma's hands.
> They were praying hands.
> Hands that held me, oh, so close.
> Hands that guided me on my way.
> Praying hands.
> Praying hands.

> I think I saw my grandma's hands.
> They were healing hands.
> Hands that comforted.
> Hands that calmed.
> Hands that eased my way.
> Healing hands.
> Healing hands.

This physical, emotional, and spiritual healing, passed down through the generations, has given the woman the strength to go through life. Three dancers take turns giving and taking each other's weight. They lift and carry each other. They protect each other, stay grounded so others can fly, and are there to catch whichever may fall. These three women, perhaps grandmother, mother, and child, stay connected throughout the piece, each always aware of what the others are doing. As the woman downstage sings "Hallelujah!" over and over again, the three women rest in a silhouetted tableau, hands interlocked, facing the singer as she walks slowly offstage.

The performance ends with "Hand to Fist," a heavy, driving piece about the Black Panthers and the revolutionary movement toward self-liberation for African Americans. The piece is an investigation of dap—the complex series of hand greeting that black soldiers brought back from Vietnam. Dap becomes an integral part of the movement—the greeting symbolized strength, power, solidarity, even in the face of the many challenges the party faced, particularly those the FBI created.

Zollar enters and recites a poem in which she recounts a time African Americans were attempting to redefine and reaffirm their place in the world. With a revolutionary posture and an African style, they resisted the forces that attempted to annihilate them. The drummer comes out dressed in black, with a black beret, and as he drums, the dancers enter the stage, checking each other out. Zollar talks about how they needed to make sure a person was an ally. The handshake became a code, a signal to let members know they were among friends. Later in the Black Power movement, as there were more and more conspiracies and the fear of infiltration and retaliation by spies increased, members of the party were put on guard, and handshakes became a means of determining who was loyal to the cause. The fist in the Black Power gesture is meant to knock down the wall of oppression, prejudice, and hate. It is a symbol of might, meant to be inspirational and hopeful and inspire fear in those who would oppose the tenets of the movement. Though the Panther party was controversial, many found power in the clenched fist. One crowning, epic moment of the Black Power movement was the 1968 Olympic Games in Mexico City, during which American sprinters Tommie Smith and John Carlos, gold and bronze medalists, respectively, accepted their medals wearing black stockings with no shoes and a black glove on one hand. Smith also wore a black scarf around his neck. When "The Star Spangled Banner" began, each of them raised a gloved fist and bowed his head. The crowd booed them. When they left the stadium, the crowd booed them again, and they, again, raised their fists. Though they became pariahs to the official Olympic organizations and were vilified in many newspapers, to many their gestures symbolized the potency of the increasingly politicized black national identity. They took a moment of allegiance to nation and proclaimed the primacy of their *black* nationality. The act meant fear for some and dignity for others. It is this complexity that Urban Bush Women taps into in "Hands to Fist."

In the dance piece, the dancers grasp hands and in unison jerk their torsos to the beat until freezing in a Black Power tableau, hands in fists raised high in the air and punching forward forcefully. They begin a rhythm section, stomping and slapping their hands against their bodies. The action echoes Zollar's use of children's games, but with their black costumes (complete with black berets) and determined attitudes the dancers convey that this is anything but child's play. The driving rhythm played out on their bodies calls others to the stage the way drums called to rebelling slaves in the antebellum South. The group repeats the greetings from "On the Black Hand Side" with slaps, snaps, bumps, grasps, and so forth, and takes them to a new level. The drumming kicks in again and the dancers move in unison, hands in fists, angrily kicking, stomping, and punching. They violently spar with one another in a capoeira-like display that breaks occasionally for the dancers to give the Black Power sign. They then chaotically move through the space—yelling at the audience until one dancer freezes the motion and brings the dancers back together, moving in step to the same beat, thereby channeling the anger back into productive energy. Warrior-like, soldier-like, the dancers move in a circle. But this is only a temporary assembly of ranks. As Zollar talks about the decline of the Black Panther Party, the rhythm slows down and a few dancers get out of step. She speaks of people leaving the movement because they were tired and burnt out. Some left because they got a little piece of the pie, others did because they thought the movement was built on shaky ground—internal conflicts, abuse of power, abuse of women, homophobia, and sexism. Perhaps the strategy of using violence by those on whom so much violence was used came to be too much for some. All of this, possibly spurred on by FBI conspiracies, weakened the force of the message and pitted party members against one another. Drug use increased and suspicions flared.

One by one the dancers leave, until only two remain, circling each other like vultures, viciously pushing and hitting each other. Soon, only one remains, and she takes off her beret in disgust. But Zollar hopes that perhaps even though people left the movement, they didn't leave the struggle for justice, and they are out in the world working to improve it, in small but powerful ways. We might take this statement (and indeed, the whole performance) as a metaphor for Zollar's work to bring about liberation and healing through dance on the concert stage and in communities.

The remaining dancer, illuminated by a single spot, continues to dance and struggle until she brings others back, one by one. Zollar reminds us to keep working and working toward liberation of all people. Individuals can inspire groups. As she and the drummer riff on the theme of "work it out," the dancers resume their circle, again moving in concert, building on each other's energy. The final moment has the dancers paused at different points in the circle, facing outward. They reach out their hands palms up, make fists, and bring the fists back to their hearts. The stage goes black on Zollar's last line: "We gotta work this out!"

Hands, like hair and butts, are vital tools Urban Bush Women uses to work audiences into working out deep-seated social issues. They are potent parts of the black female body, capable of being loaded and reloaded with symbolism. Each piece fearlessly traverses dangerous territory to do battle with disempowering stereotypes. Together, they form an arsenal in the movement to reclaim the black female body and heal the old wounds. All of the pieces analyzed in this chapter open up places for dialogue about what the state of affairs for black women's bodies looks like to all of us. Solutions are not simple, though the message is clearly that the struggle must continue.

3

The Word

Black Magic Realism

Though some contemporary dance-theater choreographers are using dramatic tension in their work, few fully explore storytelling and narrative. In the late twentieth century, the vogue was for abstract conceptual art in which dance pieces are more about lines, patterns, form, shape, theme, and variation than narrative. Even very "dramatic" choreographers like Pina Bausch preferred to riff on a concept rather than tell a story from beginning to end in a linear or even circular form. Zollar has said, "It's a tenet of postmodern dance that using stories is passé. It hasn't stopped me, though I've never felt comfortable going against the trend."[1] When I asked her about her use of narrative and storytelling, she replied, "I don't know. It's not something I try to do. It's just something that I do. And now I'm just more conscious of the fact that I like to tell stories. And I think it's something that, particularly in the '70s and '80s, was very much *not* postmodern."[2]

African and African American forms of storytelling tend to embrace both the linear and the circular and blur (or indeed simply refuse to accept) boundaries between theater, dance, storytelling, and ritual. Black performing artists have often created work on their own terms and many see Eurocentric structures as limiting. Interesting theater often comes out of African American dance.[3] Although this kind of artistic work often proves economically difficult, there remains a continuous exploration of these crossovers. This way of working appears throughout the history of African American theatrical events.

Zollar is committed to linear and circular forms of storytelling that embrace theater, dance, singing, and ritual. She is committed to using narrative and narration in traditional ways to communicate a message. Some of Urban Bush Women's works, therefore, have much in common with classical story ballet as well as black storytelling techniques. Many of her pieces are adaptations of literary texts and adhere to the basic principles of storytelling—including

Deborah Thomas, Maia Claire Garrison, Carl Hancock Rux, Trinket Monsod, Valerie Winborne, Treva Offutt, Kwame Ross, Beverley Prentice, Gacirah Diagne, Christine King, and Christalyn Wright in *Bones and Ash: A Gilda Story*. Photo by Cylla Von Tiedemann.

plot, themes, characters, and dramatic narrative structure. In this respect, one can read these dances like one does written texts.

One of the devices central to Zollar's compositions is the use of supernatural events to more clearly develop characters. Second, the dancers/characters often speak to each other as well as the audience and sometimes act as the narrators of their own stories. Third, the journeys of the pieces are often ritualistic and involve the conjuring of gods and ancestors to obtain healing. These journeys toward self-discovery and healing are directly in line with the overall goals of the company; the dances themselves not only tell the story of people who have achieved healing, but they also have the potential to be the vehicle that brings about similar responses in some audience members. The simple act of talking to the audience is a direct attempt to bring them into the story, setting up the dance as a potential sacred space in which a ritual transformation may take place.

Though the emphasis is on movement, the personalities of the performers are individualized with dramatic arcs. In the rehearsal process, storyboards are used to map out the arc of the experience and particular attention is paid to dramatic organization. Dancers go through acting and movement exercises to bring out characters. The dances use suggestive sets, props, and costume pieces (though the performers usually remain barefoot).

Urban Bush Women draws from the long tradition of storytelling in the African Diaspora. All three of the pieces analyzed here are literary in scope, and interrogating them transgresses the line separating literary criticism and performance analysis. Though most black literary theory focuses on oral and written traditions (sometimes privileging oral), corporal forms of communication are also vital to African American cultural tradition. Dance is a way of writing with and on the body. Movement becomes text with physical vocabulary, metaphors, and motifs. In this chapter, I investigate Urban Bush Women's use of storytelling, theater, archetype, myth, and the supernatural by analyzing *Praise House*, *Bones and Ash: A Gilda Story*, and *Shadow's Child*.[4] Based in African and African American storytelling traditions, these pieces show black women facing their demons, doing battle, and triumphing. I argue that by creating characters who exist in alternate realities and characters who represent entire populations, the company is attempting to rewrite master narratives. The characters push against the gaps of history and narrative and challenge us to move beyond stereotypical and limiting images of black women. These dances are exercises of agency over the stories of black women and the languages with which they are communicated. Ultimately, they are part of a long tradition of strategically employing storytelling as a means of negotiating power.

Karla F. C. Holloway offers insight into Urban Bush Women's work with her theory of plurisignant texts in the tradition of African American women's literature. These texts resist simple interpretations by making use of multiple expressions and recurring shifting language. This fracturedness often reflects the fractured psyche of the main characters, and the process of negotiating the multiplicity is the work of the text. According to Holloway, the recursive structures and strategies are part of Urban Bush Women's narrative dances: "Recursive structures accomplish a blend between figurative processes that are reflective (like a mirror) and symbolic processes whose depth and resonance make them reflexive. This combination results in texts that are at once emblematic of the culture they describe as well as interpretive of this culture. Literature that strikes this reflective/reflexive posture is characteristically polyphonic."[5]

Holloway further notes the line of continuity in texts of African American women's writings and cites many characters who see themselves surrounded by a tradition of women like them rather than reflecting in isolation. She points to Shange's *Sassafrass, Cypress and Indigo*, Brooks's *Maud Martha*, and all of the women of Gloria Naylor's *The Women of Brewster Place*. Likewise, in the three pieces I investigate in this chapter, the main characters undergo processes of (re)membrance in the company of women (ancestral, spiritual, and worldly) who give them what they need to "get over" and/or work through. These women mingle language and "speak" to each other through poetry, music, and dance, as well as dialogue, to entertain, guide, and ultimately point to resolution.

Praise House

People think I say foolish things, Sara. . . . But I know what I say. Listen to me. America is like the sea. . . . America can drown you like the sea.

Grandmother,
in Elizabeth Nunez, *Beyond the Limbo Silence*

Draw or die.

Minnie Evans,
quoted in Regenia A. Perry, *Free within Ourselves*

I seek only to forget the sorrows
of my grandmother's
silence.

Anasuya Sengupta,
"Silence"

A praise house is a traditional, informal spiritual gathering, often without a preacher. Different types of praise houses exist, but southern black Pentecostal praise houses are often the loci of very charged worship. People come together to praise the Lord with singing and dancing. Sometimes the spirit takes them and they are inspired to shake, speak in tongues, and cry. Praise dancing honors God through many different types of movement, and praise dance schools have even emerged to educate Christians on using dance to more fully worship God. Hip-hop, jazz, ballet, and modern praise dancing have all taken place in these settings.[6] The movements of mass choirs are a type of praise dancing. Praise dancing often combines symbolic gestures with more or less abstract dance. In all forms, the dancers interpret inspirational music. Another term used to describe this movement is liturgical dance, since the dancing body becomes a vessel for the spirit and the entire focus of the movement is on the deity. According to Gottschild, all praise dancing comes down to the heart of the matter: "the fact of human pain and suffering and the window of release through spiritual transcendence."[7] Praise dancing concerns the dancer's personal relationship with God and is less of a presentation for an audience. Despite this, interpretations of praise dancing have made their way to the concert dance stage.[8] In *Praise House*, Urban Bush Women examines the power of this tradition through the story of Minnie Evans, an African American folk artist.

Minnie Evans (1892–1987) was an African American artist who didn't start creating art until she was forty-three, when a voice told her to "draw or die." Her personal history was filled with strong women. One ancestor was an African slave in Trinidad who ended up in Wilmington, North Carolina. Evans was raised by her grandmother and saw her mother (only fourteen years older) as a sister figure. Although she had to leave school in sixth grade to earn a living, she loved learning and cherished the Bible stories that formed the core of her Baptist faith. As a child, she heard voices and had waking dreams and visions of prophets and religious figures, real and mythical animals, flowers, plants, and faces. She also dreamed every night. According to author Gylbert Coker, "There were times when Evans could barely distinguish between dreams and visions, as well as between dreams and wakeful experience."[9] These visions often caused her confusion, though she was conscious of having them. She was very "cautious about letting other people become aware of this phenomenon."[10] She recognized the strategic use of silence. As Foucault claimed, "There are not one but many silences, and they are an integral part of the strategies that underlie and permeate discourses."[11]

Minnie Evans did her first drawing on Good Friday in 1935 and her next on the following day. Her process was automatic and, some say, divinely inspired. Evans stated: "I have no imagination. I never plan a drawing. They just happen."[12] When she began drawing in earnest, five years later, her family feared that she was losing her mind. She gave away her drawings and then began selling them for fifty cents each. Nina Howell Starr, a photography graduate student, "discovered" Evans and became her de facto agent, showing her work in New York galleries. For the next forty-seven years Minnie Evans continued to receive divinely inspired influences to draw or die. She died at the age of ninety-five.

On folk art, Zollar has said, "I started realizing that life experience is very crucial, and many Black Americans who do folk art don't start until they are maybe 60 or older. [Some say] they are widely considered untrained. I don't think so; their training is in their lives."[13] The Urban Bush Women piece *Praise House* is a tribute to Evans and her divine messages. It is a story told through dance of ancestors and matrilineal love between a grandmother, a mother, and a daughter/granddaughter. It is also the story of being connected to the ancestors and negotiating silence. Dancers play the angels that Granny and her granddaughter Hannah see. They are kind and comforting beings, and Granny accepts them though some say she is crazy. Her granddaughter wrestles with them and is tormented with fear of repercussions.

The version of this piece for this discussion was filmed for television at different locations. This is not a filming of a stage work, but rather a piece set specifically for film. Zollar teamed with celebrated director Julie Dash to create the film version of the piece.[14] This project is in the same style as many of Dash's other works. Her 1991 film, *Daughters of the Dust*, won for best cinematography at the Sundance Film Festival, and *Filmmaker's Magazine* named it one of the fifty most important independent films ever made. *Daughters of the Dust* is a celebration of family and heritage in the Sea Islands off the South Carolina coast. Focusing especially on the women in the family, it chronicles two days in the life of the Peazants, descendants of slaves. The younger Peazants plan to leave the island for the mainland. Nana, the family matriarch, still practices African folk tradition and is displeased with the decision. Viola, her granddaughter, however, is thrilled about the family's move to modernity. Magical realism is part of the storytelling style, and the tone is ethereal. The climax happens at the going-away picnic. Nana begs the family not to forget their ancestors and their family history in their migration north. In the end, a resolution of sorts between traditional African and modern ways occurs when some of the family decide to stay with Nana while others decide to leave.

The film *Praise House* has similar themes. It also concerns intergenerational conflict over mystical old ways of understanding life and the modern issues that govern everyday living. African American women are the focus, and the tensions are decidedly female. Healing and resolution come about only with the acceptance of multiple ways of negotiating life.

Praise House opens with a black woman washing dishes in an industrial kitchen. Non-diegetic, though perhaps subliminal, African chanting begins. The performance is introduced through images of a hard-working black woman, the foundation of the family, who must remain levelheaded. The film cuts to an urban setting—cars whizz by, people rush to and fro. The camera pans to another black woman, all in black on the street corner. On a bus, she sits behind a washerwoman eating a snow cone. The scene then cuts to a more rural setting. A spiritual is sung, and on the side of a white house a young black woman squats in front of a ripped up paper bag, drawing frantically with crayons as her body convulses. She draws eyes, rainbows, angels, and lions, as if her movements are beyond her control. It is unclear whether this shaking is euphoric or agonizing. The ambiguity is important; the convulsions are vital though seemingly contradictory. The mysterious possession that terrifies some is compelling precisely because it embraces the contradiction.

The film cuts to a fan and then to an older black woman in her home. She wears a simple white dress, rust-colored housecoat, and a white floral hat. She carries white, flowing tulle-like fabric that she sweeps up into the air as she turns about herself. This is the first dancelike motion in the film. It is the light, airy movement of angels. The character, Granny Louise, looks about the room as if she sees something others don't. She says that she hears the sounds of angels' wings: "Such beautiful wings. You could be an angel but it takes 12,000 years to get your wings." The words of the spiritual become clearer: "Bring the spirit, child." Then appear the angels (the Urban Bush Women dancers) in light, airy fabric (no wings on their backs, however), leaping into the air and smiling into the camera. The girl draws the angels and shakes more vigorously, rubbing her hands frantically. The angels do African dance in Granny's home as she talks to them. The girl, Hannah, enters, sees the angels, and tries to help her granny move to the other room. The angels start sweeping their fabric over Hannah as well, and she starts to get caught up in the motion. Though they cause her to dance, they don't use violent force: it is more inevitability than compulsion. Granny talks to the angels about the trees. She states that the trees don't look so good but the leaves and flowers are coming out. "You give so much that you got to bend," Granny says. Like trees bending in the wind, we yield as much as we can, keeping some leaves and flowers without snapping. "You got to bend. You got to bend. You got to bend. You give so much that you got to bend. . . . And I thank you. And I thank you. And I thank you, oh beautiful spirits." Once she accepts them, Hannah shows delight in playing with the spirits.

In many African cultures (particularly Yoruba), guardian spirits, ancestors, and gods play important roles in the world of the living. These beings are known as Egun (also Eggun, Egungun, and Engungun). They protect, guide, and sometimes punish the living. In ritual ceremonies, masked dancers portray these beings who bless their family homes and all those who watch over them. In the Yoruba worldview, death is not the end but part of a cyclical reality.[15] As Laura Strong explains:

> Each person comes to this life, from the world of the unborn, through the "abyss of transition." And each will leave again through this archetypal realm, as they make their way to the world of the ancestors. When a child comes into this world, he or she is said to carry with them aspects of a former ancestor who is reborn in the child. This is not to say they are the ancestor reincarnate, but that there are certain features of their personality, parts of their physical make-up, and elements of inborn knowledge that come from a previous relative. When the time comes to leave this earth, it is not the end of their existence either.[16]

When ancestors have led a good life and are remembered by the living they are able to stay in the *Sasa* period (the realm and time of the living, unborn, and the ancestors). When ancestors are forgotten they move to *Zamani*, where the gods, divinities, and spirits dwell. Ancestors in the Sasa period have the ability to intervene between humans and the gods. The ancestors communicate with the living in dreams, visions, and trances. They impart messages, explain problems, give instructions, and ensure the well-being of the entire community.

This belief system survives in various forms in African American culture. According to African American spiritual writer Iyanla Vanzant, "Every living being has a God-appointed guardian spirit which walks through life with you. The good spirit unites with you at the moment you are born."[17] Some refer to it as a "guardian angel" or "protector spirit." This spiritual concept combines

African and Christian elements. Often, these spirits are thought to communicate with the living through dreams, thereby keeping the memories of the ancestors alive.[18] Some human beings are more willing or able to communicate with these spirits than others. In contemporary American society, many people are suspicious of those who claim to see visions and communicate with spirits. Seeing visions is a symptom of psychological disorder to many. And, although a lot of the culture celebrates angels, miracles, and spirituality, people who actively talk to angels in public are treated with wariness. In *Praise House*, Urban Bush Women explores this taboo subject.

Back on the bus, the woman in black leans toward the washerwoman, who looks exhausted. Neither speaks out loud, but a woman's voice projects as if in telepathic communication: "Things have a way of working themselves out. . . . Understanding comes hard. I just ask for peace." Granny's sanity is in question. Granny says, "I am a woman and stars shoot from my eyes. Some say I'm crazy, but who's to say. Time will tell. Time will tell. Time will tell, indeed. . . . So much to do. I hear the sounds of the angel's wings." The angels chant, "Time will tell."

Silence plays an important role here. For the most part in African American discourse, silence is considered an obstacle to overcome. Only by speaking will the individual be liberated. However, something different is going on in *Praise House*. Zollar moves away from the typical models, toward the strategic use of silence. Sometimes silence is necessary for survival, and alternative means of communication become more potent than intelligible speech. Zollar is certainly not the only artist to ever explore strategic silence but the steps she takes (literally and choreographically) to do this are significant.

Through the angels, Hannah and her grandmother share a sacred bond, which, because no one else shares it, leads them both to be ostracized. Because the viewers, too, see that the angels exist, they are not left to wonder if they are just crazy. Yet words are inadequate to describe the religious experience and Hannah and her grandmother's special relationship with the angels. They probably could not do the experiences justice by describing them with words alone. The only possible forms of expression are dance and drawing. When Granny speaks, she recites poetry equal to the power of the moment but nonsensical on the surface to those not privy to the celestial vision. In fact, though Zollar uses spoken English, the words are dense poetry not easily understood. Neither Hannah nor Granny can explain their reality to the washerwoman (Hannah's mother and Granny's daughter). The gift of second sight has skipped a generation; perhaps because the woman is working too hard to financially support the three of them, she cannot afford (in terms of time, money, and emotional energy) to be a part of their "reality." The story of Hannah and

Granny's bond is told through poetic text and movement. Hannah almost becomes a younger version of Granny, perhaps Granny as a girl.[19] Both are compelled to move and draw. Granny has given up our reality, possibly because she was as miserable in it as Hannah is starting to be. Neither can communicate logically and verbally. Granny has given over the narration and logical explanation to "time." She can't speak now because people think she's crazy, but "time will tell."

Historically, African Americans have had to find indirect forms of communication and strategically use silence and language to their advantage. They are a people historically denied language. Slaves were forbidden to learn to read or write; the different African languages were squelched (though retentions remain); drumming as a form of communication was outlawed. For hundreds of years, African Americans could not speak freely without fear of being lynched. To get by, they developed alternate means of communication in forms such as the dozens, coding, subversion, keeping silent, gesturing, and signifying. African Americans who have visions and speak to angels engage in a double circumvention of language and communication. Words become only one way of communicating with humans and spirits. Indirect communication is common, and particular attention must be paid to coding, subtext, and context. The story of Minnie Evans, as told through Urban Bush Women's *Praise House*, complicates the constructions of language and silence as forms of communication in a confluence of physio-rhetorical articulations. It uses supernatural beings as media for indirect communication in order to explore the strategic uses of silence in the struggle to overcome hardship.

The next short scene is also important to this examination of black women and silence. It is not clear whether the woman in black actually exists; she has an omniscient air about her. Again, no words are spoken. Instead, Dash uses a voiceover. It is unclear, then, which woman's voice says, "Things have a way of working themselves out," "Understanding comes hard," and "I just ask for peace." The woman in black is like a guardian angel, a voice in the washerwoman's head. Like Hannah and Granny, the woman in black and the washerwoman (Mama) are bonded in a way difficult to describe. Though something prevents the washerwoman from seeing the woman in black as Granny and Hannah see the angels, she holds sway over her nevertheless.

These two realities collide as Granny and Mama call out to Hannah at the same time. Mama's call snaps the girl out of her revelry and brings her back to her mother's reality. The next scene begins with Hannah asleep on a couch. In a voiceover she says that her name is Hannah and that she paints pictures of what she sees. Further complicating the identity boundaries between herself and her grandmother, Granny's voice continues the voiceover mid-thought, stating that as long as she can remember she has had this gift, the gift of second sight, which wore her out when she was a child. Following Mari Matsuda, Lani Guinier talks about this as the gift of seeing things as they are, as multiple consciousness. She calls on us to draw upon this multiple consciousness as second-sighted outsiders to find within our own voice a source of information and legitimacy. She further states, "Our gift, then, is to turn silence into insight and to make a chorus of many voices contending."[20] Like Cassandra's curse, this is a dubious gift—seeing things as they are and not being able to describe them so as to be believed.

In a scene at their home, Granny asks Hannah to comb her hair because "it ain't been combed in 300,000 years." Hannah tries to tell Granny about her visions. She says, "I see, Granny." At first, Granny mistakenly thinks Hannah sees something in her hair, but she eventually understands. "Oh girl, you got the touch," she finally tells Hannah. They are then interrupted by Mama, who, ever a force of practicality, wants Hannah to wash the household dishes. Granny tells Hannah, "There are ways that things work themselves out. You just got to have faith. You just ain't growed into yourself yet. Comb my hair so nice." Granny then sings of the strategies by which she has held on. She sings of knowledge, understanding, and the impossibility of logical explanation. She sings, "In my hair, I keeps my secrets. And you can comb them through. You'll hear them crackle out of me and go right straight to you." As in *Hair Stories*, the ritual of doing hair is powerful in African American matrilineal culture—Granny passes something on to Hannah through her hair. Intergenerational as well as spiritual connections are made. In words and with the physical gesture of doing hair, Granny tells Hannah, "You'll understand someday . . . this gift that you are given. Rising star at dawn. There is a day you will understand just where my world is gone." Granny Louise asks for her purple dress, white head scarf, and white shoes because, she says, the angels are coming this evening; she is about to die.

After Granny's death Hannah struggles between realities without a mentor. Exhausted with her, Mama finally gives up. In a voiceover, Granny says, "I know what they call me. The strangest person they ever met. Say I'd be standing in the road for a whole hour talking to a rock, staring at the air. I know." Here, she articulates the impossibility of language to communicate and explain her reality, why she has to talk to rocks. She says, "All my life I've had dreams, seen more colors than any one person could begin to know. If I could just name them, but I have no names. Such colors! My, oh my!"

Hannah goes back to working in the kitchen, washing dishes, trying to stay focused. The angels come into the kitchen, calling to her, wanting to play with her. There is African drumming. They sing, "There ain't no turning back."

Hannah tries to ignore them but can't. Mama walks through, hard at work. Hannah is afraid of the possession but can't avoid it. She doesn't want to dance, but they grab hold of her hands and tug and pull her into moving. She escapes and runs around the other side of the sink, but the angels surround her. She runs in one direction but is stopped by an angel's jerking motion. The message is that you cannot ignore, avoid, or deny these spiritual forces; just because some choose not to talk about them doesn't mean they don't exist. As the angels dance with Hannah, the angel in black comes through the kitchen on roller skates.

The next scene finds Mama in the kitchen under the table with a look of pain on her face. She finally sees the angels and is terrified that she, too, is losing her mind like her mother and her daughter. She can no longer ignore their presence. Mama starts dancing like Hannah—she becomes possessed. She and Hannah can finally move together. This brief duet symbolizes the bond that Hannah once had with Granny and can now have with her mother. Finally, Mama is in Hannah and Granny's world. The possession is not a comforting, gentle experience. Rather it is a painful, fearful transition. Though the angels are good forces, the border crossing is an agonizing journey, like a birth—a joy that only comes from pain. Indeed it is Mama's rebirth, and after her pain she will know a truth previously unknown. Throughout this transition, the angels are constantly chanting, "There ain't no turning back." Mama and the woman (angel) in black dance together. Mama is exhausted and ends up falling into the arms of this angel, who comforts Mama in an embrace.

In the last scene, Granny's voice says, "I have dreamed many dreams I have not wrote down. I did not paint them for I keep some little thing for myself. For what I know would send some people backwards. Draw. Draw or die. Draw or die." *Praise House* also sends the message "dance or die." In other words, find some way to communicate other than language if you are silenced or find words inadequate.

At the end of this piece, the viewer is not left with any assurance that Mama, Hannah, Granny, or, by extension, other black women will be able to verbally explain their world, visions, or hardships. They cannot yet speak about their suffering in a way that leads to healing. Yet, all three women have found ways to call on the spirits and allow them to intervene. Importantly, there is no sense of regret, remorse, frustration, or even anger. Rather, at the end, they are left with an acceptance of their realities. Perhaps ultimately, the piece is more about Mama's journey than Hannah's or Granny's; she finally allows herself to be "moved" by different logic, different realities, different stories. Though she tries to conform to social norms, in the end she cannot ignore alternative explanations for how the world turns.

Praise House is a dance-theater piece about telling secrets—the secrets of the angels—using praise dancing, poetry, and visual art as alternate forms of communication. It is about spirituality and the gift of ancestry to three generations of African American women. These relationships and stories are ultimately the sources of strength that allow these characters to survive.

Bones and Ash: A Gilda Story

> Dig for bones, find bones, hear the bones sing.
> Suzan-Lori Parks,
> "Possession"

> I can remake mythology as well as anyone.
> Jewelle Gomez,
> "Creating New Mythology"

The Gilda Stories, a novel by writer and activist Jewelle Gomez, is a vampire tale about a girl who escapes from slavery to acquire a superhuman power that lasts centuries. In the late twentieth century, a number of female novelists took on the trope of the vampire to reappropriate the images. These reworkings represent a transformation of the tradition, a rewriting of the rhetorical effect. The vampire is a figure in several cultural and subcultural literary genres, but the most popular is the male vampire who is eroticized yet impotent and uses sexuality only to prey on his female victims to drain them of their blood. The lesbian vampire, however, is also a rich trope, with many examples in literature, poetry, and film. She is typically a beautiful young white woman with bright red fingernails and lips. She is usually a destroyer of men and a seducer of women and often convinces women to join her of their own free will. The earliest English-language lesbian vampire is traced back to Geraldine in Samuel Taylor Coleridge's 1797 poem "Christabel." Following "Christabel" was J. Sheridan LeFanu's novella *Carmilla* (1872), a retelling of Christabel and probably the most famous and influential lesbian vampire tale. This tale establishes the breast, not the neck, as the site of penetration; sucking blood becomes synonymous with suckling.

In modern times, the male Dracula has overshadowed the female vampire. However, Raymond McNally, professor of Russian and East European Studies at Boston College and a specialist in the Dracula legend, has argued that the most famous vampire is based more on a woman, the Countess Bathory of Hungary, than on Vlad the Impaler as many have argued. Bathory was a sixteenth-century countess of Hungarian nobility who lived in Transylvania. According to legend, she wanted to stay attractive to her husband, so she sought the keys to everlasting youth. She also was addicted to biting human flesh. Once when she was sick in bed, she had one of her servant girls brought in and she bit the girl's cheek, shoulders, and breast. She also liked to have her female servants stripped nude before she tortured and killed them. Eventually Bathory was tried for her crimes. King Matthias II sealed her in her room with only a food hatch and ventilation. She died there at the age of fifty-four.

Bathory was not the sole basis for the character of Count Dracula, but her legend played a major role in the creation of the character, especially drinking blood to look younger, which does not appear in prior vampire folklore. More recently, Pam Keesey has published two popular collections of lesbian vampire short stories. *The Gilda Stories* and the film adaptation of *The Hunger* inspired her to research and collect lesbian vampire tales.

Vampire lore has also found its way into the film industry. The 1970s were the "Golden Age" of lesbian vampire films, with a large number of lesbian vampire movies made between 1970 and 1974, including *Daughters of Darkness*, *The Vampire Lovers*, *Lust for a Vampire*, *Le Frisson des Vampires*, *Le Viol de Vampire*, and *Blood-Splattered Bride*. The genre experienced a boom at this time due, in part, to the loosening of censorship laws in England and the United States. Though men created many of these films for a straight male gaze and fantasy, lesbian and feminist theorists like Andrea Weiss have argued for a possible positive lesbian spectatorship.[21] In many, like *Vampyres*, *Daughters of Darkness*, and the film version of *The Hunger*, the lesbian vampires triumph over their oppressors.[22]

Bones and Ash: A Gilda Story lies in the interstices of literature, dance, theater, storytelling, and ritual. It is yet another avenue by which Zollar and her company can assert images of empowered, whole, healed black women. The style of dancing for this piece is quintessentially Urban Bush Women. Formally, the dancing blends abstract gesturing; impassioned, dramatic lyrical dance; and grounded, strong African dance. The movement is the ritualistic process that helps bring about Gilda's awakening. Significantly, the dancers also act, and poetic dialogue furthers the plot.

Gomez served as the production's playwright, reworking the text to fit the new art form, resulting in a creation true to the original while being a distinct artistic piece. The dance piece focuses on Gilda's experiences as a slave and her years at Woodard's brothel in Boston; it does not explore several parts of the novel. In this way, the sense of journey and development remains while the plot is distilled to its essential events. Gilda acts as the narrator, thereby claiming agency over her life story and displaying or embodying the results of her self-analysis. Added to the story are the Irissas, spirit incarnations of the past

Christine King and Treva Offutt in *Bones and Ash: A Gilda Story.* Photo by Cylla Von Tiedemann.

(ancestors, guides, deities) who exist to support Gilda on her journey. Their name is derived from "iris," meaning rainbow. In the vampire community, they are the ancients, the ones who teach and guide the other family members. These characters are prototypically Urban Bush Women. The existence of these spirits strengthens the reliance on alternative storytelling devices, which translates into a call for opening up to possibilities and a resistance to a singular mode of explanation.

The dance opens with two video projections: "Bones and Ash: A Gilda Story" and "The Future 2050." On the backdrop is a picture of a slave woman picking cotton. In a voiceover a woman recites:

> There is a dream I have of cotton. Unlike what you know. Balls unskeined, unrefined, rough and tender at the same time but still white. Dreamy puffs perched elegantly in coarse leaves waiting to make me bleed. It feels much like braiding my hair but my flesh catches in the prickly fiber. That I bleed is a surprise. Such soft stubble. Blood. Spattered balls leave my load too

> light and you can't return to the rows. They move on, never waiting, never helping. The rows breathe independent. You can't return to fill up the sack. Once you've passed by. Once the blood is drawn.

Girl appears in black and dances a solo. She gathers her arms in a wide circle from the side, as if grabbing a large load of cotton. Her fingers are splayed wide as she carves her arms through the space. She attitude leaps with flexed feet, kicking them out in a martial-arts style as her hands form fists. Behind her, three women, the Irissas, enter. They each wear gauzy red material that flows freely as they move. Otherworldly, they occupy the space upstage. Girl does not overtly acknowledge them; rather, they seem like unseen influences. They travel through the space more than Girl, with fast-paced leaps and turns and extended reaches. They grunt, and their actions give a sense of urgency and purpose.

It is interesting that the piece begins in the future (the end of the book), which makes it circular—the audience experiences the person Gilda becomes before we see the events that led to her coming into consciousness. Although suspense is maintained at several moments, the audience knows that ultimately Gilda will come out the better for her travails. Thus, the process, rather than the product, is the focus of the piece. The emphasis is on *how* she triumphs, not *that* she triumphs. It is simultaneously a look back and a look forward.

After the Irissas enter, the text continues while they all dance and a woman's voice begins to hum and then speak of the crucial role of ritual dance in self-empowerment: "The shape of my life is motion through fields, through time, in blood. Each decade is woven into the next. Embroidered centuries draped across my shoulders. A rainbow of lives, every one my own. Behind me, a hundred and fifty years of those I've loved, those I've lost. All taking and giving blood. Dangerous. Vital. Blood. A thin red line. I follow down one row up the next. A rhythmic dance draws attention of the Gods, Yemanja, yellow woman and the many others. I am enamored of motion." Girl's movement is more restrained, careful, and directed here. The grunts and hums continue as the Irissas exit. A line of other women dressed in black then enters in a procession. These dancers take steps in rhythm, pause, and gesture symbolically. The line circles the stage, followed by the Irissas. When both of these groups enter the space, they turn to face the audience. These are the women of Girl's past, present, and future. Repeating Girl's opening moves, they move in unison, a community of women coming together to tell a story. The naming of Yemanja directly connects Girl and these women to African ancestry, thereby linking the mystery of an Eastern European legend with that of African divinity.

In the next section of the monologue, Girl lays out the project of the dance, namely the comprehension of the past in order to determine the future. The

Christalyn Wright, Beverley Prentice-Hall, and Gacirah Diagne in *Bones and Ash: A Gilda Story*. Photo by Cylla Von Tiedemann.

fact of slavery is just one piece of the puzzle. The more pressing matter is the longevity of slavery's legacy. Representing time—over two hundred years—Girl has lived through not only the horrors of slavery but also its aftermath. The original Gilda could not continue in the struggle and chose true death rather than the cyclical nature of inhumanity, but she leaves her hope in Girl, in whose "lifetime" the human race may rid itself of evil forces. Girl's project is to assemble a life by dealing with the past. She comes out and tells the audience that hope resides in the arts, and the performance attempts to attest to that.

> Someone said to me once, "It must be hard in this world being black, descended from slaves, 'buked and scorned, denied and neglected." I said, "No, actually, it's being over two hundred years old that pulls my patience." To live forever is a puzzle—each piece snapping into place beside the next. But the picture never fully forms. And I still don't know all I want

> to about the past. It will not lie down and die. The past follows us easy as the wind in the cold. Then sits up stiff against petals waiting for my embrace, hoping I will lay it open with a skillful blade and let the guts of memories splash onto me. Freeing blood with the stories of what really went before. When I stole away, not to Jesus, I took the knife I needed to do the cutting with. The stories that flow between us like blood are the rivers of change, are our music of struggle, are the repository of hope. The past is not just a dream. It is the place I visit on my way to my next two hundred years.

The women in black exit, leaving the Irissas, who continue their breath work while they spin through the space. They stand with their feet planted as they speak and use their arms to indicate the scope of this vision. They function as a chorus, articulating through words and dance the poetic struggle toward self-discovery. They recite in unison: "We come here for the dream. In the dreams, we find ourselves. At first, it may seem dark, nothing there. But they are here. In the air. In our bodies. In our voices. A world behind us. As large as the one ahead. In its arms lie questions, leading to our path."

This first section introduces the piece by setting up several tropes. One, the vitality of blood, is established immediately. Blood is a substance that taints the crop that sustained slavery. Much blood has been shed in the name of slavery, and it is through blood that Girl must work in order to live and understand. Blood maintains her as a vampire: by "sharing" blood, vampires are able to participate in "life." Through blood Girl will have an everlasting future. Blood is also a metaphor for her memories and the stories of her past. The concept of blood memory takes on new dimension in this tale. When vampires share in blood, they participate in its donor's memories. They can affect donors' thoughts and dreams (usually for the good) and (again usually) leave them more at peace with their lives. Blood is echoed in the red, flowing costumes of the Irissas—themselves symbols of the role of the past in the present. Blood is also inextricably linked to the violence Girl has suffered and inflicted. As she tells the audience in the opening monologue, once the blood is drawn, one cannot go back, meaning both that one cannot get blood out of raw cotton and that one cannot go back to being a human after becoming a vampire. Once she killed the white man raping her, her path was set.

Blood is very significant in traditional African religions; it is shed in sacrifices as a way to give life back to the deity, an acknowledgment that it is from the divine that all life derives. When an important member of the community dies, animal sacrifices take place, and blood is sprinkled on the coffin. Sometimes the head of the animal is placed inside the coffin. According to Kenneth Kojo Anti, "Blood is used to cleanse society and individuals and to propitiate or pacify the spiritual powers. It is used to establish links with the spirit world." The spiritual connection of women to blood is seen as very powerful. "Though they are regarded as producers of life, they are also seen as spiritual sources of danger. The ritually 'dangerous' nature of women is expressed in notions about the polluting nature of blood, especially the blood of menstruation and of childbirth."[23]

Motion, longevity, and violence also become important tropes early in the dance, which is very fluid, with few static sections, illustrating the concept of progression through life. With this flowing motion, Girl seeks to piece together the meaning of existence. She is constantly moving, constantly working things out, only able to rest once her demons are slain. Longevity, through the concept of immortality, implies possibility. It is symbolic of the perseverance of oppressed women of color. It takes over two hundred years for Girl/Gilda to find herself. Vampirism gives women the time to go on their journeys, try on different personalities, and perform different identities. Violence gets deconstructed, as the piece complicates the vampire's act of sucking blood, making it potentially a nonviolent, loving gesture. It forces the audience to reexamine the violence done to Girl as well as its judgment of those considered social pariahs. In the performance the audience witnesses Girl escaping the hardships of slavery with the help of the Irissas and other escaped slaves, her being raped, and her murdering of her rapist. Eventually, Gilda finds Girl and brings her to Woodard's bordello in New Orleans. Here she does domestic work, and the community of women here will become her refuge. She finds friendship and love and she learns about her heritage. By telling Girl her story, Gilda furthers the tradition of oral history and collective ancestral memory that connects people of African decent. These stories are in the soil, they are in the bones, and when true death comes they go back to the earth as ash. Gilda does African dancing, staying low to the ground while circling her arms like a bird and joining the singing. Girl observes and picks up the step. Soon, they dance in unison. Later, in a duet between Gilda and Bird (her companion, a Lakota woman who survived her people's annihilation by disease brought by colonists), two ancient cultures communicate. African and Native American unite against a common oppressor. Spiritual ancestors from both peoples possess the women in this ritualistic dance.

All at Woodard's seem happy, except Gilda, who expresses frustration at the continuing suffering. She frequently looks longingly out onto the horizon. At one point, Bird unfolds part of a white drop and transforms it into a bed that Girl eagerly enters. Gilda reenters, walks around herself, throws her hands up in despair, and gives a tortured monologue about humanity's long history of cruelty and the coming Civil War: "For three hundred years! For years and years and years! I've lived for three hundred years! War. War. Dead children.

Deborah Thomas and Trinket Monsod in *Bones and Ash: A Gilda Story*. Photo by Cylla Von Tiedemann.

War. It's never enough. No matter what I do. It's never enough. Three hundred years!"

We learn that Gilda and Bird are good vampires who follow the Irissas' maxim, "We take blood, not life. Put no one in danger. We take blood, not life. Leave something in exchange." They value fair trade in the exchange of life forces. Bird and Gilda take blood not in violence but as a loving gesture that not only sustains them but also leaves the human host in a better state.[24]

According to Keesey, "Vampires are representative of a number of different belief systems, but the vampire, more than anything else, represents the forbidden and taboo: life without death; killing without guilt; cannibalism in the form of blood drinking; sensuality and eroticism without reproduction or responsibility . . . the list goes on. Homosexuality in our society is also taboo, forbidden in 'polite' circles. That lesbianism would become associated with vampirism isn't too surprising."[25]

Embracing the image of the lesbian vampire has been a source of controversy. Simple questions remain: Is this icon positive or negative? Is the lesbian vampire pure evil, or in her power can we claim she is good? Many of the lesbian vampire images reinforce anti-lesbian stereotypes, and for a long time these were some of the only lesbian images available in the mainstream media. According to Keesey, "Lesbian audiences claimed those vampires, reinterpreting the stories to reflect their own experiences."[26] Gomez has commented, "I feel I can remake mythology as well as anyone. . . . I was certain I could create a mythology to express who I am as a black lesbian feminist."[27]

On the one hand, the traditional lesbian vampire is evil. She is the destroyer of men, and she is non-reproductive—which implies the annihilation of the species. Powerful women are often portrayed as evil and as castrating threats to the male hegemony. The exchange of blood has become even more taboo with the AIDS crisis. And even though the lesbian vampire would be immune to AIDS, the stigma remains—the exchange of blood in this eroticized lesbian encounter leads to death. Like other female demons, the lesbian vampire seduces young women into wicked ways. She is like fertility goddesses in whom mythology conflates the sacred, supernatural, the sexual. The lesbian vampire is a dangerous woman.

On the other hand, the lesbian vampire has been claimed as a source of empowerment for women who identify with her. She is independent and powerful and, in Keesey's words, usually chooses other women to elevate to her status: "Sexual women are often classified as demons and castrating bitches, and vampires are the most popular stereotypes of the dangerous, sexually assertive woman. At the same time, I think the female vampire is an incredibly empowering image, an example of a woman who has taken control of her life and her sexuality, not letting society dictate who she ought to be and what she ought to do."[28]

The transgressive woman as represented by the vampire is a popular image. So popular, in fact, that one of the definitions of vampire is "a woman who exploits and ruins her lover," according to the Merriam-Webster dictionary. The woman who uses her charms or wiles to seduce and manipulate men is the vamp. She is the destructive side of the goddess, part of the cycle of life, death, and rebirth in some representations but more often part of a dangerous, transgressive, and offensive sexuality of blood and death. She exists outside of accepted "feminine" behavior.[29] During the Victorian era particularly, the association of the vampire and lesbianism was a short leap. This trope of the pagan goddess threatened the Judeo-Christian order, and she was therefore made evil. She was warded off with the crucifix and holy water of Christianity. Both Lilith, Adam's first wife, and Eve, his second, defied the patriarchal order and had to be punished for their contravention; Eve is responsible for sin and Lilith is responsible for the death of children (read, the potential destruction of the human race). In Jewish folklore, Lilith left Adam after she quarreled with him over his authority, and her children were destroyed in retaliation. Later, she returns "immortal, undead, and vengeful" to kill Eve's children.[30]

In *Bones and Ash*, it is the male vampire, not the female, who is dangerous. Fox, a male vampire, kills when he takes blood. He serves as the heroines' foil by repeatedly breaking the sacred code, the ultimate betrayal of their kind. An argument with Gilda about freedom echoes postcolonial discourse about the same. Gilda tells Fox that he never learned to be free. Freedom for him means the freedom to be beaten to death like his father by white men. This is a particularly male suffering—a stripping of manhood. Gilda replies that freedom does not mean the world will be fair. Fox does not just kill whites, however: he kills indiscriminately and unnecessarily. The implication is that the system of oppression has corrupted Fox to his core.

Gilda decides to take Girl into the family of vampires. She conjures the power to entrance the girl and begin her transformation. Before her transformation is complete, though, Girl must first recount the story of her personal suffering. She tells of countering the violence of rape with the violence of stabbing. The rapist's stabbing of her is turned around and the knife becomes a phallus she can use to defend herself. Telling her story also counters the stereotype of the lascivious black woman: she becomes a victim who reclaims her life. This testimony also goes to the importance of victims being heard. In the acts of stabbing and telling, Girl reduces her attacker's power; she literally seizes the power of the phallus and turns it on her oppressor to survive.

When Girl accepts her new life, Gilda begins the ritual. African dancing fills the space as the women cry out. Gilda and the Irissas take turns dancing with the girl, each giving her a piece of herself. The lights turn red. The music slows to a pulsating drumming. Gilda brings the girl to sitting, kneels behind her, exposes her neck, and holds her in her arms as she takes the blood. Gilda exits, leaving Girl still in her trance. The Irissas remain to teach her. They say: "We point you and all our children toward an enduring power that does not feed on death. We survive by sharing blood and by maintaining connections to life. Your body will gain strength and endurance. You hold power to save someone else as you have saved yourself. There will be times of both joy and sadness. We will be here with you to experience the passage of time, moving silently through your life, finding our place closer and closer to your heart." Bird runs in, recognizes that the girl is mid-transformation and dying. She also realizes that Gilda has left. Bird hangs her head down but, as the lights fade, with the Irissas' encouragement, finally decides to finish the transformation by slicing her breast and having the girl drink her blood. Thus, the girl is a child born of three mothers—her biological mother, Gilda, and Bird.

Eventually, Gilda decides to take the true death. She appears in African dress and dances with slow, wavy steps, and, as she talks about all of the pain and suffering she has seen, her body jerks, she reaches out, and she screams, "No!" She becomes more agitated but collects herself as she talks about the integrity of nature. It is her time to complete the circle. She continues the slow movements, takes off her headwrap and necklace as a chorus of African elders (men and women) line the back wall behind her. One chorus member carries a drum, making visible the source of the sounds and spirits driving much of the action of the piece. They give her breath, and with moans they heave while keeping their focus on her. They all throw their hands up, testifying. They sing, "I believe I got to move on." One elder sings, "She is coming home!" The song becomes a blend of African music and slave spiritual, and the African drumming continues as they all clap out a lively rhythm, smiling joyously and singing, "She is coming home!" They perform in a ring shout–like circle, a slave dance with roots in African traditions. Gilda is joining her people, and the community of ancestors is welcoming her. The energy heats up and then calms down as the chorus sings about taking her to the river and dropping her into the water. Several lay hands on her. She steps into the water, represented by a gauzy backdrop that the elders open for her.[31] In this world African Americans get to choose their own paths; this moment is an assertion of self-determined identity. Not only do they need longer lives, but also their deaths must come of their own volition. And of course a community of ancestors ushers the transition. This rite of passage is an African American covenant writ large. It bespeaks a promise of salvation after a life of suffering. On the back wall, a projection of the sun appears, and in the silhouette Gilda raises her arms triumphantly and begins to shake under the sun's rays. In this way she achieves the true death and passes her identity on to Girl, who takes on her name.

The second half of the performance shows how this new Gilda survives by moving through sustaining black communities and seeking out "colored women not afraid to cry or laugh out loud." She also finds love in her childhood girlfriend, Theodora. Against the backdrop of violence in post–Civil War United States and 1950s Boston, this Gilda confronts and defeats Fox with the help of the Irissas. In the standoff, the performers use African dancing, grunts, screams, and hisses, the Irissas on one side and Fox and his followers on the other. One Irissa asks Fox why he is so mean. To the repeated refrain "I remember," he tells the story of watching his father get beaten to death by a white person, his mother being dragged in chains to the auction block, and his own torture to the cat-o'-nine-tails: "You don't know nothing about me. You better stay away. I am the king of our kind. Can you feel the heat of day? Stop preaching

Treva Offutt and Christine King in *Bones and Ash: A Gilda Story*. Photo by Cylla Von Tiedemann.

to me. I don't want to hear anymore about your giving and your sharing." Even though he has survived for so long, he remembers the pain. "I am the suffering of this world," he says. For Fox, being free means taking what one wants. The oppressors took from him; now he and the other black vampires have the opportunity to take back. To Fox, this is power. He calls upon his free choice. He and Gilda battle in a stylized fight, throwing punches across the stage. Finally, as with other lesbian vampire tales, Gilda wins the ultimate clash of powers. The image of a black woman with her head held high is projected onto the back wall.

The Gilda Stories occupies a unique niche as black lesbian fiction.[32] Gilda is clearly a good vampire. She is a quadruple threat—black, female, lesbian, and vampire. In the act of biting, she achieves penetration and power. *Bones and Ash* and the original novel, *The Gilda Stories*, are "life-affirming" tales of the transcendence of adversity by women of color. The potential for danger, however, rests just under the surface, and in the Fox character, we see what that could become. These women are still potentially threatening. Like other vampires, they hypnotize and paralyze their victims, rendering them helpless. However, they do not take advantage of their latent capabilities. Rather, drinking blood is "tender, compassionate, erotic, and, above all, 'a fair exchange' rather than a predatory act."[33] Nevertheless, they still pose a potential danger because of the injustices done to them. In an essay about her experience seeing "kill niggers" spray-painted on the sidewalk in San Francisco's Castro neighborhood, Gomez says, "Rage is always hidden beneath the surface for most people of color, even here in the postcard."[34]

Good or evil, the lesbian vampire is always an outsider, powerful yet dependent on mortals. According to Judith E. Johnson, "Gomez's vampire, thus, becomes a kind of American Everywoman engaged in a pilgrimage through our history, our society, and our changing ideas about life, love, responsibility, and the proper place of Woman."[35] These women, outsiders, are often out as lesbians but closeted as vampires. Both *The Gilda Stories* and *Bones and Ash* reexamine the outsider.

In "Tracking the Vampire," Sue-Ellen Case offers a compelling discussion in which she claims that "the vampire as the site or sight of the undead leads such feminist discourse back to the mother's right to life, where fruition becomes the counterdiscourse of exclusion."[36] In *Bones and Ash*, the girl's transformation is a loving act. Like in the traditional image of the wedding night, coupling symbolizes the relinquishment of old life and the embrace of new life. The first Gilda makes sure the girl desires the new life of her own free will. People are not taken into the "family" lightly. They learn to love.

Again, it is through blood that the lesbian vampire family is created. In heterosexual discourse, blood in the form of menstruation symbolizes the possibility of fertility and birth. In lesbian vampire discourse, blood is also a part of the cycle of life as a marker of death and rebirth or new life as the undead. In both, the loss of blood weakens and the abundance of blood strengthens: "Blood, in the dominant discourse which was writing racial laws along with such tragedies, is genealogy, the blood right to money; and blood/money is the realm of racial purity and pure heterosexuality . . . one can see such tropes operating in the anti-AIDS discourse that conflates male homosexual desire with the contamination of blood."[37]

Also important is the act that renders the lesbian vampire dangerous or transgressive. Psychoanalytic theory may render the bite on the breast as an act of taboo oral eroticism, a type of oral sex indicative of a childlike, pre-Oedipal state of arrested development. Sucking blood becomes analogous to suckling life-giving milk from a mother's breast. It may also be read as symbolic of a latent sexual awakening in women.

Additionally, the coffin is likened to a mother's womb.[38] Case uses Freud and the uncanny to discuss the desire and fear of being buried alive in a perpetual intrauterine existence. The maternal imagery supports the most compelling message in the performance—the utopian idea that one can create one's family. The women at Woodard's, the Irissas, and the ancestors all provide the belief that we can reconsider the notion of what constitutes a family.

It is usually on these created families that these women rely: "Gilda turns out to be a vampire, but a vampire with a difference, one with utopian ideas, compassion, tenderness, and a profound sense of responsibility." Throughout her long life, Gilda has found or created people to love and take care of her. Johnson explains:

> If part of the current social project with which we are all (feminist and non-feminist alike) grappling, is the redefinition of social structures to eliminate abuses of power based on race, sex, and unequal access to resources, the vampire novel, whose central metaphor contains our anxieties about these very issues, is a natural field for revisionary effort. So, for the most part, women revise the central sexual and economic metaphor of blood drinking. If the blood of vampire sexuality represents, in one of its aspects, menstrual blood, women writers tend not to see that as a source of horror but as a source of power, a source of the ability to share love and create life (other vampires).[39]

The transformative power of the vampire's bite serves as an allegory for the transformative potential of aesthetic works like *Bones and Ash* and other Urban Bush Women pieces. It indicates the quintessential, fully realized identity, or, as

Gomez has said, "who we are when we overcome our powerlessness and take responsibility."[40] And that fully realized identity, however individually defined, is central to Urban Bush Women. There is a project at hand larger than this piece, and, indeed, this company. The devastating effects of slavery and colonialism are still borne on the backs of brown, black, and indigenous peoples. The work of Urban Bush Women, through *Bones and Ash*, forces the issues. Through the dance, Urban Bush Women challenges its audiences to find that utopian new life supported by a large extended family or community.

Shadow's Child

> Krik? Krak!
>
> Call and response to begin a Haitian story

> Our lives become the stories that we weave.
>
> "Why We Tell the Story," *Once on This Island*

> We must look on the tales as a celebration of the human spirit.
>
> Virginia Hamilton,
> *The People Could Fly*

At the August 3, 2002, performance of *Shadow's Child* at Jacob's Pillow, executive director Ella Baff made a curtain speech in which she talked about the joyous preproduction week they had with Urban Bush Women. Much of this good feeling stemmed from the fact that the piece is "optimistic." This comment should not be taken lightly; "optimistic" is a rare adjective for a concert dance piece. Part of the power of Zollar's use of storytelling lies in its ability to provide guidance, hope, and idealism for the future. Zollar does not shy away from morals and messages, as is evident in *Shadow's Child.*

For this piece, Urban Bush Women combined forces with the National Song and Dance Ensemble of Mozambique, the Ford Foundation, 651 Arts (a Brooklyn-based arts organization that supports efforts in African American dance), and Lincoln Center. In 1996 Zollar met David Abilio, the artistic director of the Mozambique company, and an immediate synergy was established. They connected on the desire to tell stories through dance.

An important implication of the work of this piece is the challenge it places on our tendency to limit the African Diaspora to the black Atlantic. Oral, corporeal, and written memory ghost the past of the Atlantic slave trade, and much attention has been paid to these performative connections. However, perhaps because of the effects of the Atlantic slave trade, the African Diaspora

Sita Frederick and Francine Sheffield (foreground) in *Shadow's Child.* Puppets by Debby Lee Cohen. Photo copyright by Mike Van Sleen.

also connects all peoples of African descent. These continental bonds are ghosted as well. In other words, because the full story of the African slave trade is not (perhaps cannot be) told, the blanks are filled in by a will to community, particularly by African Americans' sense of ancestral lineage. This sense of community allows for a connection between African Americans and Mozambicans. Though Mozambique was involved in the Indian Ocean/East African slave trade, the sense of community for African Americans is not necessarily diminished. The fact that the Diasporic genealogical ties between the much older East African slave trade and African Americans have not been as well mapped as the transatlantic connections does not lessen a sense of community. Zollar talks about this sense of community along a broad African Diaspora and makes the link through storytelling. The impetus for *Shadow's Child* came from her attendance at a conference called "African Changes," intended to promote African and American artists working together. Initially she did not meet anybody whom she felt had a similar aesthetic. On the last day of the conference, she met David Abilio. "We just felt a strong community," Zollar says.[41] Through a series of exchanges and research trips back and forth they developed the story of *Shadow's Child*, and Zollar set the piece on them.

As part of their collaboration, Urban Bush Women company members learned the traditional dances of Mozambique, and they taught the Mozambicans the Urban Bush Women technique. (Urban Bush Women usually works in West African and Caribbean traditions, so southeast African dance techniques and rhythms were new to most of the company members.) They all learned new rhythms and new ways of moving based on agriculture and reverence for the earth, using movements that are mainly grounded, out of the pelvis, and fluid.[42]

Lincoln Center wanted a dance that would appeal to both children and adults; the collaboration resulted in a children's story told through dance that attempts to combine the styles of both companies. Maria Jose Goncalves, a member of the Mozambique company, testifies to this: "Jawole's great because she knew how to fuse what we already knew with what she wanted. We came up with something entirely new together."[43] In the traditions of African Diaspora cross-cultural exchange and postmodernism, the music, created by Michael Wimberly, combines traditional Mozambique songs, American pop, hip-hop, and Native American music representative of the Seminole and Creek tribes in Florida.

Also, the piece has many theatrical elements. The set is bright and colorful, like a children's book. The scenes switch from a street in Mozambique to a busy airport to a neighborhood in Florida to the woods. Some of the dancers wear giant animal puppets to portray the forest creatures. The dancers engage in dialogue and sing, dance, and play instruments.

All of this serves as an Urban Bush Women project to push our understanding of Diaspora. More than a tale of immigration, it is an exploration of the complexities of transnational identity. The piece marries movement and music styles over a shifting landscape—a simple children's tale with larger social import. In *The Ethics of Identity*, Kwame Anthony Appiah makes a convincing case for the creation of Diaspora identity based in a "rooted cosmopolitanism." Experience and narrative provide tools for individuals to claim agency in shaping their projects of making lives. The girls in *Shadow's Child* negotiate complex ideologies in order to discover themselves.

Unlike *Bones and Ash*, *Shadow's Child* is not an adaptation of a previously written story. And unlike *Praise House*, it is not based on a true story. This piece was originally titled *Night Girl*, as an allusion to a comment made by a character in Barbara Neely's teen detective novel *Blanche on the Lam*. But the similarities end there: *Shadow's Child* is not connected to the novel. Zollar took the concept of the protective night and developed a story about two little girls, difference, and triumph over adversity. One of the girls, Xiomara, is a part of a family of Mozambique emigrants to Tallahassee, Florida. After an arduous journey, they try to settle into their new life in the United States. Xiomara carefully negotiates the playground dynamics and cultural differences between her and the other children. Blue, the second little girl, is afflicted with a condition that makes it impossible for her to expose her skin to the sun. So, while the other children are jumping rope in the sunshine, Blue, covered from head to toe, remains ostracized. The girls bond over their outcast status, and when Blue becomes lost in the woods, Xiomara is able to overcome her demons and rescue her. Ultimately, both girls find a way to cultivate individuality despite destabilizing forces.

The piece opens with the calming sound of waves in the darkness. Seagulls call as the lights come up on a mother and daughter sitting on the beach. The two sing happily as the mother combs the daughter's hair. Placing the ritual of hair-combing as the opening image in this piece, Zollar connects Mozambique to her other work. In other words, the centrality of hair-combing exists in African nations as it does among African American women, connecting African women and, by extension, African women to African American women.

In a scene out of a children's storybook, corrugated tin walls break up the upstage space, a palm tree blows in the breeze, and on the horizon, a paper boat sails across the stage. As another girl enters the space, the first girl, Xiomara, hugs and kisses her mother and runs to play. The two girls play patty-cake to a Mozambican song as Xiomara's mother puts a basket on her head and dances—again, Zollar connects the children's singsong of her other work to this East African context. Next, her mother and four other women sing and dance with brightly colored cloths, their baskets filling the space with color. Xiomara's mother moves freely without holding on to the basket on her head. They pantomime a noisy marketplace. Finally the women put their baskets down, exhausted after a long day's work. This establishing moment sets the piece in a female space, an African community of support. Xiomara is clearly happy and well adjusted in this setting.

Xiomara's father then walks in with his timbila, a wooden instrument that looks like a xylophone and sounds like a marimba, as the women gather around to listen to him play and sing. One at a time, the women take turns dancing to the music. They call out, encouraging each other to dance. They begin jumping rope, establishing an important motif in the piece. In this first instance, they jump in the Mozambican way, slower and more dramatic than typical U.S. jump rope styles. The jumper only jumps every other rotation; on the other, the turners move the rope away from the jumper so that the circle happens to her side, allowing her to dance and prepare her next trick. The jumper starts out simply by jumping on one foot, dancing a bit, and repeating her jump, the dancing between jumps grounded, yet flowing. She holds her hands out and swings her head dramatically. Gradually, she moves into more challenging jumps. At one point she seems not to jump at all, keeping her body level and barely lifting her foot enough to clear the rope, as if she is on a stroll and a twig is in her path. At another point she swoons dramatically to the floor, making sure her body clears the swinging rope. Still lying on the ground, she pushes her body up to just clear the rope again. In a great example of the aesthetic of the cool, the next time around she waves to her friends, and her body jumps the rope from the lying position. From here, she also makes wide, sweeping gestures in between jumps. A third move has the jumper getting on her knees and rocking back and forth as the rope moves under them.

The pace picks up to three rotations for jumping and one for dancing. The girls line up, and each takes a turn jumping at this faster speed. These jumps, involving intricate African dance steps with the added challenge of the fast-turning rope, demonstrate the dancers' virtuosity. The game blends easily into African dancing. Xiomara's parents dance together, and her father sings. The final word in his song is "America." The women stop moving and say, "America?" He proceeds to explain that he is moving the family to America. Thrilled, the women dance as a group. They shout, clap, skip, spin, throw their hands up in the air, shake, and shimmy with excitement. Xiomara and her mother separate from the group, which dances for them, as if giving blessings and good wishes for their journey, in an embodiment of the hope and promise of immigrating to the United States. This scene extends the strong sense of community at the same time it endorses the nuclear family unit. Though gender roles are clearly carved out, the social structure is presented as sound. The family's reasons for leaving are unclear, but the atmosphere is one of promise.

The lights shift to a dim blue as the family waves goodbye to friends and enters the airport. Their emigration is depicted as a confusing negotiation of languages, signs, and systems. This scene serves not only as a transition in the dance but also as a liminal moment for the family. They are betwixt and between, both/and, and on the border. The choreography is very pedestrian and pantomimic. They walk energetically through the first airport and busily occupy themselves on the first plane ride to Frankfurt. They happily move through the Frankfurt airport with wide kicks and spins. A bit more tired, they put down their loads and rest in the terminal until they board their next plane, where they sleep fitfully. They wake up in New York, tired but still excited. In this airport they encounter a fast-paced, unfriendly, confusing world. To add insult to injury, they are ill-prepared for this new energy, having slept poorly for several days. The other dancers become the people in the airport: business people, janitors, families, et cetera. A cacophony of intercom instructions contributes to the disorder. Two dancers move through the space with signs for customs, with arrows pointing the directions for U.S. citizens and foreign nationals. The family tries to navigate through the space with no help from the others, and in a final act of cruelty the signs switch positions and go off in opposite directions, completely confusing the family. By the time they get their flight to Tallahassee, Florida, they are totally exhausted. Significantly, in this liminal space, the family cannot relate to others. The exchanges with "others" are assaults, and the family members are confused and disconnected from community. Though they start out hopeful, the reality of the unwelcoming international hubs that are airports quickly sets in. This moment of transition emphasizes not only the sense of community the family had in Mozambique but also the sense of community they seek in their new home in Tallahassee.

Several dancers then skip in as children and stare at the family members, who tentatively stare back. The girls wave to Xiomara, and she timidly waves back. A radio comes in, switching between stations; the lights brighten to a sunny day; and an announcer calls out, "Welcome to Tallahassee." Four little girls dance to the rhythm and blues music while a fifth jumps rope by herself. This second instance of jumping rope establishes the contrast between the two different cultures: in this context, it is an individual activity. Xiomara sits with her family as the American girls play. Reluctantly, she makes her way to where the other girls are dancing, clapping, and skipping around in circles. They form a circle and do a five-way patty-cake—similar to, but not the same as, the children in Mozambique. An older woman walks onto the stage, and the men stand up and bow politely. The girls stop playing, line up, and say in unison, "Good evening, Mrs. Jones." Mrs. Jones asks them if they've all been behaving themselves. They reply with drawn-out "yes, ma'ams," even though some of them shake their heads sneakily. With this scene, Zollar establishes another strong sense of place. Though this community has different rhythms from the Mozambique village, it is also a strong community. Xiomara's culture shock and the treatment she receives prove to be a challenge nevertheless, and it is not until she is called upon to test her courage that she can feel truly at home.

While Mrs. Jones talks to the girls, Blue enters upstage, her face hidden under a long hood, her hands covered by oversized sleeves, and her legs protected by a long skirt and socks. She sits on the ground dejectedly as the girls go back to dancing and playing. Neither she nor Xiomara has the courage to approach the girls, who play red light, green light and then break into a hip-hop routine as the radio changes stations over and over again. Blue continues to sulk in the corner as the hip-hop routine becomes more complex. Finally, Mrs. Jones opens her window and tells them all to be quiet. As a consolation they decide to jump rope. In this example, jumping rope is a group activity, with two turners and a jumper who stands up straight and jumps over every rotation. The first jumper manages to get a few jumps in as the turners increase the speed. The next has them slow it down so she can do a few high spread-eagles before the speed increases. One girl sees Blue and, referencing her skin condition, says, "Hey, y'all look! There goes monster girl."

The impending moment of cultural exchange between Xiomara and the girls has the potential to be nurturing and educational or to cast Xiomara as an outsider like Blue. As in "Hair Hell Moment #2," Zollar does not give audiences an easy narrative of an idealistic black female community. Here she evokes a history of transnational identity, border crossing, and postcolonialism to complicate a picture of Diasporic harmony. Xiomara has been observing all of the girls' activities from a safe distance behind one of the tin walls. She slowly emerges and after the two turners tease her, they begin to turn the rope for her. They ask her several times if she is ready. She nods, but it is clear that they are turning the rope much faster than she is accustomed to. They get frustrated with her until finally she jumps in and tries to keep up. She tries to do the kinds of tricks she knows but just ends up getting tangled in the rope. The girls have no idea what she is doing and tease her again. To further torment her, they grab her doll and play keep-away with it. They ask her if she wants her doll back, and when she nods, one tells her that she has to play hide-and-go-seek. They make her cover her eyes, and then they spin her around. As one counts, they all run off in different directions. Xiomara listens for ten, which never comes. Finally, when she opens her eyes, night has fallen and she is alone. She excitedly looks for her new friends, but as the sky gets darker she realizes that they have taken her doll. She runs off in tears.

Blue runs onstage, screaming for Xiomara to play with her now that it is nighttime, but Xiomara does not hear her. She throws her hands up into the air. Offstage, two voices sing about finding "you" in the darkness. Alone, Blue dances to the song. She moves broadly through the space, swinging her arms and legs. She falls to the ground, her legs in a wide second position and her head hanging downcast. She swings her leg around to bring herself up, shakes herself, and folds her arms over her stomach, singing about the comfort she finds in the night. In the middle of this song, she opens her arms and finds her confidence. She swings her arms through space and smiles. She finds herself in the darkness. The two offstage voices repeat their song as she takes off her outer garments, revealing her to be as normal a little girl as the others. She kneels in front of her clothes and continues her song, which ends with a call to healing.

In this piece, darkness, like silence in *Praise House*, is seemingly disempowering. However, darkness provides solace and comfort for Blue when the sun betrays her. Through story and movement, Zollar shows that one can find means of survival from unique sources. An affliction can be a blessing in disguise. During her song, she stands up and sings out to the audience. When she sings that the sun is no longer her friend, her movement is angry and agitated.

When she sings about the night, she calms down and her movement is smoother, more soothing and open. Finally, she puts her hands over her heart, then raises her arms up and chants, "Master of breath, hear my prayer."

The drums kick in as she gathers her clothes and skips offstage. In the darkness, only the drummer is lit in spotlight to the side. A crescent moon appears, and a night sky illuminates. A dancer with a giant dragonfly puppet attached to her body enters, dancing to the rhythm. The African dance makes the dragonfly move beautifully as her wings open and close and she bobs and weaves through space. A dancer dressed like a rabbit takes over while other animals of the forest congregate upstage. They all wear stylized African animal masks and echo African traditions of animal dances. Xiomara and Blue find each other and quickly become friends, with the animals guiding and protecting them. Like those in many good children's tales, these animals are benevolent guides, kind to the humans. They are like African ancestral spirits protecting the little girls. Xiomara's mother then calls her to come inside. When she leaves, Blue and the rabbit skip and leap through the forest until Blue gets caught up in vines from which she can't escape. In a voiceover, her mother calls out for her to come home for dinner, while she struggles helplessly.

In the next scene, sirens blare and flashlights weave in and out, searching for Blue. Xiomara searches the jungle while an ominous alligator follows her. Initially frightened, Xiomara eventually confronts the alligator. Five dancers dressed in light-colored unitards come out to help her. The beat increases as the dancers and Xiomara take sides against the alligator. The alligator slithers menacingly as the dancers shake their heads and form a circle around Xiomara. Like the animals earlier, the Irissas in *Bones and Ash*, and the angels in *Praise House*, these dancers act as protective spirits. Xiomara alternates between dancing with the women and hiding behind them. It is as if these spiritual sisters both shield her and teach her to defend herself. They each take a solo, confronting the alligator. They form a line and block the gator from Xiomara. Their moves are fierce, with punches, kicks, and capoeira steps. Finally, Xiomara steps forth and takes a stand against the alligator. The pace slows down, and the dancers move, ghostlike, offstage as Xiomara and the alligator face off, beginning by circling one another. They adopt the same wide stance, their arms outstretched like claws. Each circles her hips, lifts a leg up high, and takes a giant step. Xiomara summons her courage, and, to the beat of the drum, she takes powerful steps forward and throws her hands up in the air. With each step, the alligator takes one back, until it is backed offstage. This moment is an important reversal of the stereotypical image of black children being eaten by alligators. Zollar reclaims the image and gives Xiomara the strength to do battle with not only the alligator but also the centuries of negative stereotyping that cast black children as prey.

Wanjiru Kamuyu and Shaneeka Harrell (in air) and Millicent Johnnie, Liria Guambe, Maria Jose Goncalves, and Makeda Thomas (on floor) in *Shadow's Child* (Guambe and Goncalves were guest artists from the National Song & Dance Company of Mozambique). Photo copyright by Mike Van Sleen.

With new confidence, she continues her search for Blue. Xiomara cuts her arms through the brambles and reaches up to the heavens for help. A bird guides her to where Blue is trapped, and Xiomara is able to rescue her. Soon, parade whistles sound, bright lights come up, and a girl energetically dances with the bird. One by one, the townspeople come out to extol Xiomara's rescue of Blue. They sing and dance in a circle, and the girls who were previously mean to Xiomara and Blue give them sweet hugs. Xiomara's father and the dancers do a celebration call-and-response and dance. The bird hovers over the festivities, and the song ends with a tableau of the two girls holding hands, with Xiomara's mother just upstage and the rest of the townspeople looking on in admiration. The beat picks up again, and they all perform a final group dance. Xiomara and her family have found a new, supportive black community.

As *Shadow's Child* shows, Africans and African Americans can affirm their difference and connections, and storytelling can be an important Diasporic link. An African rootedness is not sufficient in the creation of a life. Xiomara and Blue connect because of experience more than skin color; Blue's skin affliction allows for a more complicated reading of her identity. Out of the materials that history and their present transnational encounters, the girls produce individual post-social autonomy.

The critical acclaim *Shadow's Child* has received confirms the power of story to still resonate with today's audiences. Zollar has said, "After seeing the enthusiastic response to our performances and the rich relationships we've built with the people from Mozambique, I have no question of [storytelling's] artistic and social value."[44] Indeed, all of the stories examined in this chapter are sustaining and inspirational. All involve crossing borders (to the spirit world, between the living and the dead, or across an ocean) that, with the help of community, lead to healing for the main character. The choreography evokes the black magic realism that creates the worlds in which these characters can transform.

4

The World

Shelter from the Heat

Much of Zollar's work with Urban Bush Women examines the lives of women in a violent and misogynistic world, the relationships they foster, their survival strategies, and their strategies for negotiating through systems that devalue them. Many of the pieces tackle difficult social issues for women, particularly women of color, and Zollar takes on the demons of domestic violence, suicide, the messages we send to adolescents, and homelessness head on. Through these staged works, she seeks to foster understanding and healing for a confused society. Dance becomes a means to constructing an empowering black female identity. The strength and work that it takes to get over is demonstrated as a process, not a given.

There are multiple reactions to suffering in the world. As part of the "culture wars" backlash in the 1980s and 1990s, artistic examinations of suffering have been labeled "victim art," and critics like Arlene Croce have disparaged the process of addressing suffering through art.[1] These commentators see the exploitation of suffering and melancholia with this kind of work and dismiss the potential healing power of art. José Esteban Muñoz provides an important counterargument in his analysis of melancholia in the face of suffering for blacks, queers, and queers of color and the role of art in these negotiations. He claims that melancholia "is a mechanism that helps us (re)construct identity and take our dead with us to the various battles we must wage in their names—and in our names."[2] In fact, one might argue that denying or trying to deny the use of suffering in art is itself a form of oppression. Zollar has articulated the importance of responding to the historical and contemporary suffering of women. The choreography advocates an interrogation of oppression and a move from suffering into self-definition. This process does not rest in the stage of victimhood but seeks to move on through it. As Zollar states in an interview with Tessa Triumph:

Dionne Kamara and Michelle Dorant in *Self-Portrait*. Photo copyright by Bette Marshall.

> The Women's Movement was very supportive for me. It was a way of rejecting what I'd been taught to be. The best of the Women's Movement was, for me, the chance to define who I was as a woman. All my life I was brought up to be a victim and when I decided that I didn't want to be a victim I had to re-define myself. So, that meant suddenly I didn't know who I was anymore. (I know myself as the victim; so if I'm not that anymore then who am I? What am I?) You're in a crisis for a while. If you can survive that and allow yourself to go through the storm it's alright and you'll find the rainbow. But first you have got to go into the darkness and be comfortable with it.[3]

According to Joseph Roach, "A number of important consequences ensue from this custom of self-definition by staging contrasts with other races, cultures, and ethnicities [and I would add genders]. Identity and difference come into play (and into question) simultaneously and coextensively."[4] Questioning the performative norms of identity by going into that darkness is the project of the pieces I examine in this chapter: *Song of Lawino*; *Heat*; *Shelter*; *Anarchy, Wild Women, and Dinah*; and *River Songs*. Rather than offering solutions to the multitude of social problems, the structures and choreography reflect the ambiguity and complexity of the situations as well as the processes through which performer and audience member must travel.

Song of Lawino

> Things fall apart.
>
> William Butler Yeats,
> "The Second Coming"

Song of Lawino is a dance piece based on a work of literature somewhat rooted in narrative, and at the same time it deals with serious social issues, specifically violence against women and cultural imperialism. Inspiration for the piece came from a long poem of the same name by Ugandan writer Okot p'Bitek. Valeria Vasilevski adapted and directed the poem, and Zollar choreographed. Though it is a long, written poem, it is not similar to Western epic or narrative poetry, and p'Bitek uses features from traditional oral songs, like repetition and multiple address. Lawino speaks to both her husband, Ocol, and the reader, to whom she pleads her case. According to scholar G. A. Heron, "This written 'Song' form was born in Uganda while Okot was writing *Song of Lawino*."[5] The poem appeals to both the general reader and the scholar, and in some East African circles the names Lawino and Ocol have become common nouns. p'Bitek was exiled for suggesting that the wholesale adoption of modern Western ideology may lead to a loss of soul. First published in 1966, *Song of Lawino* is a poem about the confrontation between Western and African ways embodied by the figures of Lawino and her husband, Ocol. The domestic dispute represents two sides of the contemporaneous debate about the cultural future of Africa. The friction is based on the practice of East African men traveling abroad and returning home with contempt for the ways of their parents and wives. In the poem, Ocol has returned home and disdains his first wife, Lawino, for her traditional ways. Lawino in turn is confused and upset about the change in her husband. Their confrontations quickly degenerate into his emotional abuse of Lawino, who struggles to understand and convince her husband to be reasonable. Lawino does not claim that Acoli ways are better than Western ways; rather, she claims that the Acoli explanations of the ways of the world are as valid as Western explanations and she has no problem with their coexistence.

The problem is that Ocol is unable to do the same; he has embraced Western culture. He has studied in Western schools, puts his trust in Western medicine, and puts his faith in the Christian God.

Urban Bush Women's interest in adapting this story for concert dance is significant on a number of levels. First, Zollar is further complicating our understanding of the African Diaspora by exploring this East African culture. She tells a Ugandan story in order to make global claims. In addition, she complicates the role of dance and the body in cultural identity. She takes an African story and asks her mostly American audiences to draw broader connections. Finally, she adds to the tale so as to make connections between the Acoli and other cultures around the globe.

The dance piece opens with dim lighting revealing a woman seated on the ground playing a kalimba. Another woman enters from stage left, moving to the music with slow, sinuous steps. Her body flows, catlike, riding the waves of the sounds. She scoops her arms around and lunges forward and backward. She moves her arms fishlike as she relevés and pliés. She makes her way to the musician and turns on the lamp of a lectern. She introduces the piece and its author and begins to recite the last chapter of the poem, in which Lawino tells Ocol how to return to their ways (that is, if he is not entirely lost). She tells him the traditional herbal and ritualistic remedies for his affliction. The performer portrays Lawino as a confident, articulate, proud woman, who clearly and persuasively tells Ocol how deeply he has wronged her and their people. Again, Zollar begins with the end of the tale, so the focus is taken off of the end product and placed on the process of getting there. Lawino has emerged from her suffering to an empowered place. The journey of the piece is her course for getting there.

The lights come up further on a woman chanting about the relationship between Lawino and Ocol and playing an African lute. She reminds Ocol that he did love their traditions once. The lights reveal an African print projected on the upstage wall and nine women seated on the floor with their backs to the audience. These women are of varied ethnic backgrounds (African American, Sri Lankan, Filipino, and Chinese), and later when they speak some reveal thick accents. They each represent Lawino. The splitting of the Lawino character into so many different parts is significant; it points to the universal scope of the issues between Lawino and Ocol and highlights the broader postcolonial issues. In this piece, the Lawinos do everything (sing, dance, act, play music). Because the character is split, the issues are repeated and reinforced with a postmodern signal difference in each iteration. The Lawinos can lean on each other (herself) for support. She becomes archetypical.

The women place their hands on the floor behind them, and each woman's arm is interlocked with the woman next to her. They take turns moving an arm out of the chain while quickly shifting their bodies to face the audience. In this position they recite lines from the poem: "My husband's tongue is bitter," "Husband, now you despise me," "Now you compare me with the rubbish in the rubbish pit," "You treat me like a little dog." Several arms raise, as one woman shouts, "Listen to my voice!" Another puts her head on her neighbor's shoulder and cries out, "Words cut more painfully than sticks!" They continue explaining Ocol's insults to Lawino and the Acoli. Their anger builds. The lights dim to blue as they each moan, "My husband's tongue is bitter," one after the other.

The piece is far from solely a diatribe by a politically empowered character: Zollar attends to the multiple possible responses to oppression by juxtaposing moments of strength with moments of weakness. While most of the dancers chant and rhythmically pound out their frustrations, a slow-moving dancer collapses to the ground, slowly huddles in a fetal position, crosses one leg over the other, and arches her head back. Locked in their places, the dancers move as if bound with invisible ropes. They speak of Ocol's new woman, Clementine, emphasizing her conceitedness. They describe her viciously, alternating between sarcastic, back-handed compliments ("beautiful one, she aspires to look like a white woman") and stinging attacks ("her breasts are completely shriveled up; they are all shriveled dry skin"). As they move and criticize Clementine, they lean on each other for support. This is a rare moment of attack on a woman. However, Clementine has clearly come to symbolize the consequences of corrupt Western ways on women.

When the women talk about how Clementine wears the hair of dead women (wigs), a clothesline of high-heeled shoes draws across the stage. The women complain about how shamelessly she dances with Ocol. In the darkness, each dancer takes down a pair of shoes. They all line up along the back wall and clumsily step into them. They examine their feet curiously and grab each other to keep from falling. When they finally feel secure, they let go of one another and stand in the line with their arms straight and their expressions blank, the anti-Rockettes.

As we'll see in *Heat*, high heels symbolize the artificiality of contemporary female identity. In the opening section of that piece, a dancer removes her high heels as one of the ritual acts she needs to perform for absolution. Later, the girls in "Lipstick" awkwardly force themselves into high heels as part of a warped coming-of-age ritual. In *Song of Lawino*, the symbolism is reinforced and taken to an international level. Not only are African American women made to conform to white, Western ideologically constructed notions of beauty, but so are women from around the globe. Lawino, on the one hand, risks losing her marriage and security; on the other hand, she risks losing herself. She stands strong against these oppressive forces by upholding tradition and leaning on other women like her, despite the uncomfortably wobbly heels.

At this moment, from underneath an altar, now bathed in red lights, a woman with ridiculously long black hair slithers. Her lower half remains underneath the altar, draped in white lace. She looks part mermaid, part snake. Her writhing on the floor—instead of, say, descending from the heavens—highlights the sympathies of the piece. She is made to be seductive yet lowly, at once attractive and repulsive. Presumably, this is Clementine.

As the dancers sing about not being able to do Western dances, they do inhabit the rhythms. They mock the styles as they execute some of the steps; in other words, even though Lawino can physically do the steps, she cannot emotionally or psychologically do the dances, because they counter her belief system and she feels ashamed.

When the drumming begins again, one dancer shuffles toward Clementine, shaking her hips. Clementine looks on disgustedly as a dancer does African dance while the others shout in encouragement. She is masterful even in the high heels and continues dancing for several minutes, playing with the audience and having a good time. Rather than conform to the high heels, she has conquered and reappropriated them. Despite their attempts to throw her off her balance, she maintains her identity. Exhausted, she makes her way back to the microphone. She and the chorus whisper, "Dancing without a song, silently like wizards. They think that nothing's wrong, silently like wizards." It is as if this information was a secret they were sharing with the audience. The process of negotiating these demands involves dissemblance and exposure. The dancers throw their shoes on the floor, and the lights come down.

The second half of the performance is filled with further examples of the disconnect between Lawino's two worlds, particularly in terms of the ways of her people, the pressure to "westernize" her hair, her experiences with the Christian versus the Acoli potter/creator explanations of the world's origins, and Ocol's disdain for her and the Acoli ways. These frustrations cause all of the women to convulse. They gather in a cluster next to a bathtub and shiver and hiss with anger.

Toward the end of part two, for the first time in *Song of Lawino*, the large group of dancers move as a unit. They start by standing up stiff, hands in fists, tapping out a rhythm. They grunt and shake their upper bodies. The intensity increases, and the movement conveys struggle and defiance in unity. Three have their hands on their hips in attitudes of insolence. One in the back points her index finger upward, diagonally, as if pointing the way. In the next series of gestures, choreographically demonstrating Lawino's trials and tribulations, the women move from being on the defensive to offensive. Their actions build in intensity and confidence as the women support each other. As the rhythm builds so does Lawino's anger and frustration at her situation. The group of women manifest the strength in community that allows individuals and smaller groups to resist oppressive forces.

A woman with a wrapped up baby enters the space and sits on a stool close to the audience. An audiotape comes on, with sound clips of interviews with women talking about sexuality, birth control, marriage, domestic violence, women's roles, wife beating, and other topics pertinent to the sexual identity of African women. Not a part of the original poem, this section is Urban Bush Women's way of pushing the events in the poem to a global perspective.

While the audio plays, the woman with the baby slowly, carefully unwraps the bundle to reveal not a child but a large red cloth with many small dolls attached to it. She treats the bundle preciously and tenderly as if it were a child. When the cloth is fully unfolded, she gently steps down from the stool and drapes the fabric over it. She exits, leaving the image of a trail of babies cascading down to the audience.

Soon several women enter from the opposite side. Some drag long pieces of fabric that hang from the ceiling. One drapes cloths over the bathtub. Another carries two baskets on her head. Others unwrap items in cloths on the floor and set up their personal spaces. As when they placed items on the altar at the beginning of the piece, here they fill up the whole space with personal items, thereby making the entire stage into an altar.

With this section, Zollar complicates the story of Lawino beyond Ocol's dislike of her traditional ways. She further opens up the dialectic on global political gender issues. She points out the disconnects between Western and African and the dangers for women when oppressive regimes are maintained. The section relentlessly points out the many ways women all over the world experience violence based on notions of domesticity and women's place in the world. When women resist, they are often met with torture or even murder. This section makes the personal political and connects the experiences of individual women into a larger story of worldwide crisis. Since the dancers are of different ethnicities and speak with different accents, they embody the global scale of this catastrophe. The piece begs for action.

A call and response develops between one woman and the others. The space seems to overflow with activities, sounds, and things. The air becomes ritualistically charged. The dancers chant relentlessly. The lone woman throws her hands up in the air and her head back. There is no neat ending to this exorcism;

it is an ongoing process. As the women attempt to reclaim their space, the lights go down on them. In the darkness, the chanting and drumming continue. Finally, the drumming cuts out, and after one more round of chanting all sound stops abruptly.

In the last chapter of the poem, Lawino is hopeful that all is not lost for Ocol. She begs him to come back to Acoli ways, to ask the ancestors for forgiveness and to let her love him the only way she knows how. The poem leaves open the question of the fate of Ocol and, by extension, African culture. p'Bitek's follow-up poem, *Song of Ocol* (1970), is a bitter and caustic attack on African culture and does not resolve the tensions presented in *Song of Lawino*. The relationship between African and Western is yet to be settled, and the balance of power (cultural, political, ideological, and personal) is still in flux.

Likewise, the dance ends without a satisfying resolution of either the relationship between Lawino and Ocol or the colonial condition between African nations and the West. In the final moments of Urban Bush Women's interpretation, a storm is brewing, churned by the sounds and movements of women who will not accept what they don't understand. The strength of their bonds prompted reviewer Deborah Jowitt to claim: "The piece—lively, finely paced—creates something beyond the poem: a powerful image of a community of women."[6] Perhaps a resolution to this violence and destruction may come, but that remains to be seen. If it does, it will be as a result of this collective effort.

Heat

> The Black female is assaulted in her tender years by all those common forces of nature at the same time that we are caught in the tripartite crossfire of masculine prejudice, white illogical hate and Black lack of power.
>
> Maya Angelou,
> *I Know Why the Caged Bird Sings*

The first part of *Heat*, titled "Life Dance 2: The Papess . . . Mirrors over the Waters," has also appeared as part of the *Life Dances* cycle, which I discuss in the next chapter.[7] The opening moment of both pieces is a ritualistic act in which a female character transforms herself from an outwardly tough but inwardly intimidated victim into a vessel of strength. The piece draws from Zollar's therapeutic spiritual influences. It starts with Zollar in a wide stance, slightly hunched over, with her back to the audience. She wears a long baby-blue overcoat, elbow-length black gloves, and high heels. Her long, bushy hair sticks out of an elaborate headwrap. As a solitary offstage female voice hums a lyrical tune, she reaches out for something and jerkily shifts her weight several times, trying to reach it. She gives a wide hip circle and extends her right arm up and her left arm to the side as she stretches her head back. She quickly draws everything in to a hunched position and tentatively reaches her hand out as if testing the air. Her body jerks several times, and she continues to test the boundaries of her space, sending out her arms and legs. Percussion kicks in as she executes a very slow extended back layout, her arms and legs wide and her head thrown all the way back so that she is almost looking at the audience. With a single hard drumbeat she collapses back, swings to the side, and casually turns around. Her stance and her large, dark sunglasses give her an instant attitude far more confident and jaded than when she faced upstage. The offstage voice starts singing an a cappella version of the blues song "St. Louis Woman"—about a woman packing up and leaving town after being mistreated by her "mean ol' man."

In the tarot, the papess means intuition, wisdom, and secret knowledge, the mysterious feminine side of the male personality—the hidden influence of women. With patience she will reveal something and suggest new solutions. Reversed, she symbolizes a lack of personal harmony and problems resulting from a lack of foresight. True facts and feelings are repressed, and the feminine intuition is suppressed, resulting in things seeming other than they are. Zollar's papess shows this duality and mystery. Holding a mirror over water produces endless reflection. Ultimately, she seeks and receives strength and feminine wisdom; she is a female symbol of the arsenal of attributes necessary for achieving accord, a trope symbolic of the work of Urban Bush Women.

Next, she takes off one glove, slaps herself with it to the beat several times, and spins it around vigorously until she tosses it aside. Arms akimbo, tapping one foot and rotating her head, Zollar confronts the audience members as if waiting for them to do or say something that will undoubtedly annoy her. She struts around to face upstage again, and as she whips about, she reveals a large knife, pulled from somewhere inside her large coat. She shows it off, twirling it about, posturing strength, threatening the audience, only to collapse from sheer exhaustion, then jerks several times and takes off her high heels. She pulls out a bright red apple and takes not one, but two big bites out of this ultimate icon of sin, an act symbolic of not only humanity's fall from grace but also woman's mythic blame. Zollar defiantly, willfully, greedily, and unabashedly seeks out the tree of knowledge; it is as if the act gives her strength to continue. She places the apple on a black cloth lying on the ground and stands on the edge of the cloth. The percussion comes back in, and she performs an undulating, ritualistic dance with her back to the audience. The sound abruptly stops, and she slowly takes off her overcoat to reveal her bare back and panties. She leans over and ceremoniously unties her headwrap and wraps it around her waist. She turns around in a series of slow undulating moves to reveal her bare breasts, then lowers herself to the black cloth, reaches into the center, and takes out an egg. She gets on her knees facing the audience and breaks the egg on her bare chest, rubs it into her skin, then pulls out the knife and circles her arm with it. She points it up to the sky and brings it back down toward the audience. Finally, she arches her back and lays out with the knife at her side.

When the piece is performed as part of the *Life Dances* cycle, an important difference occurs when she takes out the knife. In this version, she brandishes the knife, swings it to the side, and moves her arms around in a wide circle, taking control of the space. She threatens with the knife and then, in slow motion, thrusts it forward, with a pained expression on her face. Finally, she thrusts quickly, as if finishing off her adversary. Dejected or exhausted or both, she slumps forward and drops her hands. Still holding the knife, she reaches her other hand in her pocket and takes out a white flower. She crushes it until the petals fall to the floor. She staggers forward, and the song ends, then she slumps and staggers to the side. She takes a few steps forward, hunching over more with each step as the lights fade out. Like the apple in *Heat*, the white flower signifies her fall from grace; it is from this lowest point that she must rise and transform herself.

In *Heat*, the figure Zollar is portraying moves from a bound, fearful existence to one of extreme purgation that results in a devastating act from which she must obtain absolution by laying herself bare. If the knife symbolizes death, then the egg represents life. By ritualistically smearing herself with the egg, she washes herself clean of the past. Only through this rite of passage can she transform herself.

In this ritual, real strength comes not from wielding a knife or confronting the other. Rather it is a personal journey, and only when the character turns inward is she able to find strength. The character starts out simultaneously timid and confrontational. The audience member is left to decide which persona is mask and which real; perhaps there is a bit of truth to both. Items like the apple, knife, flower, and egg are charged with symbolism as she moves from ignorance to defiant awareness to absolution. This passage foreshadows the journey of the characters in the remaining section of *Heat*. Though this opening is abstract, the remaining pieces deal with specific worldly issues but similarly use symbolically charged items.

Zollar's choices in "Lipstick," the next section, stem from memories of childhood lies (Santa Claus, the Tooth Fairy), the uncertainty of not knowing the truth, and the disappointment when the truth is discovered. For many girls or women, the myth of the perfect boy or man has led to an inability to create healthy, equitable heterosexual relationships; the girls in this section are about to learn to do this. This section begins with a woman dressed in a tacky red prom dress. She starts singing "Dedicated to the One I Love," a cappella and horribly off-key. Soon, off-stage voices join her in an inharmonious rendition of the cheesy love song while she dramatically flails her arms about. They drag out and decrescendo the last word of the song, "looove." As another woman enters wearing a bright red jumpsuit, the singer exits. This new woman says, "His name is Rubio!" in a dreamy singsong while she twirls happily about the stage. Five other women in red outfits (shorts sets, dresses, skirts, and tanks) and white sneakers follow her, repeating, "His name is Rubio!" They smile, jump up and down, and push each other teasingly, like giddy teenage girls in love. The first woman claims that lipstick is her weapon, implying that she will wield her red lips to conquer Rubio's heart. Continuing the call-and-response ritual, the other women repeat the mantra, "His name is Rubio! He makes the dreams fly! My weapon is lipstick! The flash and the power!" Working themselves into a frenzy, they finally swoop down, to lounge in a clump. With a final round of the chant, the women gather enough strength to get on their knees, raise their arms in the air, focus on the audience, and scream, "The flash and the power!"

Zollar uses red clothing and all its provocative danger to her advantage. Like the apple in the first section of *Heat* and blood in *Bones and Ash*, there is dangerous power in redness. Here, Zollar removes the image's sex appeal. Red is supposed to be alluring, but instead of clothing seductive women in it, she presents giddy girls attempting to assume the sexy stereotype. This is meant to make the audience member uncomfortable; by shifting red's power, Zollar highlights how images of femininity are constructed and learned through outside forces. These girls are trying on womanhood in a heightened way that borders on the absurd. Concurrently, their chant is like a calling to the gods to assist one girl in attracting a boyfriend and like a war dance in which the communal forces create the emotional resolve to go forth and conquer. They call out the target's name, summon "the flash and the power" to go into the mating dance or battle, and select lipstick as the weapon of choice. Like the red clothes, lipstick is a crucial component in the construction. The girls revere the power it will have over Rubio. As a ritual, this is a war dance but it is also a rite of passage, ushering these girls into their expected place in the world.

One part of their constructed womanhood that remains out of place is their white sneakers. They all walk downstage left, noisily take off their sneakers, and awkwardly squeeze into high heels. Some girls walk around confidently while others wobble off-balance and try desperately to stay upright. They look as if they are attempting to walk on ice. They grab onto each other for support and giggle as they struggle to move back to center stage. Zollar uses high heels as the sine qua non of the misconstruction of femininity.

As each dancer falls to her knees, she reaches into her pocket and removes a stick of lipstick. They all hold them up like Holy Grails and stare at them reverentially. The weapons are infused with godlike power before which they humbly prostrate themselves. Because this moment is so over-the-top, there is no danger of misunderstanding Zollar's message. Rather than endorse this ritual, she challenges it and exposes its consequences. Each woman in turn speaks the name of her lipstick color—"Rio Fuchsia!" "Firecracker!" "125th Street!" "Mocha Chocolate!" "Purple Passion!" "Tip It Coral!" They all bow down, and, with their faces out of sight, they apply the lipsticks to their lips. Without mirrors to view themselves, upside down and in the dark they put the finishing touches on their ridiculous self constructions. They slowly, seductively raise their heads, and as they do they are transformed into stereotypical sex symbols. They glide along the floor until they reach a tableau that might be a picture from a fashion magazine or a pin-up calendar. The leap from silly schoolgirls to well-conditioned vixens is abrupt and shocking. Because the process was transparent, this is a tragically comic moment.

Still in tableau, the singer reappears with another one (also in a tacky red dress), and they sing, "Violins are violations . . . strings across my face." As "violins" might be heard as "violence" this could also be symbolic of the idealized romanticism associated with the sound that keeps women trapped in certain notions of femininity. Each of the six recites an alternative lipstick color—"Proletarian Pink!" "Neon Nazi!" "Bourgeois Blush!" "Radical Rouge!" "Camouflage!" "Yuppie Yellow!" They do not infuse this new litany with the same deference they did to the last. Rather, it reads like a dose of reality hitting them. They have matured, but not into the women they imagined themselves as girls. The movement of one dancer becomes spasmodic and pained. She walks about dejectedly and wearily in her high heels. She throws her arms out violently, brings her hands to her stomach, and tries to tear something out of herself. Another woman does the backstroke, attempting to stay afloat, and a third jerks her head up violently, as if she were drowning. They all shift into a tableau of boredom and inconsolable ennui.

The markers of femininity are commodities, according to this piece, to be bought and sold. These girls buy and wear desire. Soon, however, reality confronts fantasy, and the women are left with a confused sense of themselves. Violence has been done.

Next, a circular story is told about Rubio, Roman (the girl who seduces him), and Roman's niece (the narrator). The dancers portray jaded women while they tell the story of how Roman and Rubio met. The speaker goes on to explain how her own mother started dating after her first husband (the girl's father) died looking for work. Exactly what happened in this household is not

Urban Bush Women in "Lipstick." Photo by Cylla Von Tiedemann.

explained, but soon the girl is initiated into a complex relationship between sexuality and literature: "And Jimmy Baldwin slept between my legs to keep the points of my knees from causing me so much pain." After sexual abuse, the narrator keeps a novel between her legs so they don't close in and cause her pain.

Neither of these stories is satisfying. They are both choppy and confusing. In the first, the lipstick ritual succeeded to the extent that Rubio was captured by all of the trappings of constructed femininity, but the lie soon revealed itself. In the second, Aunty Roman soon refused to participate in the fiction (by cooking), and the girl has her own awakening to sexual myths.

The movement that accompanies these tales consists of staccato gestures. It is machinelike, evoking the factory where Rubio and Roman work as well as the rote lives of all of the characters. The two singers upstage move their arms in circles, like pistons, while the dancers on the floor take turns completing their gestures. The message is punctuated by their shared silent gesture—a pantomime of ripping something out of the ground.

A third woman enters upstage and joins the first two in their mechanical gestures as the dancers, facing the audience, lie on their stomachs, unwrap candy bars, and continue telling the story of the daily life of this dysfunctional family. They have become distanced from the events and thus removed adopt a matter-of-fact attitude toward the tale of Uncle Rubio chasing Aunty Roman around the house with a gun, only to end with a card game and a traumatized little girl.

This family story, full of scandals and secrets wrapped mysteriously around sexuality, is meant to intrigue in its frustrating sparseness. The dancers move slowly into different poses of reaching out. Depressed, they stand up, walk slowly back downstage right, put down their candy bars, and take off their high heels. They lean on each other and sway while they bitterly remember themselves as young girls wearing sneakers—before they became "women." The dancers begin to speak all of the lines of the piece at once when three singers come in singing the same lines in an atonal torch-song rendition.[8] The dancers move center stage into two groups of three women leaning on each other. Each group executes a series of gestures in which the dancers breathe together and reach out of the trio but end up back leaning on each other. They open out of the groups and spin lyrically with their arms wide. Breathing together, they make wide circles with their arms, take big steps, claiming as much space as possible. They all kick forward as if knocking over an obstacle, then slap themselves on their hips as they step backward. They begin slapping different parts of their bodies, as if getting rid of some contagion, grunting in frustration and pain. The intensity builds violently as the lights fade out mid-exorcism and the audience is left to imagine the types of women who will emerge from this part of the ritual. This is far from the earlier, idealized images; these women have grown, even though the ultimate outcome of this ritualistic journey is yet to be seen.

Following a dancer's monologue about a failed relationship with a man who mistreated her, all nine women reenter the stage singing about wanting to "find you, confine you, confound you." The "you" here might be either a love or their true selves. The dancers are more individuals now in their dress and their attitudes. The movement goes from urgent and frustrated to defeated. One by one, the musicians and the singers walk offstage as the music diminishes to just plinks on the piano. They leave one woman, sitting in a chair, and the piano player, who shuts off her light. The message seems to be that only one of this multitude was able to survive, but as the lights on her fade to blue and dim out, the audience is meant to realize just how alone she is.

During the pause, the jazz band plays a long set without the dancers. The mood is lighter and relieves some of the forlornness of the last piece. This becomes the link between that section and the next: if the women of the first half of the evening are struggling with sexual identity, the women in the second half are struggling to find their places in the world.

The lights come up on musician Craig Harris standing in the center of the stage and playing a didgeridoo, with the six dancers lying on their backs around him like spokes on a wheel.[9] He spins around the center while he wheels the instrument around his body, playing it and pointing it at the dancers, who start to convulse under the power of the sound. He is conjuring them, and it is almost as if he were raising the dead. They call, grunt, and groan under the strain until they pass a certain point and their movements smooth out. They all reach up, and the musician squats down. A woman walks across the stage slowly, wondering out loud: "As the world falls down around our ears, and the walls fall, why speak at all except to call out? Mothers. Our babies. Spinning our babies. What to do now? Why speak at all except to call out? If the spirits find out. . . . If the spirits find out." The musician rises and plays loudly as the women continue to reach up and the lights fade out.

The lights come up again quickly on the six women upstage right, wearing different colored leggings and T-shirts. They face the diagonal, crouched as if about to start a race. As the didgeridoo comes in, someone screams and groans, and the dancers make their way downstage left. They fling their arms back as if a force were compelling them to go no further. One at a time the dancers, thwarted from making it all the way downstage, fall to their knees and roll in a wide circle back to where they began. They end up clumped together in a line on their knees with their bodies slumped over. The music and the screaming continue to torment them. They fall to the ground, are thrown forward and backward, and are tossed up and down as if they were attached to strings being repeatedly pulled up and cut. They get themselves together and manage to form a group. Again they grab each other's hands for support and raise up on their knees stretching out as much as they can. They look into the audience searching for the source of the unbearable noises.

Eventually two little black girls from the audience stand up and walk to the stage. The younger one sits on the floor as the older one softly sings to her and the audience:

> Shelter,
> Searching for that shelter . . .
> And a place to live.
>
> Home,
> A place to call my own.
> Shelter,
> A place for me
> Where I can feel free.
>
> Lonely,
> Days and nights are lonely . . .
>
> Somewhere,
> Have to find that somewhere.
> Shelter,

A place for me
Where I can feel free

By having two real children emerge from the audience, Zollar moves the concerns raised in the piece out of the abstract concert-stage dance world and into "real life." While the performers symbolize other people and concepts, these two little girls are nothing but themselves. They are the actual recipients of the legacy of gender politics in the United States. The older girl sings to the younger one as a way of passing on what she, in her short experience, has learned of the world. Little girls of color have no place in the world. They have been misled and told myths about the world and their place in it. They are searching for a place where they can feel free to discover themselves. While she sings this song, the dancers rise up out of their cluster. They rely on one another for support, holding one another up even though they need help themselves. It is a seemingly endless struggle, and the lyrics sung by the young girl help illuminate the source of that struggle. These women are wandering in search of something—a home, themselves, a purpose.

Lively jazz music starts in, and the lights dim as the dancers spread out in the space. Facing different directions, they take in neither each other nor the audience. They are isolated in their own worlds. A new dancer runs into the space as the lights, tinged with electric blue, come up. She weaves in and out of the others, spinning around and pivoting quickly, trying to find the right direction. This woman seems lost in a crowd, working to hold on to some part of herself. The singers throw themselves on the wall as if trying to scale it and then creep along it until they too exit, leaving the jazz band playing. The band maintains a loud, tortured tune, even without the dancers and singers. One musician takes off his shoes, sits on the floor, and brings the volume down with a hand signal. The percussion continues, and the dancers slowly reemerge from offstage. For several minutes, the six dancers charge the space with a serious energy. At one point, they repeat the downstage journey on the diagonal, this time moving more freely. They regroup for one more attempt to get through; now they all move in slow motion. They finally succeed and as they all make their way offstage, the lights fade out.

This piece, particularly its ending, is very difficult to read. Humor and poignancy combine to comment on the absurd, sometimes joyous, sometimes devastating experiences of girls of color coming of age. Though gender relations and myths of sexuality seem to be at the heart of the miseducation, men are not necessarily blamed here. True, Rubio is abusive and victimizes both Roman and the girl. But the blame is laid on the social structures that don't allow Roman to leave and have a place in the world. She goes back to "playing cards" as if nothing has happened because there is nowhere she can go. She has no support and this is what the girl witnesses. The danger is that this will be replicated with the next generation if something is not done.

Although by the end the dancers seem to have overcome the various things restraining them—stifling notions of femininity, impediments to healthy sexuality, homelessness, abandonment—the ending is not joyous. These women have sought solace in each other. They have looked for the warmth—the heat—of each other's bodies. They have struggled together and given each other strength even as they themselves have needed help. They have broken through together and successfully made it to the other side, but the sense remains that the battle is not yet won and that there will be new journeys and challenges to face.

Shelter

> Life isn't about finding shelter in a storm. It's about learning to dance in the rain.
>
> Sherrilyn Kenyon,
> *Acheron*

According to the African American Planning Commission, at the time these dances premiered, women and children were the largest and fastest growing population of homeless Americans.[10] The little girl in *Heat* sings about finding a place where she can feel free, a shelter. "Shelter," in the piece of the same name, is a metaphor for a place for women in society; the term is used both metaphorically, as an emotional and spiritual sanctuary, and literally, about homelessness and its effects on women of color. *Shelter* is Urban Bush Women's most overtly political concert piece. It directly addresses the homeless problem in the United States. However, it does not advocate a clear solution, so, in that sense, it is not agitprop. Rather, through dance Zollar attempts to usher her audiences into dialogue about the issues. Zollar has said:

> I never thought of myself as making political work or political theater about the things which concern me, . . . but [this] was a place where I felt like I wanted to be real direct and say what this is about and what this means on a global scale, because I think the homeless problem that we're experiencing is part of a much larger problem. It's the same reason that that oil tanker has spilled, it's the same reason why the rainforests are disappearing. I feel like we're not connecting them. We're not connecting that they are all symptoms of the same disease. And we've got to collect ourselves and go into action about it—very soon and very quickly.[11]

Treva Offutt, Beverley Prentice-Ryan, Maia Claire Garrison, Christine King, Valerie Winborne, and Terri Cousar in *Shelter*. Photo by Cylla Von Tiedemann.

The piece opens with six women piled on top of one another. They are dressed in shades of grey and in black. A faint drum roll sounds. One woman peels herself off the top of the pile, slowly walks to center stage, leans forward, and sharply crosses her hands in front of her body in a way that says "Enough!" A drumbeat accents the action. Another woman looks up at the first as she circles her hands over her head and leans her body back, as if water is running over her head. She repeats the "enough!" gesture defiantly and walks fiercely upstage to the drumbeats and repeats the sequence facing the back wall. The repetition underscores not only the pervasiveness of the problem but also the anger and frustration wrapped around it. The dancers are piled on top of one another but do not lean on each other for support. Their bodies seem almost discarded, thrown away. Their relationships to each other are detached and cold. As the other dancers rise, in a voiceover, a speaker explains her feelings about a homeless woman she would pass on her way to and from work:

> Last winter I was working a temp job on the exclusive upper east side of New York City that lasted several months. Every day on my way to and from work I walked past a black woman who, in spite of subzero ice and snow, was living on the streets: a brown-skinned thirtyish or fortyish woman with a strong handsome face and a thick head of hair. She lived on

> top of a big square cardboard, and she never asked for money. Sometimes she would accept donations and sometimes she wouldn't. At my temp job people called her crazy and said something should be done to get her off the streets. I couldn't bring myself to walk by her and not offer her something because her silent, staring presence was powerful.

While this voiceover plays, the women all stand and walk around the space tentatively. One woman runs to the first and throws a sharp under-curved arm gesture. A second woman runs to a third and brandishes a fist. Five of the women scope each other out while one twitches and rubs herself as if tormented. She holds her stomach and folds over, disturbed and alone. This opening is a collage of gestures and hesitant interactions. Rather than seeking each other out, the women are adversarial and they channel their frustrations toward each other instead of uniting against a common enemy. At different points, one or two of them turn on their heels, walk around the space, freeze in a tableau, spin, run to a new spot, and throw their bodies off balance. The movement is a combination of wildness and control, as if these women were constantly fighting their demons for power over their bodies and their lives. They can't find solace in one another. After rising from the pile, they do not touch and only occasionally reach out to make some sort of connection. They start out huddled together for warmth, out of necessity, but, in fact, they must each make their way alone. They are unable to work together. The voice over continues: "I could see myself in her. I could see myself making a wrong turn and falling down down down off the margin, being without income too long, losing my apartment, good will dried up, savings exhausted, get up and go long gone, worn out by red tape, changes, between a rock and a hard place, at the intersection of reduced resources and reverberating rage."

To underscore their isolation, they each spin to a spot near the upstage wall so that they form a line. They individually try to move downstage, but each gets pushed back somehow when another woman rolls, spins, runs, or takes giant steps. Together, they form a tableau upstage, as if trying to get out of their skins. On the phrase "reverberating rage" they form a tight circle. Some women have their hands in fists, as if ready for a fight. They all lean forward, throwing their energies to the center of the circle. One woman begins a rhythm by stomping her feet and pounding her fists. She jumps, and another woman throws herself on the floor away from the circle, then looks back to see the one who created the rhythm fall forward as the other four catch her and place her back in a standing position. Thus begins a series of falls and brief catches. Then they all lie down in fetal positions, but before they can get too comfortable, two begin to rise slowly. They fling their arms around each other's waists and walk confidently to the downstage left corner, where they roll apart and each woman dances alone. One writhes on the floor in pain. Some try to move forward. Some collapse. The few times they touch, it is to roll off one another or toss one another aside. The drums start pounding, and one woman throws her body wildly to the rhythm. On a repeat of the phrase "reverberating rage," again five of the women form a tight circle, one pounding out a rhythm with her hands and feet. The sixth stays on the ground, writhing, in front of the group. She brings herself up and hugs herself. Again, the circle breaks apart. The voiceover continues: "Losers walking. Ain't got no place to go. Living on the streets. Them that's got, you'll get. Them that's not, you'll lose. Living on the streets. It's so easy. All for the greedy. None for the needy. Living on the streets. It's so easy. It's so easy. Living on the streets. It's so easy. It's so easy. Living on the streets. It's so easy. It's so easy. It could happen to you, too."

The dancers run through the space, searching frantically for something. At one point they all throw themselves to the floor in a line and in a round take turns throwing their bodies up and falling down, as if being kicked in the gut. The group slowly stands and begins forming a triangle, facing the audience, each dancer standing with her legs wide apart, arms straight, and face determined. On the line "It could happen to you, too," a single drumbeat sounds, and they all jump into wide second-position pliés and point their right hands to the side. Slowly and silently they cross their arms in front of them, pointing at different audience members as a way of underscoring the text. This is the first time they all move in unison. Their unison and confidence is temporary, however; they step around themselves and shrink to the floor in fetal positions. Again, before they can rest, a loud drumbeat sounds and they jump up, frightened. They scatter and take turns running forward, kicking their legs out, throwing their arms back, spinning, throwing their bodies, and rolling. They form another huddle and shiver from the cold. They use each other for physical warmth but not emotional comfort. The last woman to come to the group is up again almost before she settles down and wearily makes her way to the opposite side of the stage. Frightened and tired, the others join her, but before the last woman can settle down, she is up again and moves to another part of the stage. Again the last woman cannot join. Still these women are unable to lean on each other; finally they separate and find individual secluded spots on the floor to rest. This is the isolation of which the little girl in *Heat* sang. These women are desperately searching for that place where they won't be lonely. One gets the sense that if only they could support each other, they would be able to build up the strength to conquer their problems.

The circularity underscores the cycles of homelessness. The voiceover repeats "Keep walking" as the energy increases. The dancers gather power, strength, and momentum as a group. This energy feeds into a series of three solos, in which the group slowly figures out how to work together to fortify the individual. In the first solo, the dancer slowly and assuredly carves her hands through space, punctuated occasionally with drumbeats. She confronts something represented by a light shining on her from offstage; she is not afraid of the outside force. The second soloist boldly makes her entrance with strong high African kicks and large steps. She clasps her hands and rolls her body, kicks forward, and takes large side steps back offstage while the third soloist enters, also with bold African kicks. This dancer turns around herself with low kicks, spread-eagle jumps, shakes, and repeats. She throws an open palm at the light and jumps back, then repeats this and shakes her head as she makes her way offstage. The other dancers enter boldly, and she returns. They charge the space again. The three soloists continue across the space while the other three form a tight triangle. The voiceover repeats "Run!" four times, the last being a long scream. They look in different directions, bounce heavily in pliés, each with her hands in front of her as if holding a small ball, but they do not run away. Instead, they look as if they might attack at any moment. Finally, they throw their right hands forward in a defiant gesture and relax. For the first time, the dancers look at each other, taking each other in fully. They move closer together. One woman slowly falls backward. Two support her while the other three slowly bend forward in sustained catches. The dancers form a unit, and moving in unison they take slow steps around themselves while sending waves through their bodies. The voiceover launches into a final commentary on the sad current state of affairs in the United States, in terms of poverty, homelessness, and the legacy we are leaving our children. She likens the depletion of natural resources to the suffering of black children and points to their similar causes. As she speaks, the women move in slow motion with wide steps. They swing their arms in circles and rotate their heads as they slowly make their ways off stage. The last two women to exit turn back to face the stage and reach out their hands while backing off. Significantly, the final image is ambiguous; it lacks the devastation of the earliest moments in the piece and the energized symbols of strength just before it. Zollar shows us the possibility of overcoming these social ills, but she recognizes that we are not there yet. There is still much work to be done.

Anarchy, Wild Women, and Dinah

> I could be a maid for $7 a week or play a maid for $700 a week. I'd rather play a maid than be one.
>
> Hattie McDaniel,
> responding to criticism from the NAACP, 1940s

Anarchy, Wild Women, and Dinah is classic Urban Bush Women. It taps sources from South Carolina Sea Island folklore, songs, personal anecdotes, and African traditions. It is about women of color working together in joy and strife, a celebration and a journey. It depicts the work that has been done to liberate black women at the same time as it points to the work yet to be done. It is both playful and moving. It is about sisters "doing it for themselves," reclaiming the term "wild women" and reveling in the power of seeming anarchy. Zollar has said that she considers herself to have come from a tradition of wild women: "My grandmother left her husband and ran off with another man at a time when women didn't just do that."[12] She also sees Dinah in her mother, who aspired to be a nightclub singer but was considered "too dark-skinned" to be hired. "My mother was definitely a Dinah."[13] She recalls: "I remember her clearly, when we lived in Kansas City, taking me and my younger sister to this restaurant after the public accommodations laws were passed that blacks could go anywhere and be served. She ordered food, but told us not to eat it, because you don't trust people who hate you. She threw the newspaper down on the counter and said, 'That's the law.' And paid the bill."[14]

The piece opens with five women seated and a sixth woman bringing the others a gourd of water to drink. They all wear colorful, loose-fitting drawstring pants, brightly colored half tank tops, and headwraps. They sing joyously about drinking water as they pass the gourd among them in a ritual that is a pouring of libation, a call to the gods, and a reinvigorating act.[15] Each dancer sings a solo as the water is passed to her and the others encourage her. The last to receive the gourd is the drummer, who jokingly indicates that the gourd is practically empty, chimes in an impressively low contralto, drinks, and begins to drum.

The dancers form a procession, and as they march across the stage, they sing of going to see their friend Dinah. As they all drink from the same (African) source, there is solidarity and support in their movement and singing. This is a pilgrimage at once spiritual and playful. At one point the parade pauses, the drumming picks up, and the dancers break out singing, "I'm going away!" They leap, skip, and spin. They break into pairs, trios, and solos. Their movements weave African dancing and children's games, as the group often coaxes a solo performer to "Shake that thing! Shake that thing!" Each solo is distinctly individualized, if not improvised, and the dancers seem overjoyed to have their moments at the center of attention. Seemingly free from tension, the dancers are loose-limbed and relaxed as they execute physically challenging steps in complex, rhythmic patterns. In a singsong they chant, "Shake it to the east! Shake it to the west! Shake it to the one you love the best!"

The next section, "Moanin'," begins with just that—two women moaning. One woman stands, reaches up with both hands, moaning and keeling in struggle. The other is seated, hunched over dejectedly. While she barely moves, the standing woman physicalizes each sound with an action. Her movement is elongated, extended, and reaching. Neither looks at the audience or at each other. They seem isolated and pained, alone in their attempts to get over. In a piece mostly about strength and joy, Zollar does not ignore the challenges that remain. In these two opening sections, she depicts both the joys and the pains of black womanhood.

In the section titled "Dinah, Dinah, Dinah," Zollar appears in a head rag, tank top, skirt, and apron. Holding a washrag in her hand, the character reads domestic (a maid, slave, et cetera). As she gives a speech about who Dinah is, Zollar becomes the feisty, subversive slave, the Topsy figure who finds ways to get what she needs. She swings her arms freely, talks with attitude, defiantly picks something out of her teeth, and tells the audience the score. Dinah is that part of us that doesn't take grief from anyone, the part that has the strength to resist the worst oppression, even the bonds of slavery.

The literary figure Dinah was the head cook in *Uncle Tom's Cabin* "and principal of all rule and authority in the kitchen department." In the novel, she is compared to Aunt Chloe, also a cook, but whereas Aunt Chloe "moved in an orderly domestic harness," Dinah "was a self-taught genius, and, like geniuses in general, was positive, opinionated, and erratic, to the last degree." She marched to her own drummer and was confident that her way was always best. Even her mistress, Miss Marie, found it easier to submit to Dinah than protest. Because of her strong, assured personality, "Dinah had ruled supreme."[16] By seeming subservient while maintaining inflexibility, she was a powerful trickster figure, a master dissembler, an Esu who managed to get her way despite her position. Though her kitchen seemed like anarchy and her ways confounded, everything always turned out in her favor.

Zollar's characterization of Dinah is evocative of both the mammy stereotype and the thousands of real black women who labored in the homes of others. In a moving *Ms.* magazine article, Alice Walker talks about her reconciliation with the fact that her mother physically fit the stereotypical image of the mammy—large and dark. Also, she worked as a domestic in white people's homes. These two facts made it difficult for Walker to reconcile the image of "mammy" with the reality of her mother. She talks about how she was finally able to find the strength and power in these women who made the most they could out of their situation and paved the way for others; she found pride and inspiration in them while denying shame.[17] By evoking Dinah, Zollar builds on the same sense of pride and inspiration and turns it into confidence and attitude.[18]

After Zollar exits, four slave women enter, chanting Dinah's name and looking for her. They clap and testify as they praise her name. Afterward, they shout out a children's rhyme:

Now Dinah likes singing,
And that's for sure.
You can see her on the ceiling,
And the table, and the floor.
You can catch her after midnight.
You can catch her after dawn.
You can catch her at the juke joint,
All night long!

They continue dancing and rhyming about how much Dinah loves to dance and how she is going to dance until she is all worn out, no matter what. Though she does not go onstage, this woman, and the search for her, becomes an inspiration for the four dancers. They sing and dance in her spirit. Dinah—a figurative, inspirational, powerful woman—is what is missing in the pieces I have examined so far in this chapter. She accounts for the more positive, uplifting, satisfying tone in this piece.

The next section, "Girlfriends," is about the levels of caring and nurturing possible in a small, close-knit circle of friends and the unique nature of female bonding and the ways women use play, humor, and teasing to form close relationships. Zollar's dances are clearly meant to serve the empowerment of women, and "Girlfriends" is emblematic of that mission. In this section, a woman in pain is physically and emotionally supported by her friends. Together they go through silliness and camaraderie as well as struggles. The section's opening has the feel of a slumber party late at night, when things are pleasantly winding down. The women lounge on the floor, smiling. One of them rises up slowly, almost in slow motion, stretching first up to the sky, then rotating her upper body. She holds her head in pain as she moves her body in distress. This time, one of the other women holds on to her own head as if she too knows the pain. The standing woman turns backward in a circle, pivoting on a planted foot. She contracts her torso, her head hangs low, and her arms move in a wide circle around her head. As she continues to pivot, she moves her arms together so that she hugs herself. She opens her body up to the sky in one last rotation. As she backs away from the group, isolating herself, she rubs her forearm, pained and ashamed. She stretches out and shakes, as if she is attempting to break free of something holding her back. One by one, the other dancers stand and try to give her a new rhythm. The action stops, and the woman slowly sways, on the brink of falling. When she does fall to the side, the other women run and catch her before she lands. They bring her back to standing and lovingly attend to her, caressing her cheeks and stroking her hair. They move into a tableau, the four women clustered together facing upstage, leaning

Carolina Garcia, Jawole Willa Jo Zollar, Christine King, and Michelle Dorant in "Girlfriends." Photo by Jane Hoffer.

on each other. Just when they seem solid, the same woman breaks from the group: again tortured, she slaps at the air. The others try to bring her to her senses and pantomime reasoning with her. Again she begins to sway, but this time the others move closer, to be there for her, but let her fall. On the ground, the woman looks up at them and slowly brings herself back to standing. The other three smile encouragingly, communicating to her that they are proud she is able to stand up on her own. Knowing that they were there for her, she has found the inner strength needed to empower herself. They are relieved that she made it and pause in an embrace before they celebrate.

In the last section, "Wild Women Don't Get the Blues," the drummer pounds out a lively beat as the six dancers chant "Dinah!" over and over again.[19] They start out in a line facing the audience, stomping to the rhythm, swinging their arms forcefully. As in the other sections in this piece, the women evoke the spirit of Dinah. They open up the line, breaking at the center to provide a dance corridor, where each woman takes a turn. When each is done with her solo, she approaches another woman on the side, passing the torch. Finally,

Dafinah Blacksher, Jawole Willa Jo Zollar, Carolina Garcia, Christine King, Michelle Dorant, Kristin McDonald, Dionne Kamara, and Amara Tabor-Smith in publicity photo taken during *Soul Deep* rehearsals. Photo copyright by Bette Marshall.

the drummer, who has been the driving force for the whole performance, enters the space. She walks in with her djembe, teasing everyone by taking the volume down low before bringing it back up. She smiles as the chanting increases. Standing on one leg, continuing to drum, she slowly raises her other leg to a passé (knee bent, toes at the knee of the standing leg) and then extends her leg to the side, holding it there for several seconds as she continues to drum. She pounds on the drum once, walks proudly around the space, high stepping, and pounds on the drum again. She repeats this as the dancers encourage her and the lights fade out.

The piece developed out of company members singing their Dinah songs, and after many of the performances of *Dinah*, people from the audience came up to Zollar and shared their own Dinah songs, about the strong, rebellious woman character who has existed throughout the ages. The resulting choreography reaches out of that base to provide the strength needed to persevere through anarchy and wildness. The ethos of this piece can stand as the anecdote to the remaining struggles in the pieces examined thus far in this chapter. Evoking strong ancestors, reclaiming negative images, finding joyful support in other women, and allowing oneself to go "wild" are important tools for fighting social oppression.

River Songs

By the waters of Babylon, there we wept and there sat down.
Psalm 137:1

African and Caribbean folk traditions and the book *At the Bottom of the River* by Jamaica Kincaid inspire the piece *River Songs*. Kincaid's debut is a collection of ten highly poetic short stories depicting her childhood in Antigua. It explores two factors crucial to the development of individual identity for the narrator: the cultural expectations of a girl in this society in general and her relationship with her mother in particular. Many of Kincaid's novels explore the influence of the mother-daughter relationship on the shaping of female identity in a patriarchal society as well as the experience of female bonding. Themes of women-identified space and female relationships are also the fabric of *River Songs*. Again, the black girl is in crisis because the world is a hostile place for her and Zollar attempts to give her tools to fight oppression through choreography.

The mother-daughter relationship in *At the Bottom of the River* has been corrupted by the harsh realities of society, resulting in a complex love-hate dynamic. This relationship is an odd combination of support and oppression. It is a rite of passage, ushering the girl into her role as a woman. The mother figure is powerful, goddesslike, and omnipresent. The younger female generation is unable to develop healthily because of external adversities, and mothers must use tough love. Only after much bitterness and struggle can affection and nurturing develop.

I end this chapter with a discussion of *River Songs* because it is a good piece from which to draw conclusions about the Urban Bush Women pieces that address social issues. It reaches back to the previous chapter as it is rooted in a literary work and also provides a good transition to the next chapter, on spirituality. Though not a direct adaptation or interpretation of the Kincaid book, *River Songs* explores some of the themes and issues raised by the text. The dance starts with chanting emerging out of the darkness. In a call and response between a leader and chorus, the dancers chant patterns of "na, na, na, na." The lights come up to reveal women in white with white headwraps interacting playfully. They walk around the space, stretching as if waking up in the morning. The pace picks up, and they start stomping out a rhythm, still chanting "na, na, na, na" in a childlike singsong. Six women come out in lines from either side and dance to the rhythm they have created. The movement contains scoops and sweeping actions with hands in fists. They chant and grunt, "hi-yah!" They pantomime daily chores like milking and gathering with a sassy attitude. They are getting their work done but are not downtrodden or oppressed. They create machine rhythms and conveyor-belt actions, passing energy down the line. Each dancer takes a different attitude on the chant "eh-way" and the action that is passed to her. Then, all the dancers but two move off stage.

The two remaining sit down, one behind the other. The one in the back starts combing the other's hair. She has a difficult time getting the comb through, and the girl getting her hair done fusses about. The other chants "na, na, na, na" to calm her. The sound dies out, creating a soothing moment as she puts grease in the girl's hair. The girl relaxes with her eyes closed and rests on the knees of the mother figure while she massages the girl's temples. She gathers her hair into a bun, and they laugh and walk out together as the lights fade out. Again, the hair-combing ritual is packed with significance. Here it is played out as the complex love/hate relationship of the black girl and her mother.

In the next section a woman's voice peals in a high-pitched chanting. Blue lights come up on a single woman carrying a straw fan and purse. She wears a white tunic and colorful scarves, one around her hips and another around her neck. She mumbles to herself as she walks around hunched over. She gives her back to the audience and bends down even further to emphasize that she is giving her backside to the audience. She walks over to an imaginary river and tests the water. She shivers, as if the river were cold, turns back to look at the audience, prepares herself, and jumps in, splashing herself to get used to the water. She takes off the scarves, leaving just the white tunic. Singing, she washes herself and steps out of the water. She acts calmer, no longer muttering or appearing mad. She looks around and moves her clothes to the side. The sound of a bell causes her to look around. Three dancers walk out, one ringing the bells and carrying a basket of rocks. This dancer joins the woman and gives her the bells. The other two sit upstage. The soloist shows the one who joins her around. They squat with a basket of rocks and carefully place rocks on the stage, putting big rocks at four points and filling in a circle with pebbles. The soloist slaps down the pebbles with a breath, and the other smoothes them out into a circle. They also place smaller rocks in the center of the circle, defining a sacred space. The other two dancers look toward the horizon, chanting. One rests her head on the other's shoulder. All four move in shudders and circle each other. They circle in on themselves with their arms to the side and vocalize their shudders. They move downstage of the circle, crouch, and grab hands. They raise their hands up and with a breath throw energy to the center of the circle. They grab hands again and move as a unit around the circle, throwing energy into the center and out to the periphery. Three sit while one chants, wails, and cries out with a sound that sounds like "why?" She swings her arms and moves into a deep plié. Her arm circles are wide open as if she is letting people into her pain. She holds herself and collapses and cries out. Two others come over and pick her up. One fans her. They bring her to the water's edge and pour the water over her. They cleanse her, sweeping the bad energy from her body while she hunches over. One continues to fan her as they work the bad spirits out. She opens her mouth wide, clenches her hands, and rends her clothes. Grunting, she drops to her knees and convulses as if her body were wrenched in pain. Two women take her back to the river. One fans while the other pours water over the soloist's back, cleansing her again and drawing out the bad spirits. The soloist reaches over the two women, chanting a soothing tune. She touches their heads, raising them up. She is overcome and starts shaking uncontrollably, as if possessed through the touch. She falls to the ground, and they all feverishly try to put the stones back. They are desperate to get the stones back in the basket. It is as if the stones have taken on the woman's pain and now need to be contained. They begin to calm down as they gather the remaining stones and the lights fade out.

This ritual is indicative of a crucial part of Urban Bush Women choreography—spirituality. A sacred space to bring about healing is created with the stones, water, and touch. As in Kincaid's story "My Mother," stones and water hold the power to draw out personal hurt. Because these sacred items take on the pain, the woman is able to be cleansed and achieve peace with the help of other women.

The piece ends with five women struggling to hold on to each other while a sixth dancer lies, Christlike, on the ground. Finally, one woman places rocks all around this dying woman, echoing the ritual circle of the previous movement. The four other women huddle together, chanting and weeping softly. The woman gives her last rites by pouring liquid over her arms, face, and body. The four women move in closer, weeping and singing over their fallen sister as the lights fade out. This is the ultimate moment of sister-love and support, and the women guide their friend into the next life.

As in the ending of many of the stories in Kincaid's book, the last moments of the piece concern lost potential; a deep, complex bond between women; death; and despair. In "My Mother," peace comes over the narrator when she walks and speaks in unison with her mother, each feeling the connection with the other: "What peace came over me then, for I could not see where she left off and where I began. . . . My mother and I live in a bower made from flowers whose petals are imperishable." In the title story, the narrator and her mother speak about death. Everything ends in death and decay, including the past and the future. The mother explains the naturalness and inevitability of death to the daughter. At the end of the story, the narrator looks into the river, and at the bottom she sees a one-room house. She describes the details of the house, windows, doors, and the green, green freshly mowed grass. She also describes the white-grey pebbles beyond the grass, in direct contrast to it. By describing the green of the grass as that from which all green comes, she implies that the house at the bottom of the river is the source from which everything comes and to which everything goes: "How good this water was. How good that I should know no fear." A brown woman appears naked at the door. She walks to where the pebbles meet the grass and looks about, as if searching for something. The narrator searches as well and finally sees "a world in which the sun and the moon shone at the same time."[20] In this world without time, many things existed in truth and beauty. The narrator sees her true self at the riverbank without the burdens of feet, hand, head, or heart. This sentiment connects to my chapter 1 discussion of the burdens of body parts and the struggle to gain and maintain control over the black female body. "I was made up of my will, and over my will I had complete dominion," she goes on to say.[21] At this point the narrator enters the sea. In this moment of liberation, death, and transcendence, she can be carefree, beautiful, solid, and complete. She is bound to everything that is, was, and will be.

Thus, through death, the narrator achieves transcendence over the adversities of life. All of Urban Bush Women's characters are searching for their true selves. They all struggle; some find peace, some continue to search. These pieces call attention to the global tyrannies over women and provide strategies for understanding and conquering them with the ultimate goal of moving toward healing. The women portrayed in these pieces suffer, but they also confront, question, and sass. These pieces concern exposing issues that challenge the wellbeing of women: the beauty myth, constructed femininity, socioeconomic injustice, interpersonal relationships, cultural imperialism, and spousal abuse. Through all of the hardships, the support of other women is the ultimate weapon against these cruelties.

5

THE SOUL

The Spirit Moves

On November 21, 1998, the Brooklyn Arts Center 651 presented "Dance & Spiritual Life," featuring Urban Bush Women, the Bebe Miller Company, and Dianne McIntyre and Hannibal Lokumbe. In the program, Gerald E. Myers maps out the difficulty dance scholars have had approaching the topic of spirituality and the aesthetic: "So many modern dancers . . . insist that their art is more than technique, more than display, more than entertainment, more than vocation—and that 'more,' they often explain, is something spiritual. Writers on dance know this but for whatever reasons, perhaps because 'spirituality' seems a vague and elusive concept or because it appears too personal for public scrutiny, they give it less than deserved attention." Any study of the work of Urban Bush Women would be incomplete without an examination of the spirituality that informs the choreography's form and content. In this chapter, I explore the uses of ritual and spirituality that lead to the transcendence of adversities and healing. Siddha Yoga and Swami Muktananda guide Zollar in bringing spirituality to her daily life. As Bernadine Jennings claims, "Zollar has created a body of works that nurtures and gives voice to women and men ready to let go of both cultural and spiritual baggage."[1] On the influence of the church in black choreography, Zollar says, "The church as form runs through a lot of our work. The call and response, the peaks that constantly happen throughout a church service, may happen throughout a dance. . . . It's that drive from the church."[2] She has also said, "I'm interested in how we change and how we get to that spiritual essence and free that."[3] Jennifer Dunning, dance critic for the *New York Times*, has claimed, "Jawole Willa Jo Zollar has had a consistent and innovative interest in mining tradition and creating new ritual."[4] In this chapter, I analyze this new ritual and other spiritual dimensions of Urban Bush Women's work on- and offstage and examine the ways they use spirituality as an important tool for bringing about healing.

Part of Urban Bush Women's community engagement work is the liturgical dance workshop. Led by company members, the classes focus on dance in the Christian experience and invite all those who want to use movement to proclaim their faith. Typical dance class begins with a warm up, moves into exercises and center-space and across-the-floor combinations, and ends with a cool down. Liturgical dance class begins with prayer and a scripture reading. Warm up for the body and soul is conducted to uplifting gospel music. The dance vocabulary focuses on movements that praise God. It strives to be a moving (physically and spiritually) experience for the individual and the group.

I took part in a liturgical dance workshop led by Vanessa Manley, who at the time was the company's special projects manager and not a dancer in the company. The class was for all levels of experience. Professional dancers moved alongside complete novices. Youthful, limber dancers moved with older, arthritic ones. Some leaped across the floor. Some stayed seated and swayed. All participated. The professional dancers were not at an advantage in this setting, as is the case with standard dance class. In fact, it is probably the contrary. Unencumbered by the desire for technical mastery, the spiritual experience that provided the non-professionals the impetus for movement was perhaps more evident and in a way more beautiful than the perfect turns and leaps of the company members. There are not many settings in which these people can dance together.

There were thirteen black women and two black men in the multipurpose room in the Brooklyn arts building where the company rents office space. On the flyer advertising the class, participants were instructed to BYOB—bring your own Bible. The class was free, but donations were accepted. Some of the participants knew each other, but some were simply people in the neighborhood who saw a flyer and decided to come.

Manley talked to the group about the power of offering bodies up as living sacrifices. She called it a calling. The group introduced themselves and Manley led a prayer to guide us to worship. She encouraged each person to recognize his or her spiritual gifts and said that even if one can't achieve the technical mastery of some of the dancers, each had gifts in dance and each could achieve a place of balance through dance. Each person is in a different place in her or his life journey. She provided a profile sheet developed by Rev. M. Goosby of Jehovah Jireh Ministries. On this sheet, different roles and gifts are laid out and defined. A corresponding scripture lesson was also provided. The profiles included: apostle, prophet, evangelist, pastor, teacher, serving, helps, leadership, administration, hospitality, craftsmanship, intercession and healing. Manley directed the group to several bible passages that were read out loud and discussed.

She told her personal story, which involved being called to dance ministry as a member of the First Baptist Church in Crown Heights, Brooklyn. Following her lead, others shared personal testimonies and elaborated on their individual spiritual gifts. The group talked about the fact that there are many ways to praise God (like through dance) and many appropriate venues for worship (like a multipurpose room in an office building). They talked about the street dancers who stop traffic in Times Square and discussed the possibility of using that energy to get people closer to Christ. To illustrate the call to use the word of God as a support, the group literally stood on the bibles.

Many churches are now bringing in dance ministries, in which it is God calling the hearts of people in the arts, since dance might have the power to move when words fail. Dance can be the word in motion, the word made flesh for all to see. It is a way to communicate with and through the spirit; the arts connect us beyond language barriers. Someone in the group pointed out that this work comes from the heart and that even the word "heart" contains "art."

Next, Manley talked about "baggage" that prevents people from using spiritual gifts to glorify God, identifying specifically fear, time management, disorganization, other people, loss of a sense of control, stress, and pressures from the outside world. One woman remarked that even when we have the best of intentions, factors always seem to take us away from our spiritual gifts. Yet something happens when we let go of our excess baggage. To illustrate the point, Manley picked up all of the bags people had brought into the space and tried to walk around carrying them. She then literally let go of the baggage and walked around. She picked up the bags again, closely examined a stylish black designer purse, and remarked that even if the bag is cute, it is still baggage. She encouraged the group to be mindful of spiritual gifts, to dance from wherever one happens to be at the moment, and, above all, to dance one's own truths.

Chanon Judson, one of the Urban Bush Women dancers, led the warm-up, which was conducted to spiritual music and consisted of opening up the arms and upper torso, reaching out to grab and hold something, turning, clapping, and arching the back. This could be as simple or as intricate as the individual dancer's ability. Manley then began with spontaneous movement, while we followed along. We moved to "Fill My Cup, Lord" by Richard Blanshard, which was about enduring a hard life, pain, and suffering by trusting in Jesus:

> Fill my cup, Lord
> I lift it up, Lord
> Come and quench this thirsting of my soul
>
> Bread of heaven
> Feed me 'til I want no more

Fill my cup
Fill it up
And make me whole

People sat on their knees, lifted their hands, and improvised on the lyrics and spirit of the music. Next Manley told the story of Mary Magdalene's alabaster box, which contained her gift of oil for Jesus. Interpreting the story, the group tried to move like Mary Magdalene going through a crowd to get to Jesus. Some people pushed others, declaring that they were not good enough to appear before Jesus. Finally, they made their ways through, knelt, and mimed kissing Jesus's feet. Manley then had the participants think about their spiritual gifts and try to pour them like oil on Jesus's feet. After some meditation, she dismissed the group and people socialized for about forty-five minutes.

Liturgical praise workshops become important nexuses of the work of Urban Bush Women. Though emphasis is taken off the technical skill of concert dance work, the "work" of these workshops is nonetheless salient. From the discussion that followed and the post-class socializing, it is clear that this work deeply affected the participants. They seemed genuinely unconcerned with technique and seemed to speak honestly about personal experience to perfect strangers.

Spirituality means different things to different people, and in many respects it defies definition, which is, of course, part of its power. Too, spirituality has long been considered a path to healing and liberation. During the 1960s and 1970s, in the spirit of the civil rights, Black Power, and feminist movements, many African Americans began to loudly challenge the tenets of Western theology, and black liberation theology and womanist theology were born from these examinations. In 1970 James H. Cone published *A Black Theology of Liberation*, in which he explained, "Theology is *contextual* language—that is, defined by the human situation that gives birth to it."[5] In other words theology is personal and political, and the transformation of suffering is part and parcel of both liberation and spirituality.

Cone's articulation of the connections between community and empowered religious experience and his later adoption of womanist theory are useful for understanding much of Urban Bush Women's work. Understanding of the divine is revealed for many as part of a communal experience. Womanist theology developed during the 1980s in response to things like Cone's omission of gender issues in liberation theology.[6] This theology also asserts that theologies are constructed belief systems, faith-based explorations that have the socio-dialogical potential to shape, according to Stephanie Y. Mitchem, "personal and communal meaning in faith, to analyze church doctrines, and to challenge

Stephanie Battle in *Soul Deep*. Photo by Cylla Von Tiedemann.

ecclesiastic operations." In *Womanist Theology*, Mitchem gives a concise explanation of the history and ideology of womanist theology: "Simply put, womanist theology is the systematic, faith-based exploration of the many facets of African American women's religiosity. Womanist theology is based on the complex realities of black women's lives. Womanist scholars recognize and name the imagination and initiative that African American women have utilized in developing sophisticated religious responses to their lives."[7]

Womanist theology became a way to discuss God in black women's terms and in the contexts of black women's lives. Important issues have included slavery, oppression and violence toward black women, interrogating the roles (social, familial, and ecclesiastical) of black women, understanding the damaging work done by stereotypes, and struggling to overcome these hardships. Though it is rooted in Christianity, it also examines other forms of black female spirituality and draws from African theologies that understand faith according to the situation of communities of people, past, present, and future.[8]

Another key tenet of womanist theology is the understanding of the importance of daily life in the political and religious spheres. Daily life is necessarily linked with community life for many. According to Mitchem, African American

Urban Bush Women dancers perform a ritual. Photo by Dona Ann McAdams.

women have a long history of strengthening this communal dimension by serving as the major support system for each other as mothers and othermothers: "Mothers take their daughters to the water, and grandmothers explain the meanings of the signs." In clubs, religious institutions, and the grocery store, "'sister-power' is generated, which results in self-empowerment."[9] These everyday, communal survival skills become conduits for liberation.

I argue that womanist theology is important to understanding Urban Bush Women's work, even though the company resists labels. The pieces I examine in this chapter have in common the spiritual life of women of color. They affirm, question, and challenge many dimensions of spirituality (among them the Godhead, faith, transformation, suffering, possession, and miracles). Above all, they participate in the dialogue about the role of spirituality in the lives of women of color. They build on the long traditions of ritual dance in African and African American cultural and spiritual life. Ritual permeates Urban Bush Women choreography; the dances I examine here bring ritual to the foreground, and they work directly toward spiritual healing.

Womanist theology embraces dialogical processes and intents. According to Mitchem:

> The womanist commitment to dialogue is not merely professional good manners. Rather, four aims are reflected. First, networking is a component of black women's epistemological frameworks. Networking defines both the community and the individual: "I" becomes more distinct in community. Dialogue is a form of networking. Second, the womanist commitment to ending oppression for all requires community building, which in turn requires dialogue with all the members. Next, alliances are necessary for all those who are committed to working for justice. Finally, shaping womanist theology is a process within permeable boundaries, not just in ivory towers. This process of dialogue is not easily accomplished and can become a balancing act.[10]

Zollar speaks with similar passion about her own spiritual journey when she says, "It's part of me—the journey, the searching, the quest."[11] Zollar uses prayer for inspiration and the creative process is spiritual in its consciousness-raising and embrace of greater goods. Company members are encouraged to be conductors of light. Company member Maria Bauman says, "This company allows me to be a vehicle to express that light, so in that way to me it is really spiritual because it's really healing. [The company's work is] a vehicle through which I can be a part of somebody changing our community. In my mind it is very service oriented and for me that's spiritual."[12]

Marinesa

> Talking about spirit is like trying to catch a ghost.
> Brenda Dixon Gottschild,
> *The Black Dancing Body*

The laying on of hands is meant to bring about spiritual, emotional, and physical healing; when talking about it, many refer to the healing ministry of Jesus. The New Testament is full of stories of Jesus touching lepers and other sick people to heal them.[13] Many artists, particularly novelists, have explored the healing power of touch. For example, in Toni Cade Bambara's novel *The Salt Eaters*, Minnie Ransom lays hands on the sick to heal them. In her poem "Southern Women," Carla J. Harris writes:

> Southern women's hands—
> touch and stroke,
> hold and soothe,
> never heavy, never hard,
> always calm and sure.[14]

Urban Bush Women choreography is full of moments when one dancer touches another as a laying on of hands and a mechanism for healing. Conversely, when the choreography is meant to suggest suffering, dancers tend to refrain from physical contact and avoid each other.

In *Marinesa* five women create a ritual space by lighting candles on the side and sprinkling something (seeds?) on the floor. Goddesslike, they sit in positions of power. They move with wide torso rotations, reaching up to the sky, looking up with stretches, collapses, and rises on strong breaths. The movements initiate from the torso, particularly the expansions and contractions. They grab their heads as if in grief. They get caught up in the music, and when they finally calm down, they sink to the floor.

A woman in white seated on the floor, observing, enters the space behind the dancers and circles them. She takes out a fan and moves it in front of a dancer's face. She fans her slowly for a while, cooling her off, offering her comfort. She then gives a fan to each of the women on the ground. Their troubles eased from the fanning, each woman stands up. The fanning slowly charges the air with energy. These fans are infused with meaning; emblematic of the southern black church tradition, they are used to testify to spiritual truth, they sanctify the space, and they symbolize comfort from the spirit and from other women. Fans in *Marinesa* are also gifts that show the individual how to take care of herself. In other words, the fan has transformative powers. It gives the individual relief not only from the heat of the sun but also from intense spiritual energy.[15]

The woman in white resumes her place on the floor as the dancers begin to breathe together and move in unison in a wide circle. Like the fan, the circle is also important in African and African American custom. In these traditions, dancers stand in a circle to symbolize the communal experience. With no front or back or head or rear, the circle is inherently non-hierarchical. Everyone can see and be seen. In also creates a sacred liminal space in which transformations can occur. When one or two people step into the center of the circle she/he/they take on the energy from the others. They shine as individuals by stepping out of the group while remaining a part of it, supported by it. Often when a semicircle or arch is presented on stage, it is to include the audience as the completion of the circle.

The dancers take large steps around the circle, reaching up with their arms wide. One woman goes into the center, drops her fan, and spins, dervishlike. The others try to fan her to bring her out of this frenzied state. The woman in white returns and tries to help; finally the soloist calms down and collapses to the floor. The woman in white fans her and lays hands on her as she continues to pant.

As I have suggested, water is one of the most vital agents of African American Christian spirituality and ritual. Not only does it cleanse the body, but for many it also cleanses the soul. Baptism is a spiritual cleansing that leads to rebirth. In the spiritual "Wade in the Water," we are told to go into the water because the Christian "God is gon' trouble the water."[16] "Trouble" is a way of moving into another plane of existence. And history has shown that for social change to take place people sometimes must make trouble. The pouring of libation is a way to give back to the earth, as a gesture of thanks and praise, a bit of what it has given us.

In Toni Morrison's *Beloved*, Beloved walks out of the water, representing a return from historical and mythic ancestors.[17] An ordinary ritual that is an important part of many black women's empowering practices is "going to the water" as a place of prayer and meditation. These rivers, streams, and bathtubs offer these women assistance in focusing their prayer and spiritual journey. This touches on many parts of the African Diaspora. Mitchem explains that water "has great significance in West African traditional religions and also has lingering meanings that for some black women in the United States connect with these of 'old-time' religion, a connection that has yet to be fully explored."[18]

Water is also important in the Muslim faith. In "The Sacred Journey: The Gift of Hajj," Daa'iyah Taha, an African American Muslim woman, talks about her pilgrimage to Mecca and her spiritual experiences at the Sacred Waters of Zamzam. Waiting in line to drink from this holy well, Taha remembers the story of Hagar, an Egyptian slave woman whom God blessed with water when she and her baby were near death. The well and the city of Mecca are said to have sprung from that spot. On her own journey, after drinking from this well Taha attests the communality of spirituality: "Because of Hajj, I would never again desire to be held above or accept to be held behind another human being. I stand gratefully beside humanity in the dignity of the Circle. This is what my soul was longing for."[19]

Next in the dance, the four women each take off their sashes and wrap the woman on the floor, the soloist, then fan her as they back away. She stands and moves slowly as they move in unison behind her. She walks around the space, the others behind her, supporting her, and giving her strength. She hugs herself as she moves and then collapses wearily. The woman in white brings a cloth and lays it out. She removes the sashes from the woman on the floor and places them each on the cloth. The others gather and take off the soloist's dress as the woman in white wraps her in a white cloth. This whiteness becomes symbolic of the ancestral world, and the dance becomes more clearly a death ritual. The two women in white are the ancestors, and the other dancers are human. The woman being comforted is between these two states, and both sides are helping her cross over. A second woman in white finally rises and approaches the soloist with a large bowl of water.

Finally, the second woman in white lays her hand on the soloist's forehead and pours a libation over her, cleansing her, baptizing her. The woman cleans herself. As she reaches her head back, the four women behind her weep, mourning. The two in white finish wrapping her in the white cloth. They circle her, sprinkling her with water and seed, blessing her. The woman folds herself over, cocoonlike. She has crossed over.

By rendering a last-rites ritual into dance, Zollar does not simply present an example of or a metaphor for death, she creates a sacred space out of the stage so that some amount of spiritual awareness may be channeled to the audience. These women attempt to preserve the ties between the individual, the collective, and the divine.

Xpujla

> The most sacred place isn't the Church, the Mosque, or the temple, it's the temple of the body. That's where the spirit lives.
>
> Susan Taylor,
> quoted in Iyanla Vanzant, *Acts of Faith*

One of the first pieces in Urban Bush Women's repertory is *Xpujla*. It demonstrates the early stages of Urban Bush Women technique and of the communal energy and spirituality of Southern black women. It opens with the sounds of two calabashes and a cowbell beating out a rhythm. As the lights come up, a line of women appears along the back wall, chanting "Come home" over and over again. The women are all dressed in long white skirts, shirts, and headscarves. As in *Marinesa*, the performers' white clothing and reverent attitude indicate that this is a religious ceremony, a call for people to come home to the base of who they are, particularly those of African American heritage. This "down home" folk wisdom is often maligned in social discourse, but in this dance piece it is honored.

Three of the women play the instruments while the others chant. The line processes along the upstage wall and curves around to center stage, where three women pause as the others continue to make their way to stage left. One woman on the side riffs on the "come home" theme, telling the dancers to "come on home" and "come on back." As the three dancers move across the stage, they carve through the space with wide circles and reaches. They slide to the ground and stretch back up. At one point one chassés ahead of the others and back, and they do a round that looks like waves on a shore. Their turns with wide arms and lifted torsos make them look like women praising God. They move from side to side across the stage in gestures of praise. At one point they each place one arm behind their backs and the other across their stomachs and pulse forward and back, as if being overcome. They slowly collapse to one knee, and, one at a time, they rise briefly with a hand in the air to testify. This continues for several repetitions, until they all rise up and reach a hand up to the sky.

At this point, the chanting stops and the movement continues in silence. The three dancers move their arms in circles around their heads, then over the ground about twenty-five times. They build energy to near possession and then collect themselves. They begin to fall out of step, but then they all regroup and freeze. At last, they slowly collapse to the ground as the lights fade out.

Bells ring out in the darkness. When the lights come back up, a single dancer appears stage left with bells on her wrists. She wears a long black skirt covered by a long white sheet, draped around her shoulders and reaching to her knees. She also wears a white headwrap. Taking careful steps and flicking her wrists to ring out a rhythm with the bells, she makes her way out to center stage. While she intones notes, she flicks her wrists, circles her arms, claps, and stamps her feet. Then she recites text about how we create our world through the eternal singing in our soul and how we express cosmic yearning for answers to life's questions.

In this monologue, the speaker tells the audience a way of understanding the world and their places in it. She talks of the social construction of identity and the possibility for social change: the key is to take what is inside our souls and bring it out through song, having a voice. This process brings about wisdom and truth. We must look to ourselves for the answers to life's big questions. With a final laugh at the deceptive simplicity of it all, the dancer makes her way offstage, spinning, stamping, and ringing her bells.

Humming is heard as the lights come back up on the women walking slowly back onstage, one carrying a gourd; four, candles; one, a walking stick; one, stones; and one, a chalice of water. The four women with candles place them on an altar along the back wall draped in white. The other five sit stage right as one of them starts to sing and moan out a powerful spiritual while the others hum and rock. Some of the lyrics are "passion and wisdom," "true light from heaven," "I said, your people need you today," "a nation descending," "washing waters before me," "help me to witness change again and again," "let your people lead you today," "show the way," and "after the journey's done." The singer stands up and walks around the others. The song, like all spirituals, is also a prayer. Many of the dancers have their eyes closed. The others stand up

Amara Tabor-Smith and Craig Harris in *Soul Deep*. Photo by Cylla Von Tiedemann.

and walk to the four at the altar. The chalice is placed on the floor in the center of the stage; three dancers walk stage right and two stage left. The four dancers sitting at the altar take turns dipping their hands in the chalice and slowly cleansing their arms, heads, and bodies as the others clap and sing in canon:

> Breng the spirit, chile!
> The chile come to me in the spirit, chile.
> Breng the spirit, chile!

This cleansing ritual is sacred, communal. The dance becomes more frenzied as each dancer catches the spirit. It is the picture of a powerful revival meeting as the parishioners all get happy, moved, possessed. Some throw themselves to the ground and toss their bodies around. Exhausted, one by one they finally bring the energy back down to a calm or calming pace. Still swaying and reaching up in post-ecstasy, three dancers slowly come to standing and move toward each other, touching each other. The fourth reaches out to them, and they reach and help her to stand up. All four hug as they sway side to side as a group. Slowly, the group comes to a seated position, and they all lean on each other, rocking back and forth as the song ends and the lights come down, leaving the sanctifying glow of the candles on the altar. Again, Zollar gives the audience a ritual moment on stage—this time a spiritual possession arising from group fervor. With cleansed spirits the women raise and lower the energy together, giving themselves over to a higher power. Because of this ritual, the women can come together in an embrace that eases the soul.

Transitions

> If you want to accomplish the goals of your life, you have to begin with the spirit.
>
> Oprah Winfrey,
> Speech to the American Women's Economic Development Corp., New York, Feb. 25, 1989

As I mention in my discussion of womanist theology, it is important to emphasize that Urban Bush Women does not advocate for any particular religion. Rather, the company explores the roles of African Diaspora spiritual traditions in the lives of many African Americans. Much work has been done on the interconnectedness between black female Muslims, Christians, Buddhists, and other faiths.[20] Particularly salient are belief systems that offer an alternative to a distinctly white male God and male-controlled organized religious system. For women of color, these belief systems can offer a spirituality that centers on the individual taking agency over her spirituality and making choices about organized religion, images of God, and the role of the spirit in daily life. This continues a tradition begun by slaves who took agency over colonial religion by incorporating prior belief systems without contradiction. Gloria Wade-Gayles expresses the sentiment that black women "do not sing one song; pray one prayer; worship the same God; chant the same mantra; call on the same orisha; heal and meditate and celebrate our spirituality in the same way. . . . They have in common their belief that only when we are spiritually connected can we realize our highest selves, become one with all of humanity (as the Spirit says we must), and transform the world in which we live."[21]

Transitions examines the exploration of spirituality for black women and the multivocal conversations about the divine. It comprises testimonials, oral and physical, about both faith and the questioning of faith. It is dialogic. When I asked Zollar about the experience of creating *Transitions*, she replied that it was done at a time when the company included someone who was following traditional African spirituality, someone who was Islamic, someone who was devoutly Christian, and someone who was Wiccan.

Interestingly, in terms of dance styles, *Transitions* is one of Urban Bush Women's more "modern" and less African pieces. The dancers point their feet and extend their bodies in long lines. They hold their torsos, and though they use breath, the releases are controlled and precise. Duos and small groups dance in exact precision and are less individualistic than in other pieces. The dancers stay "in" the piece more—they break less from the world of the dance to take in the audience. The piece is pious in tone and meticulous in execution. Performed mostly to spoken word and ambient percussion sounds, it is a reflection on the many different places of God and spirituality in the lives of these women.

It opens with Zollar's voice in the darkness, in a voiceover, talking about contemplating questions about the nature of God. She goes on to interview the women in the company about the thoughts they had about God as young children. Lights come up on two women facing each other, each with her head on the other's shoulder. They slowly raise their heads and lean them back. When one of the respondents in a voiceover talks about her childhood fear of judgment day, the dancers separate with wide steps, one reaching straight up to the sky with both arms raised high and the other, in a wide second-position plié, reaching a curved arm upward. They come together again, one in front of the other, and they both lean backward, with the upstage dancer providing support for the downstage one, who shifts around the other and reciprocally provides support, carrying her around in a spin. In a voiceover, the woman states, "I was always afraid of judgment day. I thought it would come sometime soon, and I was afraid of that day. It was terrifying, and I don't want to raise my children that way." Another responds, "I remember that when it used to rain my mom used to tell me that God and the angels were mopping the floors. And they were throwing buckets of water and it was coming down." The dancers take turns giving and taking each other's weight in deep arabesques and lifts. Another woman claims, "God was always, when I was a child, this thing, this big, big thing that was in the sky. And that you never pointed your fist at God. And God was always symbolized as a man, like for most people. And was very fierce, but unknown." During the words "you never pointed your fist at God," one dancer does make a fist and raises it to the sky, less as an act of aggression toward God and more of a show of inner strength. The two dancers seem to be helping each other discover the spirit within themselves. Their gestures are wide and sweeping. Their hands are splayed wide, trying to grab onto something. Their energy is focused outward. At one point they lean on each other, side by side, and when one touches the other's torso, a wave flows through her body, as if she were being filled with élan vital. On voiceover, Zollar asks what images the women had of God growing up. One responds, "I didn't really have a visual because my parents were so adamant in saying that God was not a white male with long brown hair or blond. It was more the power. But it was still a male in my mind without being a race. But it was the power of God. The things that we couldn't predict beyond the power of humans." At this, the dancers take wide steps forward, reaching up and spinning their bodies, trying to grab onto that power. They breathe together and shift between quick spirals and very controlled held positions, which symbolize the balance needed between vitality and patience in spiritual life. On voiceover, another woman states, "The only image I ever saw was, you know, white—with the white hair, in the church. . . . Oh, we had this picture of a dinner and that's what you saw." Each dancer falls into a graceful runner's stretch and takes a few breaths, as if gathering serenity and strength to continue.

The different images of God discussed by the respondents provide an important picture of the relationships many women of color have with divinity and the influential role of social constructions. These constructions of God, particularly as a white man, have led some black women to see themselves as the farthest from "him," which, in turn, helps solidify their marginalized place in society. Zollar sets up the piece with these varying but similar images in order to lay the groundwork of common perceptions of God born of racism and sexism. This is the base of many black women's spiritual journeys; whether or not one is a believer, the image of God as a white man is omnipresent and feeds into oppression. Even beliefs that do not include this image must contend with it. The dancers' slow, gestural vocabulary at the beginning of the piece, coupled with their give and take of weight and lifts, indicate their support of each other on their journeys to understand the essence of God. Zollar layers a reverential, trancelike quality onto the movement.

Next, the dancers gather energy in with their arms, then shoot it out to the audience with their breaths. Their breathing gets more pronounced. When the voiceover speaks of God as punishment, the dancers flex their feet and make fists with their hands. They briskly kick their legs up in attitude, in contrast with the long-legged, pointed-foot graceful battements they executed earlier. They take long breaths and return to their journey with more urgency, at one point leaping high into the air and landing in a collapse. They pause to breathe and gather themselves. For the first time they step out of this world, walking around the space and prosaically looking about, taking in their surroundings. This is in sharp contrast to their previous diffused, reverent gazes. It is as if they are discovering something closer to the everyday and are waking up. Zollar's speech goes on to explain that this is a self-discovery—the discovery of God in the self:

"Every time I thought of God as something outside of myself, I couldn't breathe. I couldn't breathe and I just kept getting stuck and getting stuck and getting stuck." This is an echo of Ntozake Shange's play *For Colored Girls Who Have Considered Suicide / When the Rainbow Is Enuf*, in which the last line is "i found God in myself & i loved her / i loved her fiercely."[22] The dancers seek this love. Their actions become more fevered and their breaths more anxious. They reach up to the sky. They repeat a gesture in which they move their arms around their heads with their hands in fists. They try to take giant steps but are continually thrown off course and forced to pivot around themselves. They collapse into the runner's stretch, then try to pull themselves up, only to collapse again, repeating this several times with increasing frustration, until the lights finally fade on them in this crouched position.

At another moment in the piece, the dancers each adopt a different attitude of worship. One woman stands in a testifying pose with one hand on her heart while her other arm raises up to the sky, palm forward, and her chest is concave and shoulders raised. One opens her chest and arms in reception. One processes as if walking into the light. One raises both hands in front of her bowed head. Several bow. When they begin to move as one, they proceed in two diagonal lines moving slowly downstage, as if on a pilgrimage. Their steps originate in demi-pliés and are punctuated with shivers and forward reaches while wind chimes ring. It is a long, weary journey, and sometimes they get pushed backward. When a drumbeat kicks in, the pace of the dancing also picks up. They become less weary, spirals move through their bodies, and they take longer, bolder, more determined steps. They fix their gazes on their destination. The African drumming helps guide them, giving them the strength to continue. At one point, each shifts her focus to a partner, and in duos they repeat the part of the opening sequence in which they support each other, giving and taking weight in arabesques and lifts. They repeat the torso touch, and the wave affects those who get touched. At another point, half of the women leap backward, trusting that their partners will be there to catch them mid-leap. They are caught, the soles of their feet together and arms hugging themselves. They run around their partners and hop onto their backs, as if being carried on part of the journey. They are all on this journey together and depend on each other to reach their destination. Midway through their journeys, dancers in one of the lines step out of the piece and walk around, prosaically, as if loosing their way. On voiceover, Zollar asks, "Has anyone ever been to that place where—some people call it the dark night of the soul—where you're just at that place where you don't know if you have the will, the strength to continue forward, you just don't know?" One woman responds by discussing a time in her life when her foundation was shaken. She claims, "And what I had to learn to do was just keep eyes on the path and not try to see down the road, not try to make sense of it but trust that it was right because it is where I am." Some dancers continue working on the same path while three break away in a solo and a duo. It is as if the journey has paused so that the audience may hear some of the individual stories. At the end of the speech, the soloist leaps in a different direction from that which the group is traveling, but the duo catches her before she lands. However, she still follows a different path.

The next part of this section is a powerful solo performance done to the text of another woman speaking about a time in her life when she was sick and hospitalized and about the faith that brought her through. The soloist moves widely, with feet flexed and hands in fists. She is frustrated and angry. She kicks her legs up violently and throws her body forward so that her foot seems to kick beyond her head. Tormented, she jerks into intense contractions and throws her head back and forth. Though she gets thrown off balance, she tries to maintain composure; she tries to keep her spiritual and physical grounding. When she collapses into the same stretch in which other dancers had previously fallen, another woman enters the space to help her. She too struggles but is a positive presence for the soloist—a reminder that others have suffered and survived. The second woman becomes the rooted faith that the first is able to call upon. She clasps her hands together in front of her heart and rises up. A group of four forms upstage left, and the women strike their chests and send the energy out through their fingers. Back on the journey, they repeat the shiver steps as a sole woman slowly walks toward them. She becomes the soloist for the next story about the transformational joy of deep meditation. She touches her heart several times, then raises her leg to the side when the speaker talks of a tingling sensation. She looks at her leg suspended in air, touches it, and with her hands moves it around to the back. She touches her heart as a wave shutters through her body. The four dancers upstage also shiver. More waves pass through her, and with each shiver she throws her arms up to the sky in ecstasy. She gives in to the sweet pain, leaps for joy, and touches her heart as the wind chimes sound and the drumbeats come in.

All of the women dance joyously, filling the space with runs, skips, leaps, and turns. Their faces express their joy, and for the first time in this piece they yell out. They dance in unison as the intensity builds, and they jump straight up for joy. They break off into individual expressions of exhilaration and rapture, charging the air with apparently ceaseless positive energy. As most of the dancers leap offstage, one collapses into the runner's stretch. The lights shift back to the opening tone, and the two dancers who began the piece remain. The piece has come full circle, recalling the beginning of the journey. The second dancer walks to the fallen one and reaches up her hand, as if being touched by the spirit. The fallen dancer rises and they circle each other, move in closer, and, again, they take turns supporting each other in slow arabesques and lifts. Percussion sounds, and a man's voice hums a spiritual. As they lean on each other to carry on, three other duos enter, doing similar steps. On voiceover, a woman whispers the mantra "surrender" over and over again. The dancers pause briefly in a tableau of worship. They all walk to center stage and stand in a line facing the audience, one in back of another. They take several breaths together, and on a long, deep breath begin moving their arms to the side, up over their heads, into their chests, and out to their sides again. It presents the image of many hands moving in succession from a single being. The dancers repeat this action, gathering energy out of the ground, from the sky, and in through their common heart. They have found peace as the lights fade out.

Theology professor Marsha Foster Boyd emphasizes the importance of listening to women's stories in order to achieve transformation. She rejects the image of the wounded healer and embraces that of the "empowered co-journer" to describe the support system fostered by many black women. Her five components of womanist pastoral theology are communication, affirmation, confrontation, accountability, and healing. All of these components also comprise the work of Urban Bush Women: "WomanistCare is the intentional process of care giving and care receiving by African American women. . . . In WomanistCare, the telling of one's story and finding comfort and power in that story are essential for healing and transformation."[23] When one woman is transformed, she in turn works to transform and influence others.

This piece is a journey of transition as dancers and speakers move toward being able to surrender to a higher power—an image other than a controlling, white male God. Each person is on a personal journey rooted in community. In this distinctly female space, the women help each other even as they struggle. The voiceovers not only illuminate the dancing but also become testimonials directed at the audience. The questions Zollar asks are calls to reflect on struggle and survival and to be open to transformative experiences, especially in times of need and pain, when the road ahead seems long and hard.

The Life Dances

> The dance is strong magic. The dance is a spirit. It turns the body into liquid steel. It makes it vibrate like a guitar. The body can fly without wings. It can sing without voice. The dance is strong magic.
>
> Pearl Primus,
> "African Dance"

> and i dance my
> creation and my grandmothers gathering
> Sonia Sanchez,
> "Present"

The *Life Dances* are an ongoing journey for Zollar, at the end of which she plans to have twenty-two vignettes or sequels.[24] These solos give the audience a glimpse into the spiritual journeys of different characters and the different sides of the self contained in a person. According to Deborah Jowitt, the pieces are about "the selves that lurk within, about growth, about peeling off layers to get to the essence, about the black female ancestors who run through the blood of black women today."[25] The pieces draw on many different spiritual sources, including the tarot, shamanistic healing traditions, orishas, and Christian mysticism. These are Zollar's personal journeys, but she trusts that her audiences will be interested in joining her. There is no timeline for completion of these vignettes.[26] In this section, I analyze three of the four finished pieces in this cycle and discuss them in terms of performance and transformation. I discussed the fourth piece, *The Papess . . . Mirrors over the Waters*, in chapter 4 as part of *Heat.*

In the tarot, the fool is the symbol of beginnings and mental, physical, and spiritual journeys. In *The Fool's Journey*, Zollar presents the stages of life and spiritual awakening.[27] The piece opens as Zollar enters the stage in a crouched position. She wears a white leotard and headwrap and carries a stick with a white bundle tied to it over her shoulder. With this relatively minimal costume, her arms and legs are boldly exposed. Staying low, she slowly makes her way onto the stage, looking around and trying to safely explore the new place where her journey has taken her. Eerie mood music plays as she comes to center stage. She slowly stands and lifts her right hand as if checking for rain. She takes her bundle off of her shoulder and ceremoniously swings it toward her raised hand, then slowly swings it from side to side, lowering it with each pass until she places it on the ground. She rises up as percussion music comes in, and on each beat she looks around. It is as if the music controls her movements. Her limbs are rigid, and she moves in a jerky, robotic way. At one point, she squats down in a deep second position to the playful wind instrument that joins the rhythm. Staying in this position, she opens and closes her legs and arms and moves to the side. She swings both arms straight up and back behind her several times She kicks a leg out to the side and with a series of leaps and reaches turns her focus to her bag, getting on her knees and rhythmically crawling to it. She rolls to the side and repeats the deep second motion with the leaps and reaches, while keeping her focus on the bag. She skips, jumps, scoots, and raises her arms in praise, all to the percussive rhythm. The bag clearly holds a place of importance in the dance piece; this section is like a ritual homage to it, giving it respect and honor. Throughout this dance, the character keeps a mysterious half grin on her face, as if she knows something the rest of us do not. Her relationship to the bag and stick is at once playful and reverent. She is both honoring the bag and formally preparing to open it to allow us to experience what is inside.

The music stops. She starts a rhythm using her breath, walks proudly to the bundle, and bends down to it. She unties the knot and opens the fabric. She takes out a white pair of short pants, then sits down and puts it on. She removes her headscarf and throws it to the side, then she takes out a piece of white lace from the bundle and ties it around her head. She then takes the fabric that was the bag, refolds it, and turns it into a sash that she ties around her waist. She takes the stick and raises it in the air triumphantly, then places it on the ground, and with a final, long breath she turns to the side and pliés in a type of bow to it. After a pause, she places her hands akimbo on her hips and looks around. She takes her hands off her hips, then lowers herself to the stick in wavelike undulations as the percussive music comes back in. She swings from side to side and puts her hands back on her hips. Although she is still sprightly, she has transformed into a more secure, put-together person. She no longer looks around tentatively; she stands confidently. She is even more playful. It is important that the new clothes, symbolic of this transformation, were with her the whole time. The layers that she attaches to herself are both the form and the content of her bundle: it is as if she carried with her the person she was to become.

She reaches down and energetically picks up the stick and moves from side to side with it as if she were digging rows for planting. Satisfied with her hard work, she places the stick on her head and one hand on her hips and walks around with a swing in her step. She smiles flirtatiously as she moves, rolling her shoulder occasionally. The stick transforms into a limbo stick as she lowers herself underneath it. It is next a cutlass that she uses to clear a path through the brush. Somewhere in her swinging motion, it becomes a weapon to keep away a threat. She takes hold of the stick, focuses on the threat, and thrusts a life blow as the music stops. The stick, which she has honored, becomes everything she needs to make a way for herself in this middle stage of her life. It is a tool for livelihood, a source of pleasure, and a weapon for protection.

She calms her breath after this intense experience. She slowly places the stick on the ground, then takes off the lace headwrap and throws it to the ground. She takes the sash from her waist and ties it around her head, like an old woman's headkerchief. Her movement then slows and becomes shaky, and her breathing becomes more erratic. As the stick becomes a walking stick, she becomes an old woman. She puts her other hand on her back and hunches over.

When the percussion comes back in, she can only minimally jerk her body to the rhythm. When the playful music comes in, she takes hold of the stick with both hands and slowly swings it to the side while raising one leg in a large step. She looks around to the side, sees something, and minimally shakes her head "no." She moves her knees a little bit more, then nods her head "yes." She cannot move the way she used to. She turns back, nods with a bit of fear and awe of whatever it is with which she is communicating—something telling her she will die soon. After an initial denial, she finally accepts this last part of her journey. She places the stick on her head, and with each step, its weight slowly brings her to her knees. She then moves the stick on either side of her, as if she is rowing a boat. She raises it up in a final offering, and the music stops. This rowing to the other shore is the process of dying, leading to the final transformation.

This journey is over, and if the woman was a fool, she was so only in the trope of the wise fool who seems foolish because she is clever, the one who hides what she knows in order to survive. She is a trickster figure, and her mysterious grin is that of not a fool but of a person who knows more than she is saying. She takes what she is given (a stick and some fabric) and finds a way to get everything she needs in the journey of life.

The Magician in the tarot symbolizes mastery of the material world, creative action, self-discipline, and the willingness to take risks. In *Life Dance 1: The Magician (The Return of She)*, Zollar appears as a bootleg whiskey swigging church lady dressed in black: large hat, black dress, combat boots, and giant cross on a rope around her neck.[28] She is seated with the Bible across her lap, and in between swigs she boisterously preaches a loud, drunken, chaotic story about a bird that shall be set free. Its source is Leviticus 14:1–9, in which the Lord told Moses how to cleanse a leper. If a leper on the outskirts of society has been healed, the priest is to bring two birds. One is slain and the other washed in the blood, which is then sprinkled seven times on the leper, who shaves and bathes and after seven days is allowed to rejoin society. The living bird is set free. This, like many of the Old Testament sacrifice stories, foreshadows Jesus's sacrifice. Christians believe that, like the bird taking on illness, Jesus took on the sins of humanity. He was sacrificed so the rest of humanity could be free from sins. In African American history, this has come to mean freedom not only from sins but also from slavery and oppression. These desires are expressed powerfully in Maya Angelou's famous book *I Know Why the Caged Bird Sings*, in which the free bird knows the carefree joys of life while the caged bird knows only torment as he sings for freedom.

When she says the word "free," Zollar lifts up the liquor bottle triumphantly, leans back on the chair, and kicks her left leg out. She throws the Bible to the ground, pours out some of the liquor as libation, and gradually becomes possessed. She acknowledges the drummer and begins to move to the sound. She puts down the bottle, claps her hands several times, and clutches her chest. She looks as if something is taking over her body. She stands up, shaking all over, painfully taking giant steps toward the drummer, who sits stage left. She begins moving to the drumming. Still clutching her chest, she kicks out her leg and spins around; she kicks again and shifts frantically from side to side. The hat flies off her head, and her bushy, nappy hair gets tossed about. The drummer chants and laughs as Zollar's character gives in to her power and slowly falls to her knees.

As she gives in to the music and moves more freely, she sheds her clothes until she is left in a leotard and the combat boots. She seems intoxicated: her body is heavy, and her arms hang limply. She undulates her pelvis while she spins around, opening her arms as if taking in the world. She spins around about thirty times, then collapses before the laughing drummer.

This piece highlights the intertextuality between organized religion and spirituality and the points of convergence in Christian mysticism. The woman uses the Bible story to bring about her possession. Though a somewhat sorry sight, drunk and belligerent, when she throws away the Bible and gives in to the possession as channeled through the African drumming, she is able to free herself, like the bird in her story. It is significant that the dancer sheds the church-lady hat, dress, and cross and is stripped down to a simple leotard. Also noteworthy is that she keeps on her combat boots, since the dance (as is individual wrestling with God, perhaps) is a battle of sorts. Spiritual awakening for this woman is violent, physically demanding. The combination of the drumming, liquor, and story of the bird results in a transformative, mystic experience. As the title suggests, her return to herself is magic. She looks for God in the Bible and bottle and finds God through her own body.

In the tarot, the Empress symbolizes fertility, maternal care, domesticity, well-being, and security. Reversed, she means domestic problems, creative blocks, and infertility. In *Life Dance 3: The Empress* (*Womb Wars*), Zollar explores these themes of the roles of women in terms of childbearing in U.S. society. She directly links reproductive rights with the status of women and the Western images of God. The piece opens with Zollar sitting on top of a desk. Her arms are outstretched, and she leans toward the audience. She emits a high-pitched screech, and with labored breath and intermittent screeches, she delivers the following monologue: "I go down to the river to cleanse myself. I see the stranger dumping sewage in the river. The stranger sees me. He beat me and raped me. I go home to tell my father and my father he beat me. I go to tell my mother and my mother she stays silent. I go to tell the doctor and the doctor cut my insides out. Who gon' care 'bout the river? Who gon' care 'bout me? I'm looking for God."

Through her body language, Zollar shows that she is opening herself out to the audience. She is reaching for a connection. She is looking for not only God but also an explanation about why this has happened to her, and a way to go on. After this speech, she slowly breaks from the position and, singing to herself, retrieves a telephone from behind her and sits down at the desk. She places the phone on the desk and puts on a pair of glasses. Addressing the audience, she talks about how her mother tried to abort her when she found out she was pregnant. She stands up and walks to the side of the desk, where she adopts a wide stance and throws her arms up as if pushing against something coming at her, and then tells the story of her birth and the nurse trying to hold her in to wait for the doctor. She then claims, "I've been pushing up against it ever since." She drops her arms and sits back at the table, then starts humming a blues tune, drawing out an "oh." Her next word, "shit," comes as a surprise, as one might expect her to be singing "Oh, lord." She sings "Oh, shit" six more times with different inflections. She plays with the audience. She says, "These are probably the first words I heard from my mother when she found out she had a womb child instead of a penis child. Oh, shit!" She sings a few lines of an African song before she picks up the phone receiver and, in shock, tells her friend Marcia that New York's Cardinal O'Connor declared God a man and adds, "And you know what? I really, really, really, really think he meant to add white." She hangs up the phone. She tenses her hands toward the audience and in the stilted voice from the opening says, "I'm looking for God." She then picks up the phone and tells Marcia to reconnect with her body and find a way to get the abortion she needs.

Another connection is made between having to go underground to get an abortion and the Underground Railroad—both secret means of escape. She hangs up the phone, stands up next to the desk, and starts to run in place. She says, "Every once in a while I just have to run. I just have to run like my ancestors did. Run through Mississippi. Run up North. 'Cause I know I'm running for my life."

History repeats itself as the violence done on black women's bodies resurfaces. She walks back to the desk and places her hands on it. She assumes the same disposition she had in the opening of the piece—rigid and fighting off the pain and anger. She declares, "We have no choice but to fight!"

Zollar then recounts the story of her rape. As she tells her story, another dancer enters naked, her body straining and contorting, hands clenched in fists, and her head arched back. She then begins convulsing and begging for water. She gets under the table as if hiding from this side of herself. She searches for a way to retake control over her body.[29]

Zollar recounts her reunion with the daughter she put up for adoption. This reuniting becomes symbolic of the road to healing. Several more performers enter and surround her with lit candles and flowers. They sing, "No. No more. No. No. No. No more." The inclusion of a community of women is a vital part of this ritual; it promises to lead to the healing of body, mind, and spirit.

Indeed, all of these pieces in the *Life Dances* entail a search for healing, the divine, absolution, and peace. The empress specifically says that she's looking for God to understand how these horrible violent things could happen to her. The fool finds God at the end of her life, the papess finds God through a ritual meant to cleanse her from her sins, and the magician finds God through possession. Often, each of these women needs a weapon in her journey. Be it with a knife, a stick, combat boots, or intellect, all of them battle forces meant to keep them down. As the empress explains, from birth she has been pushing up against forces meant to hold her back.

All of these characters are women who undergo transformation. The fool goes from being a young girl to a mature adult to an old woman before the audience's eyes. The papess moves from being a troubled, wronged, dangerous woman to a cleansed woman at peace. Through reasoning, the empress is able to change from the barely communicative woman on top of the desk trying to explain her situation to a clever, articulate one exposing the myths about religion and life. Through the spirit, the magician is transformed into a free bird. The goals of these transformations are survival, healing, and ultimately, hopefully, peace.

Soul Deep

> What we play is life. . . . My whole life, my whole soul, my whole spirit is to blow that horn.
>
> Louis Armstrong,
> to his doctor, 1971

It is not a coincidence that part of the African American musical legacy comes from "spiritual," "soul," and "gospel" traditions. Anyone can draw on these lyrics and rhythms to claim a place on earth and in heaven as well as to further the collective struggle for liberation—spiritually, politically, and economically. In "Justified, Sanctified, and Redeemed: Blessed Expectation in Black Women's Blues and Gospels," Cheryl A. Kirk-Duggan talks about the transformative role of these musical genres in the lives of many black women:

> Justified, sanctified, and redeemed—what joys do these portend? African-American women live, compose, and sing spirituals, hymns, Gospels, and Blues. Sometimes they sing because they're happy; sometimes they sing because they're free; sometimes they sing from plain ol' misery. Black

> women sing what they experience. Their songs, born of an African milieu, are tempered by the pain of evil, racism, and subjugation: and their songs reflect the joy, blessedness, and beauty of spirituality and survival.[30]

Urban Bush Women uses the singing, music, and chanting of African American tradition to reach audiences aesthetically and spiritually. More specifically, the musical traditions include not only spirituals but also soul, funk, African, and jazz—all of which connect to the spirit. Though it was once called the devil's music, artists have shown how, on the contrary, jazz can lead to spiritual transformations; New Orleans jazz funerals, for instance, are the clearest example of the connectedness among jazz, transformation, ritual, and spirituality. In *Soul Deep*, musical riffs, improvisation, and passion allow the dancers to reach a level of release rare in concert dance. The piece begins with a jazz band, the David Murray Ensemble (bassist, saxophonists, trombonists, drummer, and trumpeters), lining the back wall. A male orator sits with them and speaks into a microphone, the same words as the text from *Self-Portrait*. In this new context, spoken in a soothing male voice, a jazzy, sultry attitude infuses the language. A saxophonist plays. Zollar is onstage working through some moves in a style similar to jazz improv. She swings her arms, arches her back, and contracts her torso as if warming up. She sidles up to a saxophonist who aims his music at her. They move together a bit, then Zollar resumes her stretches. She lets each note flow through her as she hops to the beat, alternating stretching with letting herself get carried away with the music. At one point, she performs an arabesque and leans on the saxophonist for support. The live music clearly influences her movement, as if the notes are passing through her body.

As the soloist walks toward the band, the other musicians come in, filling out the jazzy, bluesy sound. Another dancer enters the space, and she and Zollar boogie together, stepping lively across the stage. The lights turn from the harsh, work lights to a warmer, red tone. Zollar does another arabesque, leaning on the dancer, and then the two hold each other for a moment before making their way offstage. Several other pairs of women move across the stage, interacting with their partners in different ways: some barely notice each other, some ignore each other, some engage in confrontations, and some steal away together in secret. Soon all the couples appear onstage in simultaneous pas de deux with weight sharing, lifts, and carries. They walk across the space like friends or lovers, holding hands, leaning in to talk, laughing together. One chases her partner. Another catches her. The movement is sensual and continuous. Finally, they all come together and sit cross-legged in a downstage line, facing the audience. One by one, each touches the head of the woman next to her, who circles her head and torso before touching the next person, until the

Above and below: Maria Earle, Ravi Best, Michelle Dorant, Craig Harris, Amara Tabor-Smith, Christine King, and Michael Wimberly in *Soul Deep*. Photos by Cylla Von Tiedemann.

whole line moves in a wave. The speaker repeats the chant "om," which also sounds like "home." In response to the repetition, the dancers bounce their bodies and make their hands into fists. They stand up and confront the audience with gestures of defiance as the lights fade out.

In the dark, a voice calls out, "Wild women. Wild women do wear they blues. And they wear they blues well. Brothers, I said, wild women, they do wear they blues. And they wear they blues well." As in *Wild Women, Anarchy, and Dinah,* they evoke the power of women unafraid to stand up for themselves. The lights come back up with several of the dancers sitting casually listening to the music, calling out lines about women in the bush, while others stand around reading the newspaper. This alternating between daily life and stylized dance illustrates the effects of giving in to the spirit of the music, letting it take custody of the body. The quick return to reading the paper demonstrates the fine line between daily and heightened existence. This moment also highlights the connections between spirituality and sensuality. In letting themselves go, the dancers reject inhibition, which is a necessary precursor to discovering sensuality.

All of the women then come together in a cluster on the floor, chanting, "Women," and singing women's praises to the audience. They each stand up and make their way offstage, except one, who moans out and holds a note. The saxophonist reappears, captures her note, and, for a moment, both intone the suspended note. The soloist moans out another note as the saxophonist takes his instrument and swings it around over the dancer's head several times. The dancer shouts, pants, and goes weak-kneed, as if touched by the spirit. What follows is a soulful call and response between dancer and musician. At times playful and at times vitally serious, the interchange goes on for several minutes. Most of her singing is vocalization, but some words that she sings include "strong women," "travelin'," "bluesy," "women," "mama," "soul," and "redemption." She also touches on the tradition of soul shouting, singing as loudly as one can in praise of the divine. She "gets happy" on stage by shouting, allowing the music to influence her, and dancing. She looks at once like a church lady getting the spirit and a young girl at a night club, singing and dancing with the band. This moment highlights the similarities between the spiritual powers of religion and art. With a final, high-pitched note shouted out and held, the dancer squats low and opens her arms to the audience. The saxophonist joins the other musicians, and the dancer snaps her way offstage.

Two dancers then come out, chanting Zollar's childhood nickname, "Jody Pody Macasody," in a singsong. They snap and swing to the opposite side, where they pick up two more dancers, who chant "Zing, boom!" in the same tone. The four dancers move back to the other side, where they pick up three more. All seven sing about nappy heads as they travel across and offstage. Zollar skips on behind them and stays onstage to perform a solo. The music picks up again, slowing her movements. The orator recites text about Zollar's aunt Bell similar to the "Zing Boom" stories in *Hair Stories*. In this solo, Zollar sways with the music, keeping her head down, scratching her hair. She wanders around the space, moves into modern dancing, and then goes back to scratching her hair. She is wrestling with her aunt's attitude about nappy hair and can't quite allow herself to get caught up in the music.

With the music and the dancers supporting her, Zollar launches into a scat-rap song extolling the virtues of nappy hair while the dancers perform the electric slide in the background. Zollar chants to the audience, "I got nappy nappy hair and I'm happy. I'm happy, I'm nappy! I'm happy, I'm nappy! Hot combs, no I can't stand 'em! Hot combs, no I can't stand 'em! . . . Zing Boom! Zing Boom! Zing Boom! Zing Boom! Zing Boom! Willa Jo Jawole Jody Pody Macasody . . . got a nappy head!" Finally able to take control of her identity (through her hair), Zollar dances offstage, and the others dance jubilantly with leaps, jumps, high steps, and snaps. The music has allowed her to reach to her soul and discover pride in being the way she was meant to be. Zollar reenters, dancing jubilantly, almost out of control, throwing her arms and legs about. She squats down, swinging her head, plops down to a seated position and scratches at her nappy head, looks up, and smiles. She goes back to modern dance with wide sweeps and steps. At one point, she arches herself back and stretches her arms up as she thinks about the blue-green lavender acadia tree in her aunt's yard and how it reminds her of her mother's hair, happy, nappy hair. She then dances offstage.

The orator speaks into his microphone: "Transcendental dreams. Looking for lessons in combat and meditation. Women requesting urban survival tactics in important dance steps. And sometimes there are no sad songs at all. Just your everyday soul people redemption songs." These redemption songs for soul people are songs of freedom from oppression though the intervention of the divine. As Mitchem explains, "Salvation, then, in a womanist construction, is not found in formulaic answers but in the search for wholeness. Redemption is a journey that begins by daring to care for self in the face of repeated assaults on identity and value."[31]

The last ten minutes of the piece consist of a long group number danced to the full jazz band in which the dancers interpret the lively music. They playfully spin on stage and sashay off, and they move as a group spinning, whipping their legs around, and throwing their hands up in the air. At various times they follow different instruments in the band. The dance and the music complement each other, and the movement pauses at times to let the music take over. Each dancer

Francine Sheffield, Ravi Best, and Stephanie Battle in *Soul Deep*. Photo by Cylla Von Tiedemann.

takes some time to solo center stage. Toward the end, they all form a circle and throw their energy into the center. They charge the sacred space with their energy and take each other in as they perform the same steps. Zollar comes back onstage, and the orator calls out and riffs on the line "You don't know, but this is my dream!" All of the dancers, including Zollar, bounce up and down and throw their arms up wildly, jubilantly, triumphantly, as if at a New Orleans street party as the lights fade.

I started this book by investigating their treatment of the bodies of black women. In this, the last chapter that focuses on Urban Bush Women's concert-dance work, I investigate their treatment of the souls of black women. Some Western philosophies attempt to separate the body from the soul to promote the body over the soul. In this system, there is little room for the spirit. Works by artists like Zollar reject this binary and attempt to heal the rift and reunite body and soul through dance. As these examples show, the company works to reclaim the spirit for the body. The body and the soul are connected in many African American belief systems; for example, in *Beloved* Toni Morrison describes the Saturday afternoon gatherings at the Clearing in which Baby Suggs would call out the men, women, and children to worship together. At this spiritual revival,

Jawole Willa Jo Zollar. Photo by Dona Ann McAdams.

she teaches those gathered how to love their own flesh even though the oppressors despise it: "Love your hands! Love them. Raise them up and kiss them. Touch others with them."[32] This act of loving heals body and soul.

The analysis of the company's choreography has brought me here. To heal the old wounds, Urban Bush Women reexamines the body and celebrates the power of those parts of the black body long maligned. By celebrating stories of black women and girls, the company also rewrites the master narratives that failed to tell their tales. It celebrates the support systems provided by many black women for each other when other avenues fail in times of trial. Lastly, Urban Bush Women attends to and celebrates the spiritual life of women of color. Urban Bush Women reminds us of all the work that has been done and all the work that is yet to be done.

One final analysis is necessary to tell a complete story of the work of Urban Bush Women. The company is also committed to offstage healing work and work that leads directly to social and political change. In everyday life, as well as onstage, members of Urban Bush Women attempt to assist individuals and communities to understand and improve oppressive situations; they attempt to create kindred spirits. In chapter 6, I investigate the company's "real life" work in communities to bring about healing and change. This work functions in the spirit of Harriet Tubman, who went back to the South to free others, and Fannie Lou Hamer, who risked her life for the freedom of others. Hamer often talked about the importance of staying connected to her community, affirming African American heritage and empowering women. As Mitchem states, "Salvation in a womanist view desires transformation of self *and* society." She also writes:

> When African American women have reexamined their lives following pain, a response has often been greater dedication to the life of the community, to networking, the working for others. Salvation becomes a community event. As has happened repeatedly in the lives of black women, from Ida Wells Barnett to Fannie Lou Hamer, activism for the greater community is birthed. Each person is saved not merely for self, but for community. Each person is saved *from* socially structured limitations, saved *for* the greater good of all people.[33]

On her ordination as the first African American female Episcopal priest, Pauli Murray said, "Descendant of slave and slave owner . . . I was empowered to minister the sacrament of One in whom there is no north or south, no black or white, no male or female—only the spirit of love and reconciliation drawing us all toward the goal of human wholeness."[34] It is this human wholeness that I argue is the ultimate goal of Urban Bush Women's work. Delores S. Williams calls this "social salvation."[35] Christal Brown claims, "Collective or interpersonal transformation occurs when we reach out to others in similar situations and collaborate."[36]

Dona Marimba Richards connects many of these themes (spiritual transformation, seeking solace in others, and building community) when she says:

> We would form a circle, each touching those next to us so to physically express our spiritual closeness. We "testified," speaking on the day's or the week's experiences. We shared the pain of those experiences and received from the group affirmations of our existences as suffering beings. As we "lay down our burdens," we became lighter. As we testified and listened to others testify, we began to understand ourselves as communal beings, no longer the "individuals" that the slave system tried to make us. . . . We sang and moved until we were able to experience totally the spirit within us. We "got happy." . . . We became, again, a community.[37]

King put it well in my interview with her. Talking about working on *Transitions*, she noted how moving it was to learn something about the way other people look at life. It was like getting a glimpse of "something deeper about the person. . . . I see the spirituality as we're leaning towards a transformation, even if it is about getting to know somebody else and you need to know yourself in a different way and for me, the work leads towards healing."[38]

I call on all of these examples to illustrate the vital link between Urban Bush Women's concert work and its community work. Zollar and Urban Bush Women are at the forefront of the interrogation of spirituality, aesthetics, ethnic identity politics, and activism through dance. Black theater and community leader John O'Neal states, "Probably the central teacher I have, as I try to grasp all this stuff, is Jowole [*sic*] Willa Jo Zollar. . . . She's getting me to appreciate the way in which these things we identify as spiritual phenomena stand as complementary to physical phenomena rather than in some opposition to physical phenomena."[39]

6

THE COMMUNITY

In Theory and Practice

Who makes up a community? How can artists work within different communities to make both aesthetic contributions and effect social change? How can communities empower individuals? These questions and others inform some of the most powerful work of Urban Bush Women. Even though "community" has become a buzzword, meaning different things to different people, the members of Urban Bush Women remain committed to helping organize different communities to bring about a better world. Reviews of Urban Bush Women's concert work often highlight its community-building power. For example, in 1998 Susanna Sloat reviewed a production of *Self-Portrait* and claimed: "The line between audience and stage disappeared. . . . These pieces were about community, one that embraced the audience so thoroughly that the usual gulf between artist/entertainer and the entertained seemed to vanish. Instead . . . there seemed to be an arc from stage to viewer, one that seemed joyously two way."[1] The company also tries to create community by working in different neighborhoods, like the Dixwell section of New Haven, Connecticut; Tallahassee, Florida; and Flint, Michigan. In community sings and liturgical dance workshops, they bring together people who are interested in sharing their spiritual beliefs, organize people around political issues like voting rights, and work with children in classrooms and YMCA programs. And they do all of this work under the auspices of dance.

An eclectic look at some of the contemporary dialogue around community provides useful contextualization for discussing Urban Bush Women's community work. There are many different ways of understanding "community." Neighborhoods are communities. Religious institutions are communities. Professional associations are communities. So, too, are academic institutions and sports fans. "The community" has oddly come to be a euphemism for "ghetto," especially as far as the arts are concerned. Teaching artists go out to

Terri Cousar, Valerie Winborne, Treva Offutt, and Christine King in "Girlfriends." Photo by Cylla Von Tiedemann.

"the community" to bring culture to the underprivileged. Other euphemisms exist. Nursing homes have been replaced by "assisted-living communities." "Home" in these contexts now has a negative connotation, and "community" is the term du jour. Communes, however, are treated with suspicion in the United States—they might be taking the idea of community a bit too far. Images of hippies, cults, and tragedies like David Koresh and the Branch Davidians in Waco, Texas, are associated with communes.

To many, the United States is a nation of disconnected individuals striving to belong somewhere, looking for community, in some cases *shopping* for community. In our fast-paced modern world, the role of face-to-face contact has shifted dramatically. There are Internet communities connecting, across the country and the world, people who may never actually meet face to face. Technological communities have altered the mechanisms and forms of inter- and intra-community communication. This phenomenon has caused Studs Terkel and others to remark that there are more and more forms of mass communication and less and less communicating.

Despite the potential for international community building afforded by the Internet, we still tend to organize ourselves around national communities. In *Imagined Communities: Reflections on the Origin and Spread of Nationalism*, Benedict

Anderson offers, from a rather Western perspective, an examination of the idea of national community based on geography. These communities, he finds, are being challenged by "sub-nationalisms" that expose nationalism as a myth. He claims that "the creation of these artifacts towards the end of the eighteenth century was the spontaneous distillation of a complex 'crossing' of discrete historical forces; but . . . once created, they became 'modular,' capable of being transplanted, with varying degrees of self-consciousness, to a great variety of social terrains, to merge and be merged with a correspondingly wide variety of political and ideological constellations." He argues that the nation is "an imagined political community—and imagined as both inherently limited and sovereign." All nations create nationalism as a community in order to preserve themselves. Conversely, nationalism invents nations: "In fact, all communities larger than primordial villages of face-to-face contact (and perhaps even these) are imagined communities. Communities are to be distinguished, not by their falsity/genuineness, but by the style in which they are imagined."[2] This is not to say, I argue, that national communities are any less valuable because they may be the product of group imagination.

A discussion about the role of community in contemporary U.S. society has surfaced among intellectuals (public and academic) as well as in the general public. Suburban sprawl has isolated Americans to the point where one could go from air-conditioned house to air-conditioned car to air-conditioned office and back again without ever going outside, much less engaging with a community in person, unrelated to work. This phenomenon inspired Robert D. Putnam to write *Bowling Alone: The Collapse and Revival of American Community* (2000), in which he argues that U.S. civic society is collapsing because people are becoming more individualistic, disconnecting themselves from their families, neighbors, and government. This has led to the decline of community and civic participation in the Unites States. Specifically, since the late 1960s there has been a 40 to 50 percent decline in organization membership. We tend to know our neighbors less, spend less time with family, and give less money to charity. U.S. citizens used to bowl in leagues: now we bowl alone. Putnam concludes that it would take a galvanizing crisis to change attitudes.[3] Then came September 11.

Since the September 11 attacks, however, researchers like Putnam have identified a shift in attitude about community. People apparently took to "nesting" and sought solace in others. Right after the attacks Putnam re-interviewed some of the people he had spoken with for the book and found that many of their attitudes toward others had improved a great deal. They also tended to trust the government, police, and other individuals (even across racial lines) much more, mainly because of a perceived "shared purpose." Putnam called on progressives to seize the moment and convince Americans to invest more in issues like public health and infant mortality. In other words, since Americans were more inclined to make sacrifices now, politicians needed to ask for more in their proposals for action. Putnam noted that the shift in attitude need not necessarily lead individuals to take more action, and he bristled at the fact that in response to the attacks, President Bush asked people to go shopping.[4]

This sense of community is still unstable as administrations change. Not all New Yorkers feel reconnected. Many (especially those with small children) feel the need to flee to the suburbs. This new "shared purpose" has also created an "us versus them" attitude that has further removed Americans from the global community. The clearest examples of this are our unilateral attack on Iraq as well as the ostracizing of Muslim and Muslim-looking people in the United States and the subsequent global fallout. I suspect that if Putnam interviewed his participants again, he would find more mistrust of government and less trust across some ethnic lines than he found directly after the attacks.

An interesting experiment in citywide community building occurred in the fall of 2001 in Chicago, one of many such projects across the nation. Mayor Daley called on all Chicagoans to read the same book, Harper Lee's *To Kill a Mockingbird*, join discussion groups, and even bring it up commuting to work on the El. Oprah came on board, the 3,500 copies of the book in Chicago libraries circulated 6,000 times, one high school produced a play version of it as their fall production, and the Chicago Bar put on two dramatizations of the trial. Mary Dempsey, Chicago Public Library commissioner, claimed that the experiment was a success particularly in light of the fact that people wanted to be with other people after September 11; they wanted to be able to walk up to someone and have a connection, and the book gave them the opportunity to do so.

Perhaps the new sense of solidarity following the attacks was a blip on the radar screen of national civic-mindedness. Perhaps it was a curse in disguise. For my purposes here, these discussions form an interesting backdrop against which we can examine the community work of Urban Bush Women. Zollar often talks about work that embraces community. She looks for ways to get involved in community identity formation. Many of the communities the company works with are composed mainly of African Americans, but not all. The company builds on the work of the women's rights movements of the twentieth century and today. They also build on the long tradition of African Americans relying on each other.[5] According to Jacquelyn Grant, "The connectedness of people is the only hope of the oppressed. Western culture's individualism must yield to the profound African understanding that say, 'I am because we are.' We are defined by our community, and if our community is negated, so are we."[6]

Zollar seeks to make links with youth culture, and she embraces the stories of older people and values them as historians. According to her, the community speaks so we all may learn something about ourselves: who we are, where we're from, and where we're going. This emphasis on learning is vital to the work.

Any analysis of Urban Bush Women would be incomplete without an investigation of this extra-performance work. Much of the work toward healing communities and individuals happens in these offstage settings. Also, many of these forums provide the impetus for the concert work. An example of this is the hair parties the company held as it was developing *Hair Stories*, in which participants from different communities gathered and discussed their relationship to hair. On many occasions, this seemingly benign topic led to much more heated discussions about delicate subjects, particularly around race and gender. It soon became clear that the hair parties were more than research for a dance piece; they were doing serious community work by creating a forum for important topics. In the remainder of this chapter, I investigate the rest of Urban Bush Women's community work.

Classes and Workshops

> The power of dance is often underestimated.
>
> Jawole Willa Jo Zollar,
> interview with the author, Dec. 20, 2003

The company occasionally offers technique classes and workshops that are open to everyone as means of connecting with communities. When it is on tour it tries to organize classes for the hosting community before or after a performance. Led by a company member, Urban Bush Women's technique class starts with a forty-five- to sixty-minute warm-up that prepares the participants for full-out dancing in the Urban Bush Women style. The second half of the class focuses on the movement style and may include improvisation, phrases from repertory, and/or vocal work. In improvisation classes, company members lead exercises that encourage participants to explore the body moving through space and develop performance techniques through structured improvisation. Some classes are specialized technique training and offer social activism along with movement work. For example, in a capoeira class, the most important lesson former company member Amara Tabor-Smith, the leader, had for the participants was to go *with* the energy of a confrontation. When a force comes toward an individual, one must go with it in order to diffuse it, rather than try to meet it with an opposite force. Along with practicing the physical technique, participants discussed the ideology as a maxim for other parts of life. Tabor-Smith's goals were not just physical conditioning but also life conditioning.

The lecture-demo "Survival through Cultural Traditions" focuses on the creative process and the use of materials from African American culture and folklore in performance. Lecture-demonstrations also broaden and develop the way audiences see dance in relationship to their lives. In these classes, Urban Bush Women dancers strive to demystify the process by which art is created. The integrated process workshop is an emotion-based class for experienced actors, dancers, and singers who are interested in exploring the technique involved in Urban Bush Women's combination of voice, movement, and theater work. The acting-out workshop unites movement, music, and text to explore character and narrative. Touching on various acting techniques, participants physicalize and vocalize everything their imaginations allow. The vocalization workshop draws upon Urban Bush Women's vocal techniques. A company member leads participants in the exploration of their voices through the use of breath. Movement is also integrated with vocal work to create a more complete experience of sound. In the women's work workshop, Zollar leads a female-only exploration of current and historical attitudes about women's bodies. This workshop focuses on understanding how these attitudes can enhance or inhibit women's expression of movement. The rhythm and you workshop is a fun, participatory, community-oriented, all-ages class that explores rhythm through voice, hand-clapping, and movement.

The company also offers children creative movement workshops based on the popular and traditional dances and songs of African Americans. On her efforts with children, Zollar has said: "I'm interested in giving students a physical intelligence. . . . The cultivation of the imagination is one of the things that gets lost when there's a desire to adhere to a curriculum that gets students through tests. When the imagination is not cultivated, you don't have people like Bill Gates. You don't have problem solvers."[7] I witnessed a workshop for kids held at a Brooklyn YMCA. There were two four-week sessions. Dancer Dionne Kamara taught ten-, eleven-, and twelve-year-olds, and Francine Sheffield taught thirteen-, fourteen-, and fifteen-year olds. I observed Kamara's class, in which there were five boys and ten girls. She also had an assistant, a high school sophomore involved in praise dance at school. Kamara unrolled posters and told the kids she wanted to work on focus; he asked them what came to mind when she said, "Focus." One said, "Concentration"; another replied, "Attention." Kamara explained the difference between single-focus (focus on one spot or part of the body) and multi-focus (focus on many different things at the same time). She also discussed the concepts of space, time, force, body, movement, and form. She told her students to find a "perfect spot" in the room and began

Urban Bush Women publicity photo. Photo by Dona Ann McAdams.

a warm-up, with breathing exercises. They explored tactile perception. They put arches and curves into their bodies. They swung their arms and isolated their heads, elbows, et cetera. They spun around and inhaled and exhaled. They did a leading and following exercise. They made shapes focusing on their elbows. Kamara explained "internal focus" and had the children close their eyes and make different shapes with their bodies. Then they opened their eyes and followed her movements. Next, together they created a poem and developed a dance using multicolored scarves about their group that centered on the terms "energetic," "responsible," "skipping," "jumping," "sliding," "creative," "colorful," and "connected."

I also witnessed a hair party for kids (mostly black girls) in which dancers Kamara and Kamuyu led a group of African American children in a movement class based on hair texture. They would ask the children for different words to describe hair and would help them put those images in their bodies. For example, they might wiggle their contorted bodies when the leader called out "kinky." Or they would swirl their bodies on "curly." They talked about the different things they could do with their hair. When the leader asked what came to mind when they heard the words "beautiful hair," one little girl threw up her hands immediately and shouted, "Straight!" Other words were given, like "curly," "braided," "dreadlocks," and "wavy." It is telling, however, that the first and most enthusiastic suggestion was "straight." Throughout the workshop, the dancers tried to emphasize that different types of hair can be beautiful. This, they told the children, was the meaning behind the dances in *Hair Stories.* They performed a few segments from the piece depicting a little girl going through the trials of getting her hair done, during which the children laughed in recognition. Kamara told me that they had done a hair party for kids earlier that day in which most of the participants were white. She said these children clearly did not have the same issues about hair, and some were frightened by the depictions that amused the black children. She saw getting black children to love their bodies as one important part of Urban Bush Women's work.

Community Sings

> Meeting physical force with soul force.
> Dr. Martin Luther King Jr.,
> "I Have a Dream"

Community sings, workshops in which a company member leads participants in African Diaspora (especially African American and Jamaican) folk and spiritual singing and vocalization traditions, are also an important part of the extra-performance work by Urban Bush Women. These are workshops for choirs, choral groups, or any member of a sponsor's community and may include excerpts from the company's vocal repertory. The singing necessarily leads to movement, though choreography is not the goal. These workshops have been conducted with participants of all ages, with choirs and choral groups as well as groups of people who just come together to sing for an evening. Community sings are a valuable means by which company members and participants build coalitions. These sings allow people to gather, and singing allows them to open up physically and emotionally—important steps on the journey to empowerment. The emphasis is on allowing the group to support the individuals' needs. The community sing is an artistic metaphor. Participants are encouraged to translate the principles of call and response and chorus/soloist to their negotiations in everyday life. For example, if involved in a political debate, members should engage in call and response and try to find a collective energy that can support them when they "sing solo" and to which they can give energy to support others.

The sing I want to use as an example took place in summer 2003 during the "Dare to Go There" project. Zollar conducted the workshop, and there were twenty participants from the company and Brooklyn's Fort Greene community (eighteen women and two men). She explained that when she was doing research in Jamaica to develop choreography, she was deeply influenced by the singsongs, spirituals, and folk singing. She connected those traditions to ones from her childhood, and singing traditions of the African Diaspora took on deeper meaning in Urban Bush Women's work. Community sings, she told us, are a valuable means by which company members and participants build coalitions.

Following the introduction, she had us stand in a circle and started us off singing "This Little Light of Mine," a song familiar to all of us. She added a rhythm using hand clapping and foot stomping. She called out lines like "Early in the morning," and we responded with "I'm gonna let it shine." Some harmonized, while others took turns as soloists. This arrangement served as a metaphor for the times we want to blend and be a part of the collective energy and the times we need to rise out of the group and shine. At any given moment, however, the group supports the individual's needs. This song, in particular, reminds the participant that to let the light shine, one must be open. It is a proactive, forward motion.

Most of the songs in Zollar's repertoire come from company members, musicians, and other artists, who teach each other songs from their childhoods. For example, Junior Wedderburn, who occasionally plays percussion, taught the company the Jamaican "Gully Gully Wash Wash" song, which his mother sang. Jackie Guy, a London choreographer, taught Zollar another Jamaican tune, with the lyrics:

> Come, we just a come.
> Come, we just a come.
>
> We don't want no moderation, no!

We sang these lines a few times, then riffed on the term "moderation" to get "worry-ation" and "bodder-ation" (i.e., "bother-ation.")

We next sang some songs from the concert work. "Breng the Spirit Child" is from *Praise House* and *Xpulja*. Zollar emphasized that "bring" is not correct in this instance—there is something in the long drawn out "breng" that invokes the old church women. We sang the song again, adding three-part harmony. Then we turned it into a shout, with triple-time clapping that during slavery, when drums were outlawed, would have been done with a broom or by clapping hands. We then turned the song into a ring shout as we moved the circle around to the rhythm of the clapping, stomping, and singing.

Kamara taught us "Knocking Cumina," in which her Jamaican great-grandmother would use her knuckles to beat out a rhythm to the tune:

Rock-o, rock-o, rock-o,
Mt. Zion children, rock-o,
Mt. Zion children, rock-o.[8]

Kamara demonstrated how her great-grandmother would take small steps and accent her hips and shoulders. We then all tried it.

Next, Zollar talked about how one need not be anxious about harmony as long as one commits to a tone. In gang singing, if everyone in the group hits a different note and commits to it, it will not be cacophonous. This is an African, not Western, way of understanding tonality. She told us that Jamaican revivals are twelve hours long and during them people sing the grandmothers' songs of sustenance. She also explained that in acupuncture the heart is connected to singing; of utmost importance is that we each sing our "heARTs" out. We ended with a few more songs and then socialized over refreshments.

Summer Dance Institute: Building Community through the Arts

Every step of the way, you've got to fight.
Fannie Lou Hamer,
interview with Dr. Neil McMillen, Jan. 25, 1973

Urban Bush Women has held a number of intensive summer dance institutes, starting in 1997. According to the company's 2004 literature, "The purpose of the Summer Institute . . . is to connect concert professionals and community-based artists together in a learning experience to better maximize the possibilities of the arts as a vehicle for social activism and civic engagement."[9] The focus on these workshops is to train artist-activists as leaders.

The first Summer Institute was held in partnership with Florida State University in Tallahassee, from June 28 through July 27, 1997, and was titled "A New Dancer for a New Society." Though not offered every year, the institute has trained over two hundred artists/activists in Urban Bush Women's community engagement techniques. In my interview with her, Christine King talked extensively about the Florida institute. She told me that the primary focus was dance but that in addition to Urban Bush Women technique, participants learned about different ways to enter community and identify groups and leaders. They also learned techniques for finding out what is going on in a community and "how they can use tools that they have in their own pockets and gather people who have done a lot of community work." At the Florida institute, people from all parts of the world gathered for five weeks, and at the end there was a big community arts festival. In other institutes they have focused on issues like AIDS awareness, teen pregnancy, and undoing racism. King sees their work as "jump-starting" a community or conversation, moving them to the next level and giving the people working in each environment new tools to "keep it blossoming."[10] This jump-start is a salient concept for this work; the project of providing a forum for impetus is very different from one that remains dedicated to a community until all of its issues are resolved. Urban Bush Women makes no claims to magic remedies. Rather, it emphasizes the crucial act of providing safe creative space for working through issues. The company becomes a conduit through which community members can channel and focus their energies. The company's techniques must therefore remain somewhat open so the dancers/leaders can move in different directions as necessary. At the same time, the dancers/leaders must build on each experience learning what works and what doesn't in order to improve their approaches.

The Summer Institute has four goals: provide solid dance and choreographic training, foster participants' recognition of the cultural and historical contexts in which they live, show how research and performance can serve personal objectives and address social issues, and give participants the skills to return to their home communities and use this information to work toward community engagement. Participants are selected from across the country, based on their backgrounds in dance, research, and community work and their potential as leaders and choreographers. In addition to intensive dance and choreographic training, the institute curriculum relates research to choreography and choreography to community interest by placing traditional African forms within a social history and context and filtering those forms through modern dance and contemporary performance. Curriculum components specifically address the dynamics and mechanics of community art-making through lectures, workshops, panel discussions, and observation of community arts activities.

"Urban Bush Women has designed this Summer Dance Institute in recognition of the need for leadership training in the dance field," said Zollar. "Many university arts training programs focus on dance technique and do not promote the skills needed for successful community engagement. Over the past decade, UBW has developed a method for imbedding historical research and community engagement into the evolution of creative work. At the Institute, we will offer a new generation of dance artists the chance to learn how choreography, cultural history and community work are interconnected."[11]

The 2004 Summer Institute was held in Fort Greene, Brooklyn. In light of the upcoming presidential elections, its subject was voter education, registration, and turnout. More than forty dancers of different ages, from eighteen states and many different walks of life, participated in the ten-day workshop.[12] The professional company also participated. At the performances of *Are We Democracy?* (the product of their efforts), which took place at the Brooklyn Museum of Art, there was a voter registration table staffed by the National Organization for Women, New York City chapter, and many people connected with community groups were in attendance. There were two performances on the same day; at the first, there were about two hundred people in the audience, and at the second, there were about five hundred. The racial makeup was very diverse. There were also many children in attendance.

While audience members take their seats, dancers walk onto the stage casually and warm up. They wear white T-shirts that read "November 2" on the front and have the "I am an Urban Bush Woman" logo on the back. Songs on democracy and voting rights by Sweet Honey in the Rock play as the dancers stretch. After a while, they walk back offstage. This opening undermines the formality of a typical dance concert; house lights are up, costumes are casual, and the dancers mill about unceremoniously as the audience members are still talking and taking their seats. The intention is to make the audience feel comfortable and to move the dancers and the audience to the same plane. This will aid later in the post-show discussion. Zollar then enters and addresses the audience, explaining that she is interested in creating bold, life-affirming works that contain the stories she wants to make sure remain a part of U.S. history. She tells the audience that the piece is about process and ensuring a more equitable political process. She explains that she talked to people around the country about why they do not vote; she tried to get at why people have dropped out of the process. She is also disturbed by the ways people have been and are prevented from voting. This performance is the product of that initial research, but the piece is meant to spark further dialogue and action—it is by no means an end in itself. Zollar wants to bring people back into the process: she charges the audience to be the compassionate people at the voting booth who help citizens exercise their right. She tells the audience not to forget the little ways they can be of service to community. For example, she had heard that one of the biggest obstacles to voting was embarrassment when the polling person made fun of a name because it sounded different. She further explains that the piece is also a tribute to the life of Fannie Lou Hamer and her work registering people to vote, on the fortieth anniversary of her infamous bus ride. Last, she mentions a special guest performance by the Young Prophets Step Ministry of the First Baptist Church of Crown Heights, who prefer to perform in fatigues, which, though she was hesitant at first, she has chosen to respect and allow.

The piece opens with "Give Your Hands to Struggle" and the calling of the names of the important figures in African American history, like Sojourner

Truth and Harriet Tubman. One dancer moves slowly around the stage, her strong arms carving the space. Her fists reach out slowly, and her body rolls. The song "Give Your Hands to Struggle" comes in. She does a back extension and then leaps. Her passion builds. The larger group of dancers waits in the wings, supporting her and giving her their focus and energy. She opens her arms to them, and they begin to enter. Her energy builds as more dancers come out. Zollar reads some of the words of Fannie Lou Hamer. She reads out the ways people have been disenfranchised. When she explains that one in five New Yorkers can't vote, the dancers move into groups of five and all but one lie down. When she talks about gerrymandering, everyone shuffles to get into different groups. She tells several stories of misinformation; for example, in one town some fliers announced the wrong voting date, and in another instance, people believed they had to have their parking tickets and rent paid before being allowed to vote. All the dancers face forward and scream out, "What?!" She also tells a story about people who signed up to receive absentee ballots and then read a flier that encouraged them to walk to the polling place, only to find out that one can't vote in person if one has requested an absentee ballot. At this point three dancers walk around fiercely, trying to get help. One by one, the others turn their backs on them. Finally Zollar talks about Katherine Harris, former secretary of state for Florida, purging 57,000 names (mostly of blacks, Latinos, and Democrats) based on an inaccurate list of felons during the 2000 presidential elections. Groups of dancers walk away slowly.

From the audience, a woman stands and delivers a long spoken-word monologue about being sick and tired of being disenfranchised. The dancers move around the space, whispering, "Why?" "Why bother?" and "Why should I vote?" They stomp, pound their fists, and breathe heavily while moving as a mass. They tell stories of why people don't vote. They are stories of abuse, violence, and injustice—the most powerful of which are the stories of Martin Luther King Jr.'s struggles and Fannie Lou Hamer's beating. Hamer carried an extra pair of shoes with her when she went to Indianola, Mississippi, because she had a feeling she and the others who went to register to vote might be arrested. Afterward, the owners of the plantation on which she worked told her to leave, and she did; then the house in which she was staying was showered with bullets. Now her words haunt the space as the poet tells the audience she doesn't think the Lord brought her this far for nothing: "I'm sick and tired of being sick and tired."

Two drummers come in, and the dancers scream, "You got to fight!" then break into feverish, strong African dancing, leading up to a final, explosive moment when they scream, "Ha!" Several dancers move into capoeira, and the energy builds to the most charged I've witnessed in an Urban Bush Women performance. The dancers repeat "ha!" over and over again. In both performances, the audiences stood up clapping, stomping, and cheering. It was as if the dancers were directly feeding energy to the audience by screaming and throwing these powerful moves. It was a ritualistic moment of transformation and empowerment.

They move into a section from *Bitter Tongue*, and another spoken-word poet asks if she could ever be as strong as Fannie Lou Hamer. Then the stage clears, and a loud, clear voice shouts, "You . . . better . . . vote!" Stomping is heard offstage, and then five children from the step ministry stomp in. One young man sharply asks each of the other four if they are going to vote when they turn eighteen. Each responds with an elaborate step sequence. After more power step routines they announce a hip-hop initiative that has registered 30,000 new voters. By allowing a local group to participate in the performance (indeed, perform the finale), Zollar further underscored her commitment to community. These young men and women were not only challenged to vote themselves when the turn eighteen, but they also were given an opportunity to influence the lives of many other teens who might otherwise grow up to believe that voting will not make a difference in their lives.

The talk-back session afterward was a heated debate about what individuals could do to remain educated about injustices and make a difference. One woman asked why the theme was voting, instead of resistance. She argued that when people go outside of official programs, things happen. She asked, "What is the way forward?" A dancer responded, "Organize! Organize! Organize!" Zollar reminded the audience that Urban Bush Women is a 501(c)(3) organization, that is, they are a nonprofit, nonpartisan group and didn't advocate for a particular party during the upcoming election. But she wanted to point out (with a not-so-subtle wink) that she chose the name of her company long before George *Bush* became president. This is an important challenge for and constraint on artistic activist work. Because Urban Bush Women can take government money (though grants are scarce these days) and gets a tax break, Zollar couldn't let the discussion seem like she was provoking anti-Bush rhetoric.

A dancer pointed out that many people organize with false information and that the government should take steps to ensure that the right information is available. Another dancer claimed that we have to educate ourselves; we can't resist unless we know what we are resisting. Another dancer stated that if the people who currently didn't vote voted, the government might be very different. An audience member said this performance was a tangible step, that sometimes the task of organizing seems overwhelming, but this was a first step and we must all remember to take things one step at a time. Another audience member said that we have to be like Fannie Lou Hamer and fight tooth and nail. She claimed that the performance inspired her to fight. A dancer concurred and stated that because she was an ordinary person who was tired, Hamer can be an inspiration to us all and can lead us into action. This is perhaps part of the reason performance is particularly suited to activist work. Zollar asked if there were parts that moved the audience more than others. Someone responded that the marching made her want to move and the juxtaposition of the physicality and music was an effective way of combating the current culture of fear. Another said it was as if they were all dancing with them: "We're going to fight for democracy, our country, and our rights!" Zollar told the audience about the League of Pissed-off Dancers, in which people could get involved in a more partisan way. An audience member stated, "We have to take action into our own hands." Someone thought that a particular action of reaching out a hand read as if the dancers needed help and didn't like that. Others responded that it wasn't a "help me" move but rather "join me," because we all need to be in this together. Zollar explained that it was okay if people respond to the images in different ways. Someone was moved by the energy and strength; she thought it was about a whole group of people gathering energy, about anger and everyone moving as one: "It was about synchronizing our soul energy." Another thought the piece was quintessentially American, in that it was about power and oppression and rights and responsibilities. Some moments were performed in unison, and others were break-out moments. She saw the solos as moments in which we are looking for leadership: "We have to be the leaders we are looking for." Zollar talked about the concept of collective individualism, in which one can be an individual as well as part of a group. It is from the strength of the group's support that the individual can thrive. Then the talk-back session ended with another long standing ovation.

The talk-back session is crucial to the activist work. In fact, in some respects the performance is the lead-up to the work of the post-show discussion. The movement and texts of the performance are intended to inspire dialogue among the community of artists and audiences, which in turn begets action on everyone's part when they return to their home communities.

There are many examples of American leadership against which *Are We Democracy?* can be read. The 1930s was a particularly charged decade for dancers who wanted to use their art to effect change in the United States. Many modern dancers in New York City danced to fight for workers' rights. They danced about work and saw dance as work, and dance was the weapon with which they fought oppression. They were involved in Communist Party politics and protested the Spanish Civil War. They also worked their politics into their methods for developing choreography, trying to find more collaborative ways of creating works.[13] Another example important to understanding *Are We Democracy?* is the leadership training that prepared 1960s civil rights workers for the possible fallout from their actions. They *learned* civil disobedience. People didn't start protesting inequalities by happenstance; there was a concerted effort, and people taught each other effective ways of resisting and fighting for their ideals. Rosa Parks was *chosen* by the local NAACP to refuse to give up her seat on the bus that day. Different levels of resistance were supported, from grassroots to institutional.

Zollar doesn't let the activist work stop as the last audience member leaves. She continually analyzes and contextualizes the processes, and she continually challenges the participants to keep dialogues active. In the debriefing session she held with the participants the day after the performance, she told the dancers that they would come up against criticism meant to diminish rather than strengthen them. She encouraged them to seek community support and get a spiritual grounding. She also encouraged them to think about their communities of class, color, and ethnicity. She challenged them to ask themselves how they could work with these communities to change the world. She claimed that sometimes we go outside of our own communities because it is easier than confronting oppressive forces within them. The participants were then told to write themselves letters in which they described the kinds of things they wanted to be doing in six months and the things that they wanted to hold themselves accountable to in that time period. Zollar collected the letters and promised to mail them to the participants in six months to see if they were indeed following up on the spirit of the institute. This all speaks to her commitment to nurturing the next generation of artist-activists and not allowing the work to stop with the performance event. Community activism is ongoing work. Though she and the company can't be everywhere all the time, she tries to maintain ties and trusts that the sparks that she has helped create will light fires across the country.

Community Engagement Projects

> People are being validated.
>
> Jawole Willa Jo Zollar,
> interview with the author, Dec. 20, 2003

One of the company's most extensive forms of community work is its Community Engagement Projects, workshops that seek to engage communities through popular-culture-based activities and foster communication in oppressed neighborhoods. Though very similar to the Summer Institute, Community Engagement Projects are focused more on a neighborhood than the training of individual leaders, while the Summer Institutes prepare dancers to go back to their hometowns and foster opportunities for community engagement. In this section, I will discuss the Community Engagement model and the performance *Dixwell* that resulted from these efforts. The development of this new model for intensive community engagement has enabled Urban Bush Women to collaborate more deeply with a community on the possibilities for using culture to improve society. Urban Bush Women's model involves the company in long-term residencies designed to enrich and further an empowerment process already under way in the sponsoring community. By sharing an artistic vision informed by a broad experience, Urban Bush Women assists community members in understanding their culture in relation to a larger societal context. This process allows the community to more fully appreciate and expand upon its living cultural heritage. By no means does the company presume to go into a community and solve all of its problems through dance. According to Zollar: "We go into a community, but the creation of the stories is really a [collaboration]. We're not coming in telling the community, 'This is your story,' or 'This is how we're gonna do it.' It's really creating together and that requires a whole different kind of process of entering community and listening and working."[14]

To further elaborate the particular kind of work I see Urban Bush Women doing, I want to pause here to identify several models of performance for community service. In the first model, we have outreach, which is perhaps most typified by the League of Regional Theater's educational programs, including placing teaching artists in schools, bringing schoolchildren to the theater for performances, and providing supplemental material for teachers. In addition, the theater might dedicate a slot in the season to a play by a minority playwright. A second model can be found in the work of theater practitioners like Augusto Boal and Paolo Freire, who use theater in communities to fight oppression and provide therapy.[15] In these models, performance becomes rehearsal for revolution. In a third model, some companies work with communities without the pretext of education or revolution but rather see performance as a social experiment. A good example of this is Cornerstone Theater in Los Angeles, which was initially interested in seeing if the classics would appeal to people in small, rural towns and in other communities unused to theater.[16] Often these performances have a very powerful effect on the participants, and many members of the communities with which these companies work describe life-altering experiences, but this kind of therapy was not the original goal, and no specific reform agendas are pre-articulated.

I would like to place Urban Bush Women's Community Engagement Projects in a fourth category. Their work takes Freire's and Boal's in new directions. Like Freire and Boal, they attempt to be reciprocal—both sides (company and community) giving and taking, starting conversations, voicing opinions, and working together for progress. There is, hopefully, mutual benefit, though no one claims to have a panacea. Both sides seek empowerment, each feeds off of the other's energy, and both are committed to maintaining dialogue. In this work, the emphasis is taken off the oppressor and is placed instead on reinforcing the existing strengths of the community. Recognizing that the work needed often takes years or decades, the organization does not make any attempt to draw conclusions or solutions but instead tries to move the conversation to the next level.

The company's first residency of this kind took place in New Orleans during five weeks in January and February 1992. Planned by Zollar and educational consultant Lloyd Daniel in conjunction with the company members and community leaders in New Orleans, the project was implemented in community centers and in collaboration with organizations that were identified over an eight-month period through a series of four planning trips. During this project, each Urban Bush Women teacher shared responsibility for the five-week class with someone from the community, in an attempt to establish a learning environment. In preparation for the Community Engagement Project, the company also worked with Daniel on in-service teacher education to provide a philosophical framework for the model, as well as to further develop each member's teaching skills.

The curriculum for Urban Bush Women's Community Engagement Project, as developed by Daniel, is based on a model developed by Freire. A people's legacy and culture are considered the foundation for the development of a sense of history—and hence self-esteem—as well as for improving reading and writing skills. Participants are encouraged to assess their own knowledge, recognize it as valuable, and work to expand it, fostering an experience of education as a process that occurs in a variety of environments, not just the classroom.

In my interviews with her, Zollar discussed the impetus of Community Engagement Projects. She said that she chose the name "Community Engagement Projects" because there was something about the term "outreach" that did not sit right with her, an important point because it is indicative of a larger paradigm shift within this kind of work. I suggested, and she agreed, that "outreach" implies directionality. In other words, the organization is the base and goes *out* into a community, often to educate or bring culture to the underprivileged. Unfortunately, assumptions are often made about the level of artistic sophistication of community members, and the goal of *education* usurps other considerations like aesthetics, activism, or deep engagement. In addition, community members can perceive outreach work as condescending and alienating. While noble in intent and often very important in people's lives, they are often missing the reverse directionality—the community coming to the organization and the organization learning from the community. Community Engagement Projects are intended to be more reciprocal than other models and resist the power dynamics implicit in outreach program models. In an article she wrote for *Dance/USA Journal,* Zollar expressed her frustrations with noncommittal residency activities. She said they "are too often allowed to become almost formulaic rather than reaching the audiences of color we are seeking. It is crucial that the sites where these activities occur are visited repeatedly by incoming artists so that a sense of continuity and familiarity is developed."[17] Part of the reason that one can't discuss the Urban Bush Women formula for activism is that the company resists such ideologies. Rather, it develops many different techniques and trusts in the principles of investing in individuals and creating sensitive, nurturing, and inspiring artistic leaders. Over the years, the company has explored different ways to bring about the kind of community work Zollar would like dance to create. Resisting the potentially alienating power dynamics of outreach programs, Urban Bush Women's Community Engagement Projects are intended to be more reciprocal than other models. Zollar claims: "It is not us as artists coming in and bringing our expertise to this community that doesn't have any culture. It's really being engaged with a group of people. They're learning. We're learning. To the mutual benefit of both of us."[18] Zollar points to the power of a community's culture: often more is going on than meets the eye, and these projects are intended to help bring these deeper issues to the surface.

The Community Engagement Projects process is evolving as the group learns from each experience. The company is building up the background needed, and its goals are clearer each time. Though the issues are different with each project, company members are getting more adept at identifying and working with them. Zollar wants her work and the company to move more in this direction. Urban Bush Women has been solidifying its methodology and discovering more and more effective approaches. Zollar wants the members of the company to become community specialists and wants to use art as a catalyst for social change. She would also like children to feel empowered through the arts. Hair parties, for example have afforded the company an important connection to different societies. Manley was a mentor for the Children's Aid society and a leader in her church's dance ministry; in this spirit, Zollar would love to initiate a grassroots organizing wing of Urban Bush Women.

Part of what Zollar receives in this exchange is the maintenance of her own artistic and personal connections to these communities. At one point in her widely acclaimed career, Zollar realized that in the concert dance world the people coming to see her shows were not necessarily the ones who inspired the work. Now, with Community Engagement Projects, the company can more directly connect with these groups. In any city on the company's dance tour, there may be a sizable black community, but often there is no relationship between a city's major theater and its African American community. Urban Bush Women's concert dance audiences are about 80 percent white—which, Zollar wants to emphasize, is great. She doesn't want to alienate that audience base, because the company is happy for the support. However, the community work allows Urban Bush Women to be in touch with African Diaspora communities, to draw on that power and to give its energy back to these communities (to which most of the company members belong). During my observations of the *Dixwell* workshops, rehearsals, and performances, I could sense the power of community that Urban Bush Women wishes to tap. Even with a very diverse audience, this sense was tangible and based in a knowledge people had that they were a part of the creation of the piece. The feeling in the air was "This is about us! We recognize this as coming out of our efforts." The atmosphere was thick with solidarity and neighborhood pride. It was a communal remembering and commitment to celebrating a strong history and an even stronger future. As intern André St. Clair Thompson stated, "They invest a lot of time and energy in helping other communities find their strengths and create [everything] from that strength that they can."[19] The *Dixwell* project provides an important case study in community and African American identity. For example, one piece illustrated the move to the North and the hope that it brought. Another was about living in the neighborhood and the strong extended family relationships. One section that got a lot of attention was about the Monterrey, a former popular nightclub in the neighborhood. In all, the performance highlighted the positive aspects of this community as well as the areas for improvement.

The Dixwell Community Engagement Project

From June 14 to June 30, 2001, the sixth International Festival of Arts and Ideas took place in New Haven, Connecticut. Local officials hoped the annual event would help secure New Haven's place on the cultural map, aid in the cohesion and revitalization of the once thriving community, and provide summer entertainment and enrichment for locals and visitors alike. Festival organizers prided themselves on having one of only a few venues for regular international work, along with the Brooklyn Academy of Music, Lincoln Center, and Miami's International Hispanic Theater Festival. For seventeen days each summer, New Haven becomes a cultural Mecca, an aesthete's playground.

A few highlights of the 2001 season included works from many different cultures. That year, the Italian puppet troupe Teatro Minimo presented a piece based on the work of Maurice Sendak. There was also an aerial dance by an

Argentinean company, complete with ropes, harnesses, and bungee cords. The Royal Shakespeare Company and the Young Vic coproduced Carlo Goldoni's *A Servant of Two Masters*. Ireland's Abbey Theatre performed Brian Friel's *Translations*. The Taganka Theatre performed *Marat/Sade* as a Russian musical about what happens when we can't tell aesthetic genres apart. Cole Porter's *Kiss Me Kate* went up at the Shubert. The New England Academy of Theater performed a series of short pieces written by up-and-coming playwrights of the Northeast.

On the music front, the Metropolitan Opera performed Puccini's *Tosca*. Bands included Femi Kuti of Nigeria, the Jamaican reggae band Third World, the Robert Cray Band, and the Camut Band from Spain (which presented a fusion of African drumming, tap dance, and flamenco). Bebel Gilberto of Brazil performed a bossa nova, and Trilok Gurtu of India performed from a new album, *African Fantasy*, which is an exploration of how two cultures can share and exchange musical traditions.

In visual arts, the Yale Center for British Art placed a hundred of its eighteenth-century drawings and watercolors on display and sponsored a series of lectures examining developments in British art, film, and theater. It also held a retrospective of the Earl of Snowden, the twentieth-century innovative photographer, and a conversation with the artist. The Great Kinetic-cut Sculpture Race took place again that year. And local arts showcases included the Architects of the Air exhibit and Heart of the Matter, a series of science and art workshops for families. The New Haven Arts Council hosted Art of the Edge, a smaller curated visual art, dance, and poetry exhibition, and Dancing under the Stars, an evening of music and dance for everyone.

Coupled with an exploration of contemporary art from around the globe is the embrace of the dialogue on aesthetics—the "ideas" part of the International Festival of Arts and Ideas. That year, in a series called Inwords/Outwords, more than twenty poets explored ideas about place, nation, and self. How is place poetic? How can words bridge worlds? Also, artists who have confronted censorship in their home countries came together to discuss the repression of the arts and the influence of politics on lives and art. The New Haven Colony Historical Society housed an exhibition about the role of family and community in New Haven during the twentieth century. And the 1901 Project explored the relationship between New Haven and the world in terms of culture and art.

According to literature on the Dixwell project, in 1999 the International Festival of Arts and Ideas and the Regional Cultural Plan, through the auspices of the Greater New Haven Arts Council, began a cooperative project with the Dixwell neighborhood in New Haven's largely middle- and lower-middle-class

Dixwell building project. Photo by Nadine George-Graves.

African American community.[20] The Regional Cultural Plan was then beginning to establish a Cultural Development Team in Dixwell. One of the team's first tasks was to select a nationally recognized artist who would spend several weeks as a resident in the neighborhood and work collaboratively with community members to create a new work for the 2001 festival, thanks to several grants, which funded the residency and commissioned work. In a six-month review process, the team ultimately selected Urban Bush Women for the project. Over the next year and a half, the company visited the community and began to develop relationships and interact with various groups there to learn about the rich history of the community. In May, ten members of Urban Bush Women took up temporary residence in New Haven, delved more deeply into the community issues, conducted workshops, recorded oral histories, and began working with a group of Dixwell artists and apprentices to develop the piece *Dixwell*, which premiered at the festival that summer.

The Regional Cultural Plan of New Haven was instituted in 1999 to foster the long-term cultural health of the region. One of the major programs of the plan is the establishment of cultural development teams in the inner-city neighborhoods of New Haven. The teams were charged with mapping the cultural assets of their communities, envisioning the future of their neighborhoods' cultural life, and taking concrete steps to realize that vision. As its first community project, the Dixwell Cultural Development Team participated in selecting Urban Bush Women to be artists-in-residence. This was the company's first piece specifically about the history of a particular neighborhood; its pieces have always reflected the community, but there was something powerful about including its (uninterpreted) voices. Zollar was inspired by the works of Anna Deveare Smith to tap into the power of hearing people's own words.

So, the plans of the festival combined with Urban Bush Women's model for community engagement to create *Dixwell.* Kwame Ross (the project's residency coordinator) came to New Haven a few times a month before the six-week residency, meeting with different groups, conducting workshops, and brainstorming ideas, which he brought back to Zollar. Zollar spent the first few weeks of the residency looking at videos, developing ideas about how to tell the story of this neighborhood, and looking at the company's own repertory for pieces that might help tell the story. She used these because there was not enough time to develop all new work, but she only chose work that made sense in context, or could heighten emotional response and make larger connections. For example, they used the "Hand to Fist" section about the Black Panthers from the larger work *Hand Singing Song* because the Panthers have a particularly strong history in New Haven, and she knew it would work well with the prevailing concepts for *Dixwell.*

One of the workshops Urban Bush Women organized in New Haven was a tea party, which became the prime stimulus for the initial vision for the piece. Originally called "pink teas," tea parties were a tradition in Dixwell. In Urban Bush Women's tea party, seniors came up to the microphone and told stories about the community. Zollar thought this was a powerful moment, and she realized how important it is for the youth of Dixwell to know that the community existed at a time when people could leave their doors unlocked. She wanted to assure them that this could again be possible. "They need to understand that this is not a mythological history," Zollar said. She initially devised the idea of the performance as a flashback tea party. This idea later changed, but many ideas that did make it into the final performance came from stories at the tea party. The company also did a community sing, liturgical dance workshops, and praise dance workshops, but it was really the tea party that provided the impetus for the project.

During auditions, Zollar looked for people with talent as dancers whom she felt could work in the Urban Bush Women style. She claimed that the audition was really about connecting with people; however, she was less interested in seeing people who might be less talented artistically but perhaps important to the work of the community. This is symptomatic of a tension between the goal

Monterrey Café scene in *Dixwell.* Photo by Nadine George-Graves.

of engaging the community as participants and audience members and the desire to maintain a very high level of professionalism and expertise in order to put on a good show. In other words, to participate, one needed to be a very talented performer. This also challenges the process versus product goals of the collaborations. What are the implications involved with such expectations? What would suffer if talent expectations were lower? At the same time, she did succeed in finding committed and talented local performers, which speaks to her unwillingness to compromise on artistry simply because she is doing community work.

Zollar claimed that above all she wanted to provide a forum through which the community can "take voice." She believes she was able to do that in a small way and hopes she has helped inspire the community, and the people who want to support it, to continue the work. When it takes on a project like this, Urban Bush Women gets new ideas, and Zollar hopes that the community gets new ideas. The company gets reinvigorated and refreshed, and Zollar hopes that the community does as well. On the most fundamental level, these projects bring members of a community together around a common goal. In many communities, this is a very important first step. For example, two drill teams performed together at the end of the program, though they had been in fierce competition with one another. When they came together for this event, it became clear that they are a force much more powerful united than divided. Zollar also talked to the two teams about incorporating an afterschool literacy program into their practice. In this kind of work, according to Zollar, people just feed off of new energy and new ideas. She wanted to use the drill teams in part because she was in a drill team as a little girl and thinks they provide a powerful way for people to see the community's youth performing in a highly disciplined form.

I asked Zollar how she would define her role in this project, because as I saw it, she was more than just choreographer. The terms I came up with were "community builder," "griot," "narrative historian" (giving us a glimpse of life in Dixwell), and, finally, "social therapist." She responded that she hopes her role is "community builder," because the work is about healing—about not running away from the things that hurt us or have hurt us but telling the story no matter how painful it is. It is a healing process toward moving forward. Alliances are made, and people are allowed to voice their opinions and perhaps start working toward problem solving. For example, it became very important to talk about the tearing down of the Q House (a very strong community center in the neighborhood) and the building of a new Q House; a lot of people had problems with the whole process of creating the new one. During Urban Bush Women's residency, the issue kept resurfacing. The company members didn't profess to have any solutions but it was something that clearly needed to be talked about so that people could understand the problems created through *development*. The specifics seem relatively minor, but as the conversation kept building, it became clear that the issues were vital for some. For example, the new building has a lot of steps, difficult to maneuver for some of the older residents, who feel excluded—thinking that the house was not built with them in mind. This seemingly small issue came up in discussion again and again. Zollar used her forum to push the dialogue forward. This discussion then became the basis for a moving section of the performance in which performers (including company members and adult and child residents) danced as an ensemble. At one point, interviews with residents about the Q House were projected onto the back wall while each member of the group simply, yet powerfully, stretched a hand out, symbolically reaching for reconciliation. Some of the people on the screen were in the audience. They were not just out to see a show; they came to be witnesses, to learn, to be validated, and to be given the spark to keep the dialogue alive. It is not difficult to imagine a resident coming away from the show feeling better about the Dixwell neighborhood and having a renewed commitment to improving the neighborhood. Though Urban Bush Women opened a forum for working out the issue, it is up to the community to take the next step.

Another important example from the performance is the opening up of the conversation about the Black Panthers in New Haven. This was tangentially a part of a larger discussion going on in the "Ideas" part of the International Festival of Arts and Ideas. But locally, people responded very differently from the ways they did to the Q House issues. People would not talk about the Panthers. Zollar thinks this is because it is still a very painful memory and people are angry and confused. There are so many negative portrayals of the Panthers that we lose sight of the good work that they did and why that good work became a threat. Zollar wanted to convey the important message that, like the Amistad Rebellion, the Panthers illustrate a strong history of resistance by black people in New Haven. Zollar wants to keep the spirit of the Panthers alive. They are part of a history of black people taking charge of their lives and destinies: the Amistad Rebellion, the Underground Railroad, the Black Power movement, civil rights. And the message of this part of the performance is that black people can take charge again.

Zollar has subtitled this work "When Lions Tell History." "When the lions tell history, it is a very different story from when the hunter tells history," she says. The image of the lion is a strong one. The lion is not weak prey, yet the hunter (oppressive regimes) is domineering. When history is told from the lion's perspective, a more accurate picture is created. "The power of dance is often underestimated," says Zollar. She would like to show that when people come together through movement they are touched in places that words can't reach. But of this work we must ask: What happens when the emphasis is taken off the oppressor and reclaiming power from the oppressor and placed instead on reinforcing the existing strengths of the community? What happens when the organization does not make any attempt to draw conclusions or solutions? Is jump-starting the conversation enough?

I asked Zollar what it was like stepping into a community she knew nothing about in order to create a piece about the community. Since she travels so much, she said, she always feels like she's stepping into communities. From the community's point of view, the outsider's perspective can be very important, she thought, especially to identify valuable stories, information, and specific details that people might not have realized were valuable. I don't think Zollar is insinuating that she can make herself a member of any community, but she has pointed out the similar histories among middle- and lower-middle-class African American communities. Because the stories are so similar, she cannot dismiss them as coincidence. Getting the little stories out as part of larger national trends is an important initial step toward social justice and healing. And art is a particularly good means of getting at these stories. For example, hearing stories about houses in minority neighborhoods getting torn down for highways helps us understand institutional racism and the government's lack of concern about dividing these communities.

Zollar claimed that she took away a lot to fuel her choreography from the experience. Particularly, Zollar found in the Dixwell community the same sense she gets from a lot of African American communities—a strong past and the mixed blessing and sometime curse of urban development. Zollar sees the possibilities for communities like Dixwell to be powerful again. And she sees artists as keys to the equation. Through this work, Zollar is starting to come to her own conclusions about what is happening in African American communities. She sees the benefit of creating empowerment zones. However, empowerment often leads to the cycle of gentrification; Starbucks moves in, and the older residents and artists get pushed out. Then, low-income housing, which is promoted as the solution to urban blight, is built on the outskirts of this community; slums and poverty and the lower classes are moved out. Zollar hopes this cycle will be broken in New Haven. Awareness through continuing the conversation is vital to preventing disempowerment.

We must investigate the history of cities like New Haven and redevelopment efforts that took place in the mid-twentieth century and had devastating and lasting effects on these communities. My research into some of the early redevelopment efforts in Dixwell produced several newsletters written in the 1940s, edited by M. Yolles. On October 5, 1948, the Dixwell Inter-Racial Group put out the first edition of the newsletter in which they detail their efforts to combat racism and discrimination, promote cooperative efforts between the races, and improve the overall conditions of the "Negro." The group opened the year with an informal talk by Professor Kennedy of the Yale sociology department. He contrasted the progress in the political, legal and civic arenas with the work still to be done in the social arena, which, he thought, could improve conditions only when the attitude of the average changes. He pointed out that the housing situation was "perhaps the most pressing problem facing the Negro today with public housing the only answer in sight."[21] Now, over sixty years later, the same problems concern the mostly African American Dixwell population. Public housing in the form of towering high-rises is no longer considered the answer. Now, the experiment is with smaller structures that look more like houses and with stronger community building. But the question remains: Will the community be redeveloped out of the neighborhood?

Of the past, we must ask ourselves: How much was redevelopment and how much was displacement or "urban removal"? How did this affect the neighborhoods, and how are the arts responding? We are at another moment in time when these issues and efforts are resurfacing. When Zollar began the Dixwell project, she did not know much about the new redevelopment efforts in the community, though when I told her about them she expressed the hope that it does not end up being the same old story. Space does not permit me to detail these efforts but suffice it to say that they are wrapped in a mass of politics and controversy. It would have been interesting if the performance touched on these current issues. Ironically, the company hired to build community did not even get to know greater New Haven, as Zollar put it, "not even to go shopping." They lived in month-long rentals in Hamden, Connecticut (the next town over), and their rehearsal schedule was very tight. So they did not learn much about how Dixwell fit into the rest of New Haven or about white flight and the community's bitter history with Yale University. Rather, the work focused on intra-community efforts.

I asked Zollar what she wanted the audience to take away from this type of work. She claimed that she wants the audience to be committed to how this community rebuilds itself—spiritually, economically, and emotionally. "It might even be about saying a prayer every day because prayer is very powerful," she said. And from the experience she has taken away a desire to do more of this kind of work. She loves storytelling and dance, and even though she has gotten criticism she embraces these methods. This community work and the stories that arise from it inform her concert work. But the concert work is not as interesting to her anymore; she wants to have the younger voices do that so she can concentrate on the community projects. Her other goal in doing residencies is to provide opportunities for younger choreographers to work: for this project, she mentored three company members and Dixwell residents as choreographers.

Zollar says she can't determine the next step for the *Dixwell* performance, nor can she say what will happen in the community, but she hopes the festival will continue its commitment to the neighborhood. Throughout all of Urban Bush Women's community work, Zollar has emphasized that the company's work cannot be the whole story and only through longstanding commitment can progress be made.

CODA

By Blood, through Dance

Dance is my medicine.
Pearl Primus,
Dance Magazine interview, 1968

As a coda to this work I want to talk about Urban Bush Women's twentieth-anniversary season and the piece created for it, *Walking with Pearl.* Pearl Primus was a mid-twentieth-century dancer, choreographer, and anthropologist. She traveled to Africa and the U.S. South to research African Diasporan culture. She was a champion of dance not only for entertainment's sake but also to help people better understand their lives and struggles. In addition to performing, she formed a school with Percival Borde in the early 1950s and developed a technique to educate dancers about African dance. Primus's choreography might have been lost had she not built some of her dances on Philadanco, the Philadelphia-based African American dance company, before her death in 1994. Primus's body, like those of most Urban Bush Women dancers, was very muscular and powerful. She became more of a symbol of strength than her contemporary Katherine Dunham. As I stated in chapter 2, Zollar can be seen as an heir to Primus's legacy, and in this twentieth-anniversary project, she looks back and builds on Primus's work.

The *Walking with Pearl* project makes for a fitting end to this study because it is a piece that deals with many of the ideas I discuss herein. The piece was developed in part from an intensive community workshop in which participants learned Primus's choreography as well as Zollar's technique. Moving stories from African Diaspora culture were the impetus for the creation of many of Primus's pieces, and she (as well as those who teach her dances) uses backstory and narrative as motivational cues to help dancers execute the choreography.

Like those of Urban Bush Women, the subject of most of her pieces was the suffering, resistance, and plight of black people. Finally, the dancer of a Primus piece must also go to a deep spiritual place—soul deep.

In summer 2003 Urban Bush Women organized "Dare to Go There," a week-long series of community workshops in Fort Greene, Brooklyn. In addition to some smaller community workshops, they also held a "Walking with Pearl" intensive, in which about thirty-five individuals (including company members) participated in a week of classes and activities honoring Primus. The class was comprised of one white man, three black men, and three white women, and the rest were women of color. The participants learned original choreography by Primus for *Strange Fruit* and *Hard Time Blues*. Scholars taught about Primus's life so that participants could work knowledge of the historical figure into their dancing. The motivational emphasis was on breath and fists. Kim Bears-Bailey, a dancer with Philadanco, taught Primus's technique, which she learned directly from Primus. Learning the steps of this choreography was only the beginning, though. The dancers practiced silent screams to access an emotional place important to the choreography. For example, in *Hard Time Blues* there was always a "power movement" before a run. "Something" compelled the dancers to move. They ran and, with a leap, threw their fists up in the air. They reached their arms behind them holding one fisted hand in the other hand. As the dancers executed the steps, Bears-Bailey called out their motivation. She would say that "someone" was calling them and "something" took them. The unspecified "something" and "someone" referred sometimes to the inner voices that drive one to move, seek freedom, and resist suffering and sometimes to an imaginary character, like a slave master. She would say, "Come back to where you came from! The fight isn't over yet! You still can't get away! You're in bondage! You're restricted but you still have fight in you! Even though they have you in bondage!" She had the dancers imagine that they were being captured by a master. They had to feel the pain and find a way to fight back. They had to search for the strength to continue. Then they went back to the work of the day. They were to feel the floor and imagine someone having power over them, controlling when and how they moved. They were asked to emotionally go to a place where they did not get so twisted inside that they couldn't survive. They had to imagine trying to stay with their loved ones as the oppressors tried to separate them. They had to feel the weight of something heavy on their backs. "It never gets easier, because fighting oppression never gets easier," she told them. They put their wrists forward in submission, then got slapped to the floor. They got doors shut in their faces. They used a sense of groundedness in order to rebound. Something always brought the dancers back to the harsh reality. These were the quieter moments of the piece, the

Carolina Garcia, Michelle Dorant, Allyson Triplett, and Joy Voeth in *Transitions*. Photo by Cylla Von Tiedemann.

moments in which resistance could be built up in order to be released in more explosive moments. At one of these moments, they would jump up with their hands in fists and one knee up high, jump again with the other knee up, roll onto their backs, and then quickly jump up again another two times. Bears-Bailey said, "By the time you get to this part of the dance, you want to get your everything up—your butt, your legs—everything! The power is going to the Gods." They had to imagine pulling back on the reigns that were used to control them. They had to have a clear idea of what they were pulling against. There was power when they hit the floor. In the final moments, Bears-Bailey told the dancers that it was their last chance to get "it" (their frustration) out. They bent forward, shook their heads, and violently crossed their arms back and forth as if crying out, "No!" The rehearsal emphasized an extreme emotional and physical experience. There was no release, no resolution, no exhale, no relief. Even the quieter moments were fraught with tension in order to build up energy needed to fight. There was an almost unbelievable amount of energy needed to do the dance—emotional and physical. It was excruciating for the dancers, and even though each group collapsed after finishing a practice of the whole piece, many told me that they felt themselves in a powerful place. Letting go of the tension was difficult. This tension was Primus's tool to protest oppression through dance; one could see the faces and bodies of slaves struggling and fighting. Bears-Bailey also stated that marking or walking through a sequence was not in Primus's vocabulary. She always danced full out. "It's like a conversation that never ends. There is no place where I want to stop. You can't mark it emotionally. You have to go there," Bears-Bailey said.

In the rehearsal for *Strange Fruit*, Bears-Bailey began by reciting the words to a poem written by Primus to help set the psychological space the dancers needed to inhabit. Interestingly, the image was not of black bodies swinging but of white women in a lynch mob. This "woman" was a universal subject and was intended to be neither male nor female. She was a concept, a statement. Bears-Bailey admonished the dancers against holding back emotionally; she told them that only when they could imagine what it was like to be the last white person to leave a lynching could they attempt the choreography.

The right hand slithered, serpentlike. The feet were like roots of a tree growing out of the earth. She told them to look, fall, reach, collapse, move like a serpent, reach, collapse, crawl, and roll. When they were on their backs, their feet scurried around. Lifelessness entered their bodies. They swung from trees and collapsed as if being cut down. They jumped up and ran, then rolled on the floor. They reached out and ran in a circle around the whole space two times, their arms out wide and faces in silent screams. They collapsed into lifelessness, physically and emotionally exhausted. They walked around the space, slicing their arms like machetes through crops, thinking, "I've had enough. I'm not going to take it anymore."

At several points during the workshop the participants talked about Urban Bush Women continuing this legacy—of black women in performance, strong and inspirational. Pictures of Primus almost always depict her in the air—moving, fighting. Bears-Bailey told the dancers that Primus danced so high she didn't need to come down. She advised them not to think about the steps, to let it be natural and use the support of other people to keep going through to the end. One gets the sense that anyone who has known extreme suffering can do the choreography. There were no counts: the dancers had to feel the choreography in their bodies against the music. After all the groups had practiced it all the way through, there was a deafening silence and a different energy in the room. One woman was crying. Bears-Bailey broke the silence and asked everyone if they heard the scream, because she had heard it: "Give in to that scream. No! I'm not going to allow them to get to me. Even though they got me in bondage." Indeed, at the end of the piece the dancer's struggle is not yet won but he or she is still standing—this is a fitting image for all of the work of Urban Bush Women. Afterward, to let their bodies recuperate, they took a long cool down that involved many release moves.

This work all fed the choreography of the two sections of *Walking with Pearl* (*Southern Diaries* and *African Diaries*) for Urban Bush Women's twentieth-anniversary season. Each section is based on a different journey Primus took to feed her self-discovery as well as academic and artistic research. In *Southern Diaries*, which premiered at the American Dance Festival, the dancers are dressed in plain brown dresses with beige aprons and beige hats. The piece is accompanied by old-time blues and Southern spirituals. Zollar recites selections from Primus's diaries about her research trip to the U.S. South. The opening words concern Primus making a connection with the slaves of this land: "I could see the chains that fell off the people's feet. . . . All of that went into the dance." Zollar then speaks the words of Langston Hughes concerning the power of Southern black church services. The dancers pantomime testifying before the Lord and other movements found in these services. The language draws a connection between shouting and dancing. Both are a kind of release, an outlet of pent-up emotions, "a savior from the psychiatrist": "Rhythm is healing, music is healing, dancing and shouting are healing." This is a way for oppressed people to feel better. Hughes sees the same thing in the work of Pearl Primus. The dancers move into a stylized ring shout, pounding out a rhythm with their hands, feet, and voices. As the music shifts into blues, their movements alternate between strong kicks and punches and fatigued pedestrian releases. They evoke the weariness of oppression and the strength that many find to get through. The movement shifts, and the dancers walk hunched over in slow motion while their left hands jerkily reach to the ground and scoop up something from the earth. They move their arms into the shape of a basket. A soloist performs Primus's *Hard Time Blues*. And then, shaking off the pent-up anger that Bears-Bailey demanded, she joins the other dancers on the side. Another dancer comes out and also performs part of *Hard Time Blues*. The other dancers then come out, grunting in disgust and shaking their fingers no. They take turns spouting homegrown aphorisms. The tone shifts, and with handkerchiefs flying, the dancers walk around the space, swinging their hips with iconic Southern black female attitude. The next segment takes this movement style and abstracts it. The dancers lean forward and push out their chins and buttocks. From here they sashay, boogie, place their arms akimbo, and testify. The isolations of the hips are not cheap; instead they celebrate these women. Next, a dancer walks around the space, putting on white gloves and a white headkerchief while Zollar recites, "I discovered in the Baptist churches, the voice of the drum, not in any instrument but in the throat of the preacher." As she walks slowly to the upstage corner, other dancers follow behind, forming a procession. The second dancer stops and dances in a lyrical modern style that evokes praise and spirituality, as women's voices sing about going to waters. Other dancers come in in the same style. Some shake with possession, others move reverently and joyfully. Some embrace and lift others. They briefly walk piously around in a circle. The energy picks up with leaps and spins and arms thrown up to the heavens. They run in the circle, kick, and spin. They hold one another in couples and threesomes. As the music fades out, two dancers lean forward, with others holding their feet. A dancer begins chanting the words "feels like" while the others pound out a rhythm with their feet and pick up the chant. The dancer who began the chanting then sings about what this world "feels like." She sings of an old woman rocking on a porch looking to Primus and saying, "Hey, chile. When you go. And we know you gonna be the one what go, chile. Tell 'em what we know. Tell 'em what we know down here, chile!" This is a powerful call to continue the oral traditions of knowledge and historiography: what Primus did, what Zollar is doing.

The lights dim so that only silhouettes of the dancers are visible. The song "Strange Fruit" comes up as the dancers simply look off into the distance. They move solemnly. One woman breaks down into tears as the others surround and comfort her. It is as if her son has been lynched and the women are there to support her. They hold on to her as she moves through her pain. She jerks free and throws her body into convulsions. The others move into a semicircle while she vigorously dances out her pain. Others then take turns in the center. They begin to clap, stomp, and grunt, and more dancers take their turns in the center. Through dance, these women exorcise the pain of tragedy. They tighten the circle and, shoulder to shoulder, let out a deafening scream. They continue the rhythm, move into a triangle facing the audience, and dance out an intricate pattern of claps, spins, and stomps. Zollar's voice comes back in, speaking Primus's words: "I got a deep drink of our African American people. What they did to physically endure. I discovered material in the South for dances. I found certain rhythms, patterns, incantations, songs—all allied African culture. I found a well of culture and hope and belief." The dancing and chanting build up as the lights fade out.

On a warm June Tuesday in 2005, Urban Bush Women capped its twentieth-anniversary season with a week of performances at the Joyce Theater in New York. On opening night, audience members were dressed to the nines. Many former Bush Women were in the house. Film cameras were set up, interviewing Ruby Dee. Members of the diverse audience greeted each other with enthusiastic hugs and kisses. Though the show was not quite sold out, the buzz from Urban Bush Women fans more than made up for the few empty seats.

The actress Lisa Gay Hamilton came on stage and talked about how moved she had been by Urban Bush Women's work, particularly when she was new to the city and struggling in her own nascent career. It was empowering, she said, to see women who looked like her creating such inspiring work, too long undervalued by dance and theater scholars. At many times during this twentieth-anniversary run (I saw the show five times), audience members were moved to stand up, testify, and speak back to the dancers. They laughed and sighed as they recognized truths in the choreography.

For the first part of the show, Zollar reprised "Give Your Hands to Struggle" from *Hand Singing Song*, "Girlfriends" from *Anarchy, Wild Women, and Dinah*, and parts of *Batty Moves*. A new piece by a guest choreographer, Bridget L. Moore, was also presented. As part of its effort to support young female choreographers, Urban Bush Women sponsored a competition called Project Next Generation. The winning piece, Moore's *Sacred Vessel*, fit into the Urban Bush Women aesthetic, as it concerned struggle, spirituality, sassy attitude, and reaching to the past.

Opening the evening with "Give Your Hands to Struggle" was a fitting invocation of a litany of ancestors and elders to continue to inspire the present and future generations. Other highlights include Zollar dancing in a big, fluffy, pink negligee in "Girlfriends" while two other dancers lovingly tease her. One evening, an audience member shouted out "No! You look good!" when Zollar's character began to put on her robe in embarrassment. Though different dancers performed with Zollar for the different performances, they all evoked the tones of playfulness, seriousness, comfort, battle, teasing, conversation, and love that are characteristic of deep friendships.

Perhaps the pinnacle of the run came during the opening night performance of the piece from *Batty Moves*. Zollar introduced the piece by talking directly to the audience about what inspired her to make the dance. As a young dancer, she would go to her ballet classes, where she was "explaining, holding, tucking, and apologizing," and then to her African dance classes, where she was "loosening, freeing, and empowering." She wanted to bring her two worlds together. Later, in her travels, she noticed that all over the world, in people of African descent, one sees the movement of the batty. She then talked about learning about Sarah Bartmann and connecting with her shame. *Batty Moves*, she said, therefore, was about "how and where we see beauty and how we celebrate that beauty. . . . I see beauty in the different body types." On opening night, during a rap in which all of the dancers extolled their own physical virtues (e.g., one dancer rapped, "I'm an African American of the Seminole tribe. They call me coffee 'cause I grind so fine!"), all of the former Urban Bush Women in the house stood up and danced onto the stage. They also rapped about their positive qualities. Lisa Gay Hamilton also came out on stage and rapped about herself. The dancers then chanted out, "Big Mamas coming down. Lord, big mamas! We're everywhere." Finally, the dancers called out to the audience: "Big Mamas in the house, stand up!" It didn't take much coaxing for the women (and some men) to stand up, clap, scream, and shake their rear ends. *That* probably doesn't happen too often at the Joyce. That spirit of celebration and empowerment is valuable and not to be taken lightly. When the audience finally sat back down, the current Urban Bush Women dancers continued the piece. During one particularly powerful solo, Zollar peeked her head in, winked at the audience, and said, "I taught her everything she knows!" During another moment, an audience member called out, "Dance, girl!"

The last piece of the performance was the second part of *Walking with Pearl. African Diaries* opens with sounds of the wind blowing. Seven dancers in earth-toned draping fabrics line the upstage wall in profile while Zollar moves slowly through the space, carving with her hands and undulating her body. She raises her hands up to the sky and dips them back down, as if picking up water. Chimes come in as she walks across the stage and sits down at a microphone. There, she introduces the piece. The lights come up on the dancers as Zollar recites from Primus's diary. The movement is sparse, modern. The dancers' faces are dreamlike. They do not take each other in. Instead, each looks off onto her own personal horizon. No music accompanies the opening section, and as the audience listens to Primus's thoughts about her personal journey to discover herself through the dance traditions of her people, the dancers onstage move through a series of gestures that show their journey. The attitude is serious. Zollar says, "Mother, speak to me. Tell me you love me." As Jack Anderson, reviewer for the *New York Times*, stated, "The dreamlike manner of the dancers suggested that they were on a journey of exploration that was spiritual as well as geographical."[1]

African music comes in as the dancers begin to interact with each other with embraces and touches. The words speak of leaving mother Africa with newly found strength and precious memories. Two dancers come together, give and take each other's weight. As the music cuts out, the dancers crouch down, embracing themselves. Using breath, they bring themselves to standing as Zollar speaks Primus's words: "Dance is my medicine. It is the scream which eases, for a while, the terrible frustrations common to all human beings who because of race, creed or color are invisible. Dance is the fist with which I fight the sickening ignorance of prejudice. . . . Instead of growing twisted like a gnarled tree inside myself, I am able to dance out my anger and my tears." The chimes come back in, and the dancers change from being dejected to summoning strength. There are leaps and held tableaux of strength, like holding a leg in midair and staring defiantly at the audience. Several of the dancers pulse up and down with their hands in fists, shifting their weights from side to side. One raises her fist up to the air, throws her head back majestically, and opens her mouth in a wide, proud smile.

The dancers freeze as Zollar continues: "If a mask came alive for me, I shall tell of it." She speaks of knowing herself to be an artist and not a journalist or scientist. The dancers stand in a semicircle, and several perform for one who appears more timid than the others. Eventually, she summons strength to dance. The lights dim as the sounds of night come in. The dancers move slowly in the dark, and when the music comes back in, the movement is lighter and faster-paced, as Zollar speaks of African sunsets. One dancer starts to shake as Zollar talks about the "blood in ocean." It is a nightmare in which the dancers move in torment. The blood is from her ancestors who call to her: "The sky bleeds into the ocean!" The dancers reach out in torment and finally fall to the ground. A dancer begins to sing, "I must take myself to the ocean." She evokes a baptism by blood, through dance, so that she may connect with her ancestors in order to find herself. The dancers sing of going to the sacred mountain of Ife, "soaked in the tears of my people." Zollar says "Africa, I know I that can never scrape the red clay from my feet or tear the leopard of sorrow from my back or dry the tears which fall upon my face" as a dancer puts her hands in the "ocean" and cleanses herself in the blood of her ancestors. Primus has been forever changed by her journey: "My body still dances with the unquenchable fire that is Africa!"

On creating this piece about Primus, Zollar has said,

> This is not about me telling her life, it's about me connecting my artistic heart to her artistic heart, through her writing. . . . What I really appreciate about Pearl Primus is that she became a dancer against all odds. . . . She was this thick, dark-skinned black woman who had started training in dance late. She had been an athlete, so she had this incredibly powerful jump. She had a vision of dance that was bigger than the concert stage and that was about a kind of personalization of experience and letting it come out in a very rough-hewn manner, which I absolutely identify with.[2]

As a last word, I want to return to the "work" of Urban Bush Women. I asked the dancers I interviewed if they thought the work was about healing.

Christal Brown told me: "Yeah, the whole thing is about healing. I think it's about healing. It's about understanding. It's about learning. It's about teaching. It's about accepting. It's about sharing. We were given these talents not to keep to ourselves. I believe artists are the closest people to God. If we didn't suffer, there would be no art. If he didn't suffer, there would be no us."[3]

Maria Bauman said: "I think in the end it is largely healing because the overall message is that we're all okay, and the idea is that hopefully we want to leave the wounds behind and just be able to enjoy our physical manifestation for what it is. I really think that that's Jawole's intent. I have a feeling that it's purposeful but I also think it's just sort of the person that she is and where she's coming from, that that comes through in her work. I definitely think it's healing for the audience, then also, in various ways, for the performers."[4]

Christine King recounts an audience member's response to *Praise House*: "After that piece, a woman came up and said she was just so thankful that it was there because something on the stage really addressed something that's inside of [her]. She had such a connection to it."[5]

As Christal Brown describes it:

> We have this thing where we go out and talk to the audience sometimes, like even if we don't have a post-performance discussion, we go out and talk to them in the lobby and a lot of them are just deeply touched. It's just that movement. It moves. I feel like any time you see something different or you're moved spiritually by something different, a new neuropath is opened up in your heart. There's a point of compassion that you get to where you're so open, you can see everything for what it is. You can feel everything for what it is, and for a brief moment . . . you feel compassion. For that brief moment we've touched you somewhere where only the most intimate people you know touch you. And when people feel that, they don't even know what to say about it. It took me a long time to understand that people are really that moved.

Vanessa Manley told me a story of a woman who saw *Hair Stories*. During the post-show discussion she talked about the fact that she was going through chemotherapy and was wearing a wig since her hair had fallen out. She stated that she didn't know why she was doing that and took the wig off. Her daughter, seated next to her, gave her a hug and told her that she was proud of her. I reminded Zollar of this moment, and she agreed that it was very powerful. I asked her if she thought about the healing possibilities for others in her work. She commented:

> Sometimes I think about it because I think at my core it's about healing. Yeah, it's about the different journeys, about the aesthetic and it's about how you put the piece together and the colors that you use and all of those things but I don't know that I could make a work that is not about healing. What would that be about? Being? Well, you know, it's interesting, a European director said to me, he says, you know, your work is old-fashioned because you have this obsession with hope, . . . and I said, you know, the values in my community that I've also internalized are that. So no, it's not about nihilism for me or this train-spotting angst. No, that's not my culture. So it can be corny to you. That's fine.

Joy Voeth, Michelle Dorant, and Francine Sheffield in *Transitions*. Photo by Cylla Von Tiedemann.

I then asked her if she thought about her audience. She replied:

> No, I think it's more about myself, to be really honest. I mean I want my works to be provocative, but I can't really determine what's gonna be a healing moment for someone. I can only determine what's a healing moment for me. Or sometimes a dancer will talk about what a healing moment is for them in a piece. The audience is too big and too vast and too unpredictable and too multilayered to figure that out. I want the audience to walk in one way and to leave in some kind of transformation.

When I asked her what she wanted for the next twenty years of the company, she responded: "I want to be able to do works on an operatic scale—that large-scale theatrical work where it's gonna take me two to five years to develop. I also want to have a place for younger choreographers to really be able to work. We don't have places where the dancers just sit out in the hallway and talk art and politics. We've lost some of those centers. I'd love to be able to have a center like that."[6]

Jennifer Dunning, of the *New York Times*, said of the twentieth-anniversary season: "What connects all of Ms. Zollar's pieces most strongly is the fierce intensity she and her dancers have always poured into the work, performing as if it were not just their own lives but also the lives of those they portrayed that depended on them."[7]

They do.

According to the narrator in *Soul Deep*, the dancers of Urban Bush Women and the audience members they dance for are people "requesting urban survival tactics in important dance steps."

Notes

Introduction

1. Brenda Dixon Gottschild, *Digging the Africanist Presence in American Performance* (Westport, CT: Praeger, 1996), 57.
2. Nancy Goldner, "Urban Bush Women at the Painted Bride," *Philadelphia Inquirer*, May 2, 1987, D5.

Chapter 1. Development

1. Jawole Willa Jo Zollar, "Jawole Willa Jo Zollar: A Self-Study," in *Black Choreographers Moving*, ed. Julinda Lewis-Ferguson (Berkeley, CA: Expansion Arts Services, 1991), 31.
2. Ibid., 32.
3. For a fuller discussion of Zollar's use of African dance, particularly Wolof-based Senegalese movement, see Angela D. Gittens, "Hands, Eyes, Butts, and Thighs: Women's Labor, Sexuality, and Movement Technique from Senegal through the Diaspora" (PhD diss., New York University, 2008). See also Ama Oforiwaa Konadu Aduonum, "Urban Bush Women: Building Community and Empowering the Disempowered through a Holistic Performing Arts Medium" (PhD diss., Florida State University, 1999).
4. Jennifer Dunning, "Rough, and Proud of It," *New York Times*, June 19, 2005, C8.
5. For an examination of the parallels between Zollar's choreography and black women's written autobiographical work, see Veta Goler, "Life Dances: Jawole Willa Jo Zollar's Choreographic Construction of Black Womanhood," *Choreography and Dance* 5, no. 1 (1998): 25–37; Alison Lee Bory, "Dancing with My Self: Performing Autobiography in (Post)Modern Dance" (PhD diss., University of California, Riverside, 2008); and Veta Goler, "Dancing Herself: Choreography, Autobiography, and the Expression of the Black Woman Self in the Work of Dianne McIntyre, Blondell Cummings, and Jawole Willa Jo Zollar" (PhD diss., Emory University, 1994).
6. Zollar, "Jawole Willa Jo Zollar: A Self-Study," 33.
7. On several occasions when I have told people unfamiliar with dance that I am researching Urban Bush Women, the response has been, "I didn't know there were urban bush women. You mean natives living in cities?" Because the name of the company is

open to interpretation, Urban Bush Women dancers are able to stage resistance before they even step foot onstage.

8. Madhavi Sunder, "Urban Bush Women: Dancing Their Politics," *Ms.*, March 1994, 85.

9. Zollar, "Jawole Willa Jo Zollar: A Self-Study," 34.

10. Ibid., 91.

11. Jennifer Dunning, "Dance: Urban Bush Women Troupe," *New York Times*, July 2, 1984, C11.

12. Jawole Willa Jo Zollar, interview with the author, December 20, 2003, Brooklyn, NY.

13. Kwame Ross and Michael Wimberly, in particular, have held important positions as musical directors and performers.

14. Zollar, interview with the author.

15. Zollar says that when men have toured with the company they have tended to take the attention away from the female dancers.

16. Alice Walker, *In Search of Our Mothers' Gardens* (New York: Harcourt, Brace, 1983), xi–xii.

17. Zollar, interview with the author.

18. Ibid.

19. Jawole Willa Jo Zollar, interview by Jennifer Donaghy, tape recording, April 1989, Hatch-Billops Collection, New York, transcript page 6.

20. Joseph Roach, *Cities of the Dead: Circum-Atlantic Performance* (New York: Columbia University Press, 1996), 5.

21. Zollar, interview with the author.

22. Zollar credits an early teacher, Winifred Widener, with encouraging her to study dance despite her body type. See Elizabeth Zimmer, "Parallels in Black," *Dance Theatre Journal* 5, no. 1 (Spring 1987): 6.

23. Brenda Dixon Gottschild, *The Black Dancing Body: A Geography from Coon to Cool* (New York: Palgrave, 2003), 177.

24. Zollar, interview with the author.

25. Christal Brown, interview with the author, December 2003, Brooklyn, NY.

26. Maria Bauman, interview with the author, December 2003, Brooklyn, NY.

27. Zollar, interview by Donaghy, 5.

28. Zollar, "Jawole Willa Jo Zollar: A Self-Study," 35.

29. Bauman, interview with the author.

30. Zollar, interview with the author.

31. The poetic text for this piece was composed by Carl Hancock Rux.

32. Bory, "Dancing with My Self," 87.

33. Gottschild, *The Black Dancing Body*, 90.

34. Zollar, interview with the author.

35. Ibid.

36. Christine King, interview with the author, December 2003, Brooklyn, NY.

37. For an interesting discussion of the muscularity of contemporary dancers, see chapter 2 of Ann Cooper Albright, *Choreographing Difference: The Body and Identity in Contemporary Dance* (Hanover, NH: Wesleyan University Press, 1997).

38. For testimonies on the perceived strength of black dancers' bodies, see Gottschild, *The Black Dancing Body*, 51.

39. Zollar, interview with the author.

40. Ibid.

41. Ibid.

42. Ibid.

43. Gail Hanlon, "Homegrown Juju Dolls: An Interview with Artist Riua Akinshegun," in *My Soul Is a Witness: African American Women's Spirituality*, ed. Gloria Wade-Gayles (Boston: Beacon, 1995), 1.

44. For more on the aesthetic of the cool, see Robert Farris Thompson, "An Aesthetic of the Cool: West African Dance," in *Signifyin(g), Sanctifyin', and Slam Dunking: A Reader in African American Expressive Culture*, ed. Gena Dagel Caponi (Amherst: University of Massachusetts Press, 1999), 72–86. See also Gottschild, *Digging the Africanist Presence*.

45. Zollar, interview with the author.

46. Jacki Apple, "Urban Bush Women," *High Performance* 10, no. 3 (1987): 36.

47. Brown, interview with the author.

48. King, interview with the author.

49. Zollar, interview with the author.

50. Brown, interview with the author.

51. Bauman, interview with the author.

52. Zollar, interview with the author.

53. Paul Carter Harrison writes extensively on nommo, mojo, and sayso in *The Drama of Nommo* (New York: Grove, 1973).

54. Beverly Robinson talks about the African Diaspora heritage for many of the tropes I discuss: ritual, storytelling, games, coded performances, and spirituality. See Beverly Robinson, "The Sense of Self in Ritualizing New Performance Spaces for Survival," in *Black Theatre: Ritual Performance in the African Diaspora*, ed. Paul Carter Harrison, Victor Leo Walker II, and Gus Edwards (Philadelphia, PA: Temple University Press, 2002), 332–44.

Chapter 2. The Body

1. Zollar, interview with the author.

2. Raul Rabinow gives an excellent summary of Foucauldian theory in his introduction to *The Foucault Reader* (New York: Pantheon, 1984), 3–29.

3. Though African American men have had similar struggles, it would be a mistake to assume that the effect on the social control of the black male body is the same as on the black female body.

4. Judith Butler, *Bodies That Matter: On the Discursive Limits of Sex* (New York: Routledge, 1993), 12–13 (my emphasis), 15.

5. These principles hold for class as well but it is beyond the scope of this work to delve too deeply into class.

6. Coco Fusco, *The Bodies That Were not Ours: And Other Writings* (New York: Routledge, 2001), xv.

7. Ibid., 5.

8. See chapter 5 for more on community work.

9. For other examples of interesting artistic interrogations of black female hair, see *A Raisin in the Sun*, a play by Lorraine Hansberry; *School Daze*, a film by Spike Lee; *Funnyhouse*

of a Negro, a play by Adrienne Kennedy; and *The Colored Museum*, a play by George C. Wolff.

10. Alternatively spelled "dreadlocks" or "dredlocks," many drop the "a" because of connotations from slave trade when Whites declared that matted hair looked dreadful. Others drop the "dread" altogether and call them locks or locs.

11. Ayana D. Byrd and Lori L. Tharps, *Hair Story: Untangling the Roots of Black Hair in America* (New York: St. Martin's Griffin, 2001), 2.

12. Of course, black women are not the only subsection of the U.S. population to have meaningful hair care issues. One thinks of white women and the buxom blonde-haired, blue-eyed beauty ideal and Malcolm X's cringing description of conking his hair for the first time. However, the particulars of black women and their hair give important clues about race and gender relations in the United States.

13. Lissa Brennan, "Urban Bush Women," *Essence* 33, no. 5 (September 2002): 112.

14. In the film *Nappy* (1997), directed by Lydia Ann Douglas, a real professor is interviewed and postulates on the African-centered political and social agenda of people who chose particular hairstyles. One's appearance is a way of making a political statement, she says.

15. Whoopi Goldberg, *Live on Broadway*, VHS (New York: Lions Gate, 1991).

16. I interrupt here and discuss the fact that I've been describing possible audience experiences by implying that the piece brings back memories of personal hair stories and allows black women a space to think about the ways they construct their own identities in terms of their hair. Though I believe this is the audience base for which Zollar developed this piece, in reality the piece is open to analysis by multiple spectatorships. For those not traveling down memory lane, laughing together with their sisters in solidarity, getting indignant, and reevaluating personal decisions, the piece becomes a history lesson and education. There are a few places where Zollar invites other perspectives (a white woman and a black man are interviewed), but the space of the work is largely black-female identified. She does not actively exclude others (the Jacob's Pillow audience is 80 percent white, and she has that constituency to serve as well), nor does she define black women by their relationships to white women, white men, or other people of color. She tries to create an inviting space (mostly through humor) for this public ritual—no simple task.

17. Audiences are asked to suspend their disbelief about race here. Before entering the elevator, the dancer tells the audience that the elevator is filled with white people in moment #1 and black people in moment #2. They are the same dancers. This moment is illustrative of the performative work this meta-theatrical forum can provide as a "rehearsal" for everyday life. The dancers exist on stage as white women, black women, black women commenting on white women, black women commenting on black women, and white women commenting on black women.

18. "Batty" is a Jamaican patois word for buttocks.

19. Gottschild, *The Black Dancing Body*, 177.

20. Quoted in Thomas F. DeFrantz, "The Power of the Drum," *Attitude* 11, no. 3 (Fall 1995): 80.

21. See Tessa Triumph, interview with Jawole Willa Jo Zollar, *New Dance* 41 (Summer 1987): 1–4.

22. *Batty Moves* contributes to the body of artistic work that addresses, explicitly or implicitly, the legacy of Sarah Bartmann and attempts to move the image of the black

female buttock in affirming directions. Many contemporary artists and writers have tried to come to terms with this legacy, particularly the fact that Bartmann was probably never able to exercise agency in the definition of self. For example, see Suzan-Lori Parks's play *Venus*, the art of Kara Walker, the short story "Black Venus" by Angela Carter, and Willie Bester's sculpture *Sarah Bartmann* for the University of Capetown. In *The Couple in the Cage*, a piece by Coco Fusco and Guillermo Gómez Peña, the performers re-create exhibitions like Bartmann's to surprising responses—many of which approximated the power dynamics of the original. Less overt examples can also be found in contemporary culture. For instance, in August Wilson's *Ma Rainey's Black Bottom*, the title character, the great blues singer, is working on a song with the lyrics "Ma Rainey's gonna show you her black bottom." This is reminiscent of Clay in LeRoi Jones's *Dutchman*, in which he claims that "Bessie Smith is saying, 'Kiss my ass, kiss my black unruly ass.' Before love, suffering, desire, anything you can explain, she's saying, and very plainly, 'Kiss my black ass.' And if you don't know that, it's you that's doing the kissing." Pop culture has not escaped this conversation but not always in the affirming way advocated by works like *Batty Moves*. In the fall of 2002 the VH1 *All Access* series aired a special, titled "Booty Call," in which hosts reported on the national obsession with the rear end. In June 2000 *Ebony* claimed that "fashion trends may come and go, but a well-shaped bottom line will never go out of style" and tells us how, in just six to eight weeks, following ten simple exercises, black women can improve their rear view. In 2006 the Oxygen network put out a call for full-figured beauties to enter a new pageant hosted by Mo'Nique titled *Mo'Nique's FAT Chance*. Janell Hobson writes about several black female artists who attempt to create affirming aesthetics surrounding the black female body, particularly the buttocks. See Hobson, "The 'Batty' Politic: Toward an Aesthetic of the Black Female Body," *Hypatia* 18, no. 4 (Fall 2003): 87–105.

23. Gottschild, *The Black Dancing Body*, 153.

24. Her origins have been debated by scholars as either Bushman, "Hottentot," Khoikhoi, Khoekhoe, or Khoi-San. Some place her birthplace on the Gamtoos River in 1789.

25. The black male body did not garner similar scientific curiosity in terms of sexuality, though many were also displayed in circuses. For more on ethnological show business and further examples of the practice of displaying the black body as a circus attraction, see Bernth Lindfors, *Africans on Stage: Studies in Ethnological Show Business* (Bloomington: Indiana University Press, 1999).

26. Roland Barthes, "The Man-Eater," in *Critical Essays on Emile Zola*, ed. David Baguley (Boston: G. K. Hall, 1986), 92.

27. Anca Vlasopolos, "Venus Live! Sarah Bartmann, the Hottentot Venus, Re-Membered," *Mosaic* (*Hygieia: A Special Issue on Literature and Medicine*) 33, no. 4 (December 2000): 129, 139.

28. Napoleon's chief doctor, Cuvier was considered a significant scientific mind. He played an important role as a founder of vertebrate paleontology and created the comparative method of organismal biology. He also dismissed the theory of organic evolution and argued that there were past life forms that no longer exist (extinction). His most devastating theories, however, were those on racial superiority based on his biological experiments.

29. Blacks were considered the missing link connecting apes to humans; thus, they were considered the lowest form of human or the highest form of ape. Black sexuality

was thought to be more animalistic than white sexuality, as demonstrated by the "large" genitals in specimens such as Bartmann.

30. Sander Gilman, *Difference and Pathology: Stereotypes of Sexuality, Race, and Madness* (Ithaca, NY: Cornell University Press, 1985), 89. Gilman also provides several examples of conclusions about the separation of races based on this kind of study. One writer even ranks the races according to the size of the female pelvis.

31. The legacy of the Venus Hottentot has surfaced in many arenas since the nineteenth century. Josephine Baker, Jeanne Duval (Baudelaire's mistress), the profession of prostitution (also linked to race—white prostitutes were considered closer to black sexual "animality," and their buttocks were used as evidence), Manet's *Olympia*, Picasso's *Olympia*, and Zola's *Nana* can all be linked to the Venus Hottentot as a governing symbol of black sexuality.

32. Vlasopolos, "Venus Live!" 133.

33. Ananya Chatterjea, "Subversive Dancing: The Interventions in Jawole Willa Jo Zollar's *Batty Moves*," *Theatre Journal* 55, no. 3 (October 2003): 451–65.

34. Thomas F. DeFrantz, "Booty Control," in *Dancing Many Drums: Excavations in African American Dance*, ed. Thomas F. DeFrantz (Madison: University of Wisconsin Press, 2002), 25.

35. See Jacqueline Jones, *Labor of Love, Labor of Sorrow: Black Women, Work, and the Family, From Slavery to the Present* (New York: Vintage, 1985), 14.

36. Ibid., 15, 16.

37. Michele Wallace, *Black Men and the Myth of the Superwoman* (New York: Verso, 1978), 91.

38. Jones, *Labor of Love, Labor of Sorrow*, 21.

39. The snap has also permeated mainstream culture, especially black female gesture-coding as is evident in the "Hair Hell Moment #2" section of *Hair Stories*. There are many different types of snap, each with its own nuanced meaning. For examples, see the play *The Colored Museum* by George C. Wolff, the film *Tongues Untied* by Marlon Riggs, and episodes of the television show *In Living Color*.

Chapter 3. The Word

1. Valerie Gladstone, "Telling a Story That's African and American," *New York Times*, July 7, 2002, 25.

2. Zollar, interview with the author.

3. For example, see Bill T. Jones's *Last Supper at Uncle Tom's Cabin* and Rennie Harris's hip-hop operas.

4. Many of the other Urban Bush Women pieces also deal with story, but these three are the most narratively structured.

5. Karla F. C. Holloway, "Revision and (Re)membrance: A Theory of Literary Structures in Literature by African-American Women Writers," in *African American Literary Theory: A Reader*, ed. Winston Napier (New York: New York University Press, 2000), 388.

6. See chapter 6 for a brief discussion of a step-dance praise dance group.

7. Gottschild, *Black Dancing Body*, 277–80.

8. The most famous example is Alvin Ailey's *Revelations*.

9. Gylbert Coker, "Elephants around the Moon: The Art of Minnie Evans," *Raw Vision* 11 (Spring 1995): 29.

10. The Anthony Petullo Collection of Self-Taught and Outsider Art, http://www.petulloartcollection.com/artistprofile.asp?refArtistID=17.

11. Michel Foucault, *The History of Sexuality* (New York: Vintage, 1990), 27.

12. Holland Cotter, "Visionary Images That 'Just Happened,'" *New York Times*, March 3, 1995, B4.

13. Zollar, "Jawole Willa Jo Zollar: A Self-Study," 34.

14. There is also a stage version of this piece.

15. See Wole Soyinka, *Myth, Literature, and the African World* (Cambridge: Cambridge University Press, 1976).

16. Laura Strong, "Egungun: The Masked Ancestors of the Yoruba," *Mythic Arts*, http://www.mythicarts.com/writing/Egungun.html.

17. Iyanla Vanzant, "Guardian Spirits," in *My Soul Is a Witness: African-American Women's Spirituality*, ed. Gloria Wade-Gayles (Boston: Beacon, 1995), 332.

18. See Rosalyn Terborg-Penn, "The Spirit Keeps the Memory of the Ancestors Alice," in Wade-Gayles, *My Soul Is a Witness*, 65–70. See also Margo V. Perkins's interview with black women, "Exploring New Spaces: A Dialogue with Black Women on Religion, Culture, and Spirituality," in Wade-Gayles, *My Soul Is a Witness*, 171. bell hooks also discusses listening for God and the role of dreams as guides to the spirits in *Sister of the Yam* (Boston: South End Press, 1993).

19. In some stage versions of the piece Granny is also named Hannah instead of Louise.

20. Lani Guinier, keynote address, Conference on Black Women in the Academy, MIT, Cambridge, MA, January 13–15, 1994 (transcript published in *Toledo Law Review* 25 [1995]: 875–90, quote on 883).

21. Andrea Weiss, *Vampires and Violets: Lesbians in Film* (New York: Penguin, 1993).

22. For further discussion, see Pam Keesey, "Interview," *Vampire Information Exchange Newsletter* 74 (March 1996).

23. Kenneth Kojo Anti, "Women in African Traditional Religions," presentation, Women's Center, Eastern Washington University, Cheney, WA, May 1996.

24. Judith E. Johnson calls this an "economy of the erotic," in which both partners must be satisfied. Judith E. Johnson, "Women and Vampires: Nightmare or Utopia," *Kenyon Review* 15, no. 1 (Winter 1993): 74.

25. Keesey, "Interview."

26. Pam Keesey, *Daughters of Darkness* (San Francisco: Cleis, 1998), 14.

27. Jewelle Gomez, "Writing Vampire Fiction: Re-Casting the Mythology," *Hot Wire* 4, no. 1 (November 1987): 42–60.

28. Keesey, "Interview."

29. For more on the association of the vampire and the otherness of the lesbian, see Bonnie Zimmerman, *The Safe Sea of Women: Lesbian Fiction 1969–1989* (Boston: Beacon, 1990) and "Daughters of Darkness: Lesbian Vampires," *Jump Cut*, no. 24–25 (March 1981): 23–24.

30. For more examples of the lesbian vampire in world lore, see the introduction to Keesey, *Daughters of Darkness*, 8.

31. In chapter 5, I talk more about the importance of water and the laying on of hands in African and African American culture.

32. In 2005, a year before her death, Octavia Butler published *Fledgling*, a novel about a black female vampire who, similar to Gilda, negotiates racial identity politics

and sexuality in order to discover herself. However, Butler's novel lacks the lesbian story that makes *The Gilda Stories* unique.

33. Johnson, "Women and Vampires," 72.

34. Jewelle Gomez, "San Francisco: Still Mighty Real," *Gay & Lesbian Review Worldwide* 9, no.3 (May–June 2002): 13–15, reprinted in *Out in the Castro: Desire, Promise, Activism*, edited by Winston Leyland (San Francisco: Leyland Publications, 2002), 259–63.

35. Johnson, "Women and Vampires," 73.

36. Sue Ellen Case, "Tracking the Vampire," *Differences: A Journal of Feminist Cultural Studies* 3, no. 2 (1991): 9.

37. Ibid., 6.

38. See Raymond T. McNally, *Dracula Was a Woman: In Search of the Blood Countess of Transylvania* (New York: McGraw-Hill, 1983), 96.

39. Johnson, "Women and Vampires," 73, 78.

40. Gomez, blog entry, April 3, 2002, http://www.jewellegomez.com (blog no longer available).

41. Zollar, interview with the author.

42. Gladstone, "Telling a Story That's African and American," 25.

43. Ibid.

44. Ibid.

Chapter 4. The World

1. In 1994 Arlene Croce criticized choreographer Bill T. Jones for creating the piece *Still/Here*, which dealt with terminal illness and included footage of survival workshops held with terminally ill people.

2. José Esteban Muñoz, *Disidentifications: Queers of Color and the Performance of Politics* (Minneapolis: University of Minnesota Press, 1999), 74. See also David Gere, *How to Make Dances in an Epidemic: Tracking Choreography in the Age of AIDS* (Madison: University of Wisconsin Press, 2004), 91–137.

3. Triumph, interview with Zollar, 3.

4. Roach, *Cities of the Dead*, 6.

5. G. A. Heron, introduction to Okot p'Bitek, *Song of Lawino, Song of Ocol* (London: Heinemann, 1966), 2.

6. Deborah Jowitt, "Lift and Uplift," *Village Voice*, February 9, 1988, 91.

7. In this chapter I will discuss the choreography in terms of its position on violence, and in the next chapter I will discuss it in terms of spirituality.

8. The three singers are Thought Music (Robbie McCauley, Laurie Carlos, and Jessica Hagedorn).

9. Harris's Dirty Tones Band provides musical accompaniment for the piece. This section has also been performed separately as *Four Moments of the Sun*. In this version, the women's faces are painted, and the image is of primitive women coming of age. They use sticks to draw on the floor, carve through the air, and explore the space. It is an evolutionary story, as the women learn to stand and use their sticks as weapons. The piece ends with the women pointing their sticks at the audience. The women in *Heat*, however, have not yet reached that position of power.

10. African American Planning Commission, Inc., http://www.aapci.org.

11. Zollar, interview by Donaghy, 12.

12. Quoted in Craig Bromberg, "Ailey: Merging Song, Dance, Theater, Soul," *Los Angeles Times*, September 17, 1987, 2.

13. Zollar, interview with the author.

14. Quoted in Sasha Anawalt, "Bush Women Bring Urban Poetry to Life," *Los Angeles Herald Examiner*, September 18, 1987.

15. I will discuss the significance of water in African and African American spirituality further in the next chapter.

16. Harriet Beecher Stowe, *Uncle Tom's Cabin* (1852; repr., London: Oxford University Press, 2002), 213, 214.

17. Alice Walker, "Giving the Party: Aunt Jemima, Mammy, and the Goddess Within," *Ms.*, May–June 1994, 22–25.

18. There have been other powerful images of black female domestics in dances choreographed by black women. See *Cry* by Judith Jamison and *Chicken Soup* by Blondell Cummings.

19. The section includes a dance that is also performed as the solo *The Magician* (*The Return of She*). As it is a part of the *Life Dances* cycle, I leave the discussion of this work for the next chapter.

20. Jamaica Kincaid, *At the Bottom of the River* (New York: Farrar, Straus, Giroux, 1983), 60, 61, 79, 77.

21. Kincaid, *At the Bottom of the River*, 79.

Chapter 5. The Soul

1. Bernadine Jennings, "Eye of the Hurricane," *Dance and Spiritual Life* program (Brooklyn, NY: 651 Arts, 1998).

2. Zollar, "Jawole Willa Jo Zollar: A Self-Study," 74–75.

3. Triumph, interview with Zollar, 3.

4. Jennifer Dunning, "The Stage: Jawole Zollar in 'Song of Lawino,'" *New York Times*, January 24, 1988.

5. James H. Cone, *A Black Theology of Liberation*, Twentieth Anniversary edition (1970; repr., Maryknoll, NY: Orbis, 1990), xi. This edition includes articles by contemporary scholars responding to the original work and discussing the significance it had over the previous twenty years. For example, Gayraud Wilmore tries to assess black theology during the prior two decades. He describes and accounts for some of the failures of the movement. Pablo Richard analyzes the influence of black liberation theology on theological work in Latin America. For more on Latin American liberation theology, see Gustavo Gutiérrez, *A Theology of Liberation* (Maryknoll, NY: Orbis, 1988).

6. For more on early womanist theology, see also Katie G. Cannon, *Black Womanist Ethics* (Atlanta: Scholars Press, 1988); Jacquelyn Grant, *White Women's Christ, Black Women's Jesus: Feminist Christology and Womanist Response* (Atlanta: Scholars Press, 1989); Renita Weems, *Just a Sister Away: A Womanist Vision of Women's Relationships in the Bible* (San Diego: LuraMedia Press, 1988).

7. Stephanie Y. Mitchem, *Introducing Womanist Theology* (Maryknoll, NY: Orbis, 2002), ix.

8. For more see John S. Mbiti, *African Religions and Philosophy* (New York: Anchor, 1970).

9. Mitchem, *Introducing Womanist Theology*, 49, 53.

10. Ibid., 86.

11. Zollar, interview with the author.

12. Bauman, interview with the author.

13. See Luke 6:19 and Matthew 8:3, 9:18–29.

14. Carla J. Harris, "Southern Women," in Wade-Gayles, *My Soul Is a Witness*, 18.

15. Anyone who has seen Alvin Ailey's seminal work *Revelations* knows the symbolic power of the fan for African American women. In that piece, church ladies enter fanning themselves. The fans connect the dancers to the hot South. Later, the fervor with which the women fan becomes linked to the juiciness of their gossip (no words are actually spoken). They also use their fans to chastise their men for their wayward behaviors. When testifying, they fold up their fans and point them to heaven and then to the audience.

16. Alvin Ailey also choreographed this spiritual. It is a tour de force baptism. For a detailed discussion, see Thomas F. DeFrantz, *Dancing Revelations: Alvin Ailey's Embodiment of African American Culture* (Oxford: Oxford University Press), 2004.

17. For a larger discussion of this, see Karen Baker-Fletcher and Garth Baker-Fletcher, *My Sister, My Brother: Womanist and Xodus God-Talk* (Maryknoll, NY: Orbis, 1997), 89–90.

18. Mitchem, *Introducing Womanist Theology*, 48.

19. Daa'iyah Taha, "The Sacred Journey: The Gift of Hajj," in Wade-Gayles, *My Soul Is a Witness*, 271.

20. For more on this, see Wade-Gayles, *My Soul Is a Witness*.

21. Ibid., 7–8.

22. Ntozake Shange, *For Colored Girls Who Have Considered Suicide/When the Rainbow Is Enuf* (New York: Collier, 1975), 63.

23. Marsha Foster Boyd, "WomanistCare," in *Embracing the Spirit: Womanist Perspectives on Hope, Salvation, and Transformation*, ed. Emilie M. Townes (Maryknoll, NY: Orbis, 1997), 198–99.

24. Her early collaborators in this series were Tiye Giraud and Edwina Lee Tyler.

25. Deborah Jowitt, "Witch in Women," *Village Voice*, November 25, 1986.

26. Zollar has run into difficulty touring these pieces. In an interview, she told me: "They were very highly personalized and edgy, and as I was developing them, that's right when the whole Helms thing and NEA [exploded]. Most of them were not tourable because they're way too provocative for the kind of touring that we do. Most producers are not going to touch them. But I have been thinking about doing something called the Evocative Workshop for DTW, something that's not going to tour."

27. *The Fool's Journey* is not numbered because it is the alpha and omega, the beginning and end of things.

28. *Life Dance 1: The Magician* (*The Return of She*) has also appeared in *Anarchy, Wild Women, and Dinah*.

29. For more on how this piece ends with a celebration of women's ability to re-find peace in order to resist social controls, see Ananya Chatterjea, *Butting Out: Reading Resistive Choreographies through Works by Jawole Willa Jo Zollar and Chandralekha* (Middletown, CT: Wesleyan University Press, 2004).

30. Cheryl A. Kirk-Duggan, "Justified, Sanctified, and Redeemed: Blessed Expectation in Black Women's Blues and Gospels," in Townes, *Embracing the Spirit*, 140.

31. Mitchem, *Introducing Womanist Theology*, 111.

32. Toni Morrison, *Beloved* (New York: Plume, 1988), 88.

33. Mitchem, *Introducing Womanist Theology*, 111,112.

34. Pauli Murray, *Song in a Weary Throat* (New York: Harper & Row, 1987), 435.

35. Delores S. Williams, "Straight Talk, Plain Talk," in Townes, *Embracing the Spirit*, 98.

36. Brown, interview with the author.

37. Dona Marimba Richards [Marimba Ani], *Let the Circle Be Unbroken* (Lawrenceville, NJ: Red Sea Press, 1992), quoted in Wade-Gayles, *My Soul Is a Witness*, 96.

38. King, interview with the author.

39. Kate Hammer, "John O'Neal, Actor and Activist: The Praxis of Storytelling," in *A Sourcebook of African American Plays, People, Movements*, ed. Annemarie Bean (New York: Routledge, 1999), 141.

Chapter 6. The Community

1. Susanna Sloat, "Urban Bush Women," *Attitude* 13, no. 2 (Spring–Summer 1998): 68.

2. Benedict Anderson, *Imagined Communities: Reflections on the Origin and Spread of Nationalism* (London: Verso, 1983), 14, 15.

3. Robert D. Putnam, *Bowling Alone: The Collapse and Revival of American Community* (New York: Simon & Schuster, 2000).

4. See Robert D. Putnam, "Bowling Together: The United States of America" *American Prospect* 13, no. 3 (February 11, 2002): 20–22.

5. Jacqueline Jones discusses post-Reconstruction self-reliant black communities in *Labor of Love, Labor of Sorrow*.

6. Jacquelyn Grant, "Faithful Resistance Risking It All: From Expedience to Radical Obedience," in Wade-Gayles, *My Soul Is a Witness*, 206.

7. Kate Mattingly Moran, "Incubating Classroom Creativity," *Dance Teacher* (February 2001): 66.

8. This song also appears in *Nyabinghi Dreamtime*.

9. Urban Bush Women, "Summer Institute: Building Community Through the Arts" promotional flier, March 2004, Urban Bush Women Archives, Brooklyn, NY. See also http://www.urbanbushwomen.org/summer_inst.html.

10. King, interview with the author.

11. Urban Bush Women, "Summer Institute: A New Dancer for a New Society" promotional flier, May 2000, Urban Bush Women Archives, Brooklyn, NY.

12. Attendees included Americorp and Vista volunteers, young dancers and musicians, recent college graduates, teachers, folk artists, a doctor, and an engineer.

13. For more on this see Ellen Graff, *Stepping Left: Dance and Politics in New York City, 1928–1942* (Durham, NC: Duke University Press, 1997).

14. Zollar, interview with the author.

15. See Augusto Boal, *The Rainbow of Desire: The Boal Method of Theatre and Therapy* (New York: Routledge, 1995), *Legislative Theatre: Using Performance to Make Politics* (New York: Routledge, 1998), and *Games for Actors and Non-Actors* (New York: Routledge, 2002).

16. See Sonja Kuftinec, *Staging America: Cornerstone and Community-Based Theater* (Carbondale: Southern Illinois University Press, 2003).

17. Jawole Will Jo Zollar, "A Constant State of Premiere," *Dance/USA Journal* (Fall 1993): 18.

18. Zollar, interview with the author.

19. André St. Clair Thompson, interview with the author, December 2003, Brooklyn, NY.

20. The *Dixwell* project told stories decidedly from an African American perspective—other communities in Dixwell didn't get their stories told in this piece. This outlook is in part because African Americans make up the majority of the population of Dixwell and in part because of Urban Bush Women's African American focus. Most of the performance concerned the strong history of the African American part of the neighborhood.

21. M. Yolles, "Professor Kennedy Speaks at First Group Meeting," Dixwell Inter-Racial Group newsletter, October 5, 1948, Yale University Archives, Sterling Memorial Library.

Coda

1. Jack Anderson, "Troupe Celebrates Spiritual and Geographical Journeys," *New York Times*, June 23, 2005, E4.

2. Dunning, "Rough, and Proud of It."

3. Brown, interview with the author.

4. Bauman, interview with the author.

5. King, interview with the author.

6. Zollar, interview with the author.

7. Dunning, "Rough, and Proud of It."

Index

Page numbers in italics refer to illustrations.

Studies in Dance History
A Publication of the Society of Dance History Scholars

Titles in Print

The Origins of the Bolero School, edited by Javier Suárez-Pajares and Xoán M. Carreira

Carlo Blasis in Russia by Elizabeth Souritz, with preface by Selma Jeanne Cohen

Of, By, and For the People: Dancing on the Left in the 1930s, edited by Lynn Garafola

Dancing in Montreal: Seeds of a Choreographic History by Iro Tembeck

The Making of a Choreographer: Ninette de Valois and "Bar aux Folies-Bergère" by Beth Genné

Ned Wayburn and the Dance Routine: From Vaudeville to the "Ziegfeld Follies" by Barbara Stratyner

Rethinking the Sylph: New Perspectives on the Romantic Ballet, edited by Lynn Garafola (available from the University Press of New England)

Dance for Export: Cultural Diplomacy and the Cold War by Naima Prevots, with introduction by Eric Foner (available from the University Press of New England)

José Limón: An Unfinished Memoir, edited by Lynn Garafola, with introduction by Deborah Jowitt, foreword by Carla Maxwell, and afterword by Norton Owen (available from the University Press of New England)

Dancing Desires: Choreographing Sexualities on and off the Stage, edited by Jane C. Desmond

Dancing Many Drums: Excavations in African American Dance, edited by Thomas F. DeFrantz

Writings on Ballet and Music by Fedor Lopukhov, edited and with an introduction by Stephanie Jordan, translations by Dorinda Offord

Liebe Hanya: Mary Wigman's Letters to Hanya Holm, compiled and edited by Claudia Gitelman, introduction by Hedwig Müller

The Grotesque Dancer on the Eighteenth-Century Stage: Gennaro Magri and His World, edited by Rebecca Harris-Warrick and Bruce Alan Brown

Kaiso!: Writings by and about Katherine Dunham, edited by VèVè A. Clark and Sara E. Johnson

Dancing from Past to Present: Nation, Culture, Identities, edited by Theresa Jill Buckland

Women's Work: Making Dance in Europe before 1800, edited by Lynn Matluck Brooks

Dance and the Nation: Performance, Ritual, and Politics in Sri Lanka by Susan A. Reed

Urban Bush Women: Twenty Years of African American Dance Theater, Community Engagement, and Working It Out by Nadine George-Graves